Bandelier

Bandelier

THE LIFE AND ADVENTURES OF ADOLPH BANDELIER

Charles H. Lange and Carroll L. Riley

University of Utah Press   *Salt Lake City*

Library of Congress Cataloging-in-Publication Data

Lange, Charles H.
Bandelier, the life and adventures of Adolph Bandelier / Charles H.
Lange and Carroll L. Riley.
p.   cm.
Includes bibliographical references and index.
ISBN 0-87480-499-X
1. Bandelier, Adolph Francis Alphonse, 1840–1914.
2. Indianists—United States—Biography.
3. Indianists—Switzerland—Biography.   4. Archaeologists—United
States—Biography.   5. Archaeologists—Switzerland—Biography.
I. Riley, Carroll L.   II. Title.
E57.B36L36   1996
970'.007202—dc20
[B]   96-910

Contents

Illustrations

MAPS

PHOTOGRAPHS

Illustrations

Preface

Adolph F. Bandelier (1840–1914) has long been recognized as a significant figure in the early history of anthropology, not only in the American Southwest but also in Mexico and South America. Celebrations in 1940 of the centennial of his birth and in 1980 of his first trip to Frijoles Canyon, New Mexico, along with frequent references to Bandelier and his work in scholarly and popular publications and the continued attraction of Bandelier National Monument in New Mexico, have served to keep his name in the public awareness.

It seemed to us that a faithful biography, making liberal use of Bandelier's own journals and letters, would be a logical, challenging, and worthwhile venture. Together, these sources reveal much of his determination and complexity; they go far in portraying Adolph F. Bandelier as an important early contributor to several fields of study. His career also has importance because it paralleled so closely the founding and growth of the discipline that was to emerge as anthropology.

In 1981 we completed editing and annotating the last of the four volumes of *The Southwestern Journals of Adolph F. Bandelier,* covering the years 1880 to 1892. These volumes were issued by the University of New Mexico Press between 1966 and 1984. After nearly a quarter of a century of research and writing related to Bandelier, we thought our involvement with him had come to an end.

Yet just before our fourth volume went to press, new and significant biographical material came to our attention. A part of this material came from a 1982 biography of Bandelier by Eric Rufener, published in French. Other new information had been collected by Madeleine Turrell Rodack of the Arizona State Museum, University of Arizona, Tucson, through correspondence with Rufener and Madame Simone Bandelier Sarasin in Switzerland. In addition to the Rufener and Sarasin data, we obtained, through the courtesy of Jeffrey K. Colville and Ruth R. Olivera of the Latin American Library at Tulane University, a copy of a biographical interview with Bandelier recorded early in this century by George H. Pepper.

Fortunately, we were able to incorporate certain of these new data into our final volume of Bandelier's journals. But because much was left out, we began to consider the possibility of writing a full-fledged biography of Adolph F. Bandelier, using the remainder of the new material generously provided by Dr. Rodack, Mr. Colville, and Mrs. Olivera.

Despite our long-term research into and publication of Bandelier's journals, and despite long-standing public interest in the man and his work, there was still no comprehensive published biography of Bandelier. Furthermore, the existing biographical sketches suffered not only from incompleteness but also, and more importantly, from numerous inaccuracies that continued to be repeated in the literature. Accordingly, it seemed important for us to write a biography based on the wealth of data gathered in the course of our research and at the same time correct and, we hope, lay to rest the oft-repeated inaccuracies. Another point in our deliberations was that all four volumes of Bandelier's southwestern journals were already out of print.

In working with his journals, we had repeatedly been impressed by their richness as a source for revealing Bandelier in his varied activities as archaeologist, ethnologist, historian, naturalist, and scientist. In addition, although we have found very few letters written to Bandelier, a wealth of his own correspondence with colleagues and friends still exists.

Much of this correspondence has not previously appeared in print— and when it has been published, it has often been in scattered places and in excerpts aimed at readers with particular interests. This considerable correspondence, often as candid as his journal entries, supplements the journals and provides a broader base from which to view Bandelier and come to know him.

Bandelier's journal entries and, especially, his voluminous correspondence with academic and scientific colleagues are also of value in another, broader sense. They provide on-the-scene insights into the early days of American archaeology and ethnology as well as the beginnings of historical studies of the Southwest and the remainder of Latin America. The establishment of institutions such as the Bureau of Ethnology (subsequently Bureau of American Ethology) and the American Association

for the Advancement of Science in Washington, D.C., and the Archaeological Institute of America in Boston took place during the period
when Bandelier was embarking on his investigations. Correspondence
files and records such as annual reports and the minutes of meetings of
these organizations provide the broader context within which Bandelier's
contributions to the study of the culture history of the Southwest and
Spanish America may be appreciated and accurately appraised.

A greater understanding of Bandelier as a scholar may also be gained
through an examination of his bibliography, which appears as an appendix in this book. The dates of his publications extend from 1858 until his
death in 1914, and there are several posthumously published titles as well.
In many years Bandelier published multiple works, and a number of his
publications have now been reprinted. His writings covered a considerable range of subjects and appeared in English, French, German, and
Spanish.

Our earlier research was directed primarily toward Bandelier's southwestern experiences, and we gave relatively little attention to his earlier
and later years. We have now incorporated material from his year in
Mexico (1881), from his South American years (1892–1903), from his
life in New York City (1903–13), which included a visit to Mexico
(1909–11), and from his final months in Spain (1913–14). Again, we have
drawn much of this material from letters written by Bandelier and also
from his post-southwestern journals, which continue to provide insights
into his personal thoughts and professional views.

Acknowledgments

This biography of Adolph F. Bandelier had its beginnings in the four volumes of Bandelier's southwestern journals (1966, 1970, 1975, 1984) that we edited and annotated with Elizabeth M. Lange. Betty Lange's collaboration was of great value in the project, and her unexpected death in the spring of 1986 deprived the world of a dedicated scholar in Bandelier studies.

In the course of our research and writing, we benefited from the assistance of many friends and colleagues in the United States, Mexico, and Europe. These people have been thanked in the four journal volumes and we will not name them again here—but the collective aid they rendered has been significant and is greatly appreciated.

Neither of us ever expected that our work on Bandelier would take up as much time and effort as it has. Balancing this observation, we can only add that the work has provided us with many rewarding experiences and brought us many new friends and much satisfaction.

Charles H. Lange
Carroll L. Riley
Santa Fe and Las Vegas, New Mexico
September 1995

ONE

The Family Bandelier

. . . he will try to make a place for himself, if not a brilliant one, at least a solid and modest one.

—Marie Senn Bandelier, 1848

O N THE PATIO WALL of the visitors' center at Bandelier National Monument, New Mexico, there is a simply worded memorial plaque that reads:

ADOLPH F. BANDELIER
ARCHAEOLOGIST ARCHIVIST HISTORIAN
BORN IN BERN SWITZERLAND
AUGUST 6 1840
DIED IN SEVILLE SPAIN
MARCH 18 1914
A GREAT AMERICAN SCHOLAR

This plaque was placed in conjunction with a memorial conference sponsored by the Museum of New Mexico in Santa Fe on August 6, 1940, to commemorate the one-hundredth anniversary of Bandelier's birth. Adolph Bandelier was well known in the American Southwest, but people elsewhere may ask, "Who was this person?" or "What did he do?"

Adolph Bandelier has been called anthropologist, archaeologist, archivist, ethnographer, explorer, geographer, historian, and scientist. He was a leading figure in the anthropological and historical study of

American Indians that was nascent in the late nineteenth and early twentieth centuries. Although he had almost no formal education, Bandelier succeeded in blending the data and methods of disparate academic disciplines to paint a rich portrayal of prehistoric and protohistoric American Indian life—a truly unique contribution for his day. His interests were well ahead of his time; even if he had sought professional instruction in his fields of interest, he would have been hard-pressed to find it.

In the years following Bandelier's field investigations and writings, other scholars largely ignored his unique approach to culture history. It was not until about the time of World War II that researchers and writers began to urge that disciplines such as archaeology, ethnography, and history be combined in order to present a more inclusive picture of past eras.

Adolph Bandelier was a true pioneer and explorer—academically as well as in the field. He had no manuals or handbooks to tell him how to proceed. Many times he was naive or aggressive or willing to settle for less than the whole story. Shaped by his early years in rural Illinois, he willingly walked many miles, rode horseback, or hitched a ride with a passing wagon or buggy to get to the next fieldwork site. In the endless hours he spent searching for and copying old manuscripts and documents, he endured dim candlelight, freezing or sweltering rooms, and a host of other inconveniences.

A major influence on Bandelier's career was Lewis Henry Morgan, the "Father of American Anthropology." Morgan brought Bandelier to the attention of prominent scientists in the 1870s, as well as fashioning Banelier's thoughts from the time of their first meeting in 1873, in Rochester, New York, until Morgan's death there in 1881. An equally valid claim could be made for Baron Alexander von Humboldt, the world-renowned German anthropologist, geographer, and historian whose writings were known to Bandelier before he ever met Morgan. As long as he lived, Bandelier paid homage to Humboldt and his thoughts.

Bandelier's father, Adolphe Eugene Bandelier, was born in Sornetan, Switzerland, on August 18, 1812, the youngest of four children of Simon Bandelier and Marianne Juillerat Bandelier. Little is known of Adolphe Eugene's early life, but in October 1830 the young man began studying law at Lausanne. In November 1831 he moved on to the law school at Bern, eventually receiving a degree in law. At Bern, he also joined the Swiss military, rising in later years to the rank of first lieutenant.

While in Bern, Adolphe Bandelier took rooms with a small-scale *hôteliere,* Marie Senn Ritter, who was sixteen years his senior and who would eventually become his wife. Marie Senn, the daughter of Emmanuel Senn and Elizabeth Scheurer, was born on November 1, 1796. She had met her first husband, Adrian Louis Ritter, while serving as a governess in Russia and had married him in 1816. Ritter, thirty years her senior and the son of the well-known Bern architect Erasmus Ritter, had been a military officer in Holland and had later gone to Russia as some sort of tutor. He adopted a Russian form of his name (Rutovsk?), which may have had aristocratic overtones. Adrian Ritter died in 1830, leaving no children and apparently very little money.

This Russian adaptation of the name Ritter may be the basis of a persistent claim that Marie Senn had married a Russian nobleman. This idea was apparently firmly held by Fanny Bandelier, the second wife of Marie's son, Adolph, who may have told this patently false story to impress her. More likely, Fanny, an incurable romantic, was simply trying to glamorize her husband and his family.

Marie Senn Ritter and Adolphe Eugene Bandelier were married at Seedorf on March 8, 1838, with Bandelier's older brother, Pastor Alphonse Simon Pierre Bandelier, probably performing the ceremony. Following their marriage the couple lived in Bern, where their son and only child, Adolph François Alphonse (Adolph F.), was born on August 6, 1840. About the same time, father Adolphe was appointed to the military tribunal in Bern, and he occupied various positions in the canton government throughout the early 1840s. The elder Bandelier, however, stood opposed to a radical new constitution adopted by the canton of Bern in 1846, which caused him to break with the government party and retire to a private law practice.

Meanwhile, young Adolph F. Bandelier had been growing up in troubled political times. Very little is known about his Swiss childhood, but one may surmise that both parents were concerned with and able to contribute to his upbringing and education. In 1940, Hulda Hobbs of the Museum of New Mexico wrote a sketch of Bandelier's early years:

Adolph's parents tutored him until he was old enough to attend school. Even after that, they stimulated in him the spirit of scientific inquiry. They had a telescope, through which Adolph and his father used to study the heavenly bodies. They had a custom of reading aloud in the evenings.

The remarkable breadth of Adolph's knowledge thus appears to have been built up from his early childhood. He and his father spoke French together, unless others were present. They spoke perfect "Paris French"— not the Swiss patois. They were equally at home with German.

We do not know why the senior Bandelier turned away from practicing law in Bern and chose to emigrate to the New World. It was a decision probably based on several factors, foremost among them the fact that Bandelier's career in government had come to an end. In addition, he very likely believed his son would have a better future in a country other than Switzerland.

In August 1846, a Mr. Meyrat was visiting in St. Imier, Switzerland, the community where Bandelier's brother, Alphonse Simon Pierre, was a pastor. Meyrat, a planter in Brazil who was about to return to that country in the spring of 1847, spoke with Adolphe about South America. He suggested that Bandelier accompany him and offered to make all the necessary arrangements. Adolphe then persuaded John Balsiger, a good friend, to join him in the venture.

Marie Bandelier and young Adolph F. were to remain temporarily in Bern. There is little to indicate how Marie felt about her husband's plans for Brazil and whether she played any real part in his decision to leave Switzerland. In any case, Bandelier and Balsiger sailed from Le Havre, probably in mid-April 1847.

A letter written by Marie Bandelier to her brother-in-law on September 5, 1847, tells of A. E. Bandelier's arrival in Brazil: "Thanks be to God, Adolf arrived safely at [?]. Yesterday I received [a] short letter announcing his arrival. He was not sea sick. The crossing was a good one and lasted 70 days; they had no mishaps except that in the Channel they were thrown first into the coasts of France and into those of England."

This letter from Marie also reveals she had health problems. She wrote, "My eyes are a little better." Later letters also referred to eye difficulties. In addition, the letter contains one of the few references to Adolph F. as a young boy. Written a month after the child's seventh birthday, it said, "The little one is weak, having again fallen ill, which forces me to go to the country with him to avoid the bad effects of winter."

On the other side of the Atlantic, Brazilian government officials were so impressed with A. E. Bandelier's credentials that they offered him a government position, but he refused it. Together he and Balsiger visited the Swiss colony in Rio de Janeiro and then traversed vast areas of Brazil. Although Bandelier found that some plantation owners treated their slaves better than European masters treated their servants, he was distressed by the contrast between the very wealthy and the abjectly poor.

By the autumn of 1847, A. E. Bandelier had become disillusioned with Brazil. The country indeed offered opportunities, especially in agriculture, but they necessitated a heavy initial investment in land, equipment, and slaves. The elder Bandelier had certain reservations about the institution of slavery, but he mainly disliked the idea of bringing up young Adolph in the moral and religious climate of Brazil. In his later years Adolphe was strongly anti-Catholic, and he probably felt that way in the 1840s as well. With his friend Balsiger, Bandelier decided to leave Brazil for the United States.

Many years later, in an interview with the archaeologist George H. Pepper around 1906 or 1907, Adolph F. Bandelier supposedly stated that he and his mother had joined his father in Brazil. It is possible that this completely false statement resulted from a misunderstanding on the part of Pepper, but the interview contained several other dubious and misleading claims as well. For once in his life, Bandelier seems not to have been particularly interested in accuracy.

Marie first learned of her husband's plan to go to North America from the elder Balsigers, who shared a letter from their son. On January 4, 1848, she wrote her brother-in-law about "the news I have just learned." By that time, Bandelier and Balsiger, along with a St. Louis, Missouri, man, M. Adolph Renard, were already on ship for New Orleans.

In January 1848, Marie wrote to her brother-in-law with a revealing statement about young Adolph (and probably about herself as well). "My little one, as a result of a cold drink one evening . . . almost got an inflammation of the chest or the [?]; the rash little one causes me cruel anxiety; when will he be good?" Another letter written on January 25, 1848, from Marie to Alphonse tells us something about the personality of A. E. Bandelier.

My dear brother,
. . . The news of Adolf's [Adolphe E.'s] departure for the North, his rashness in sailing again on the same ship, that, added to my weakness, has dealt me a blow which I was unable to ward off. . . . Now that he has

seen the widely touted El Dorado he can judge it seriously and make correct comparisons, and tired of roving about, he will try to make a place for himself, if not a brilliant one, at least a solid and modest one suitable to his needs. Adolf never aimed at anything brilliant anyway, I knew that. A quiet corner was what he sought.

A. E. Bandelier and John Balsiger reached New Orleans on the tenth of January, 1848. Bandelier probably reached Highland in late January, assuming that he was forced to spend a few days in New Orleans arranging for the trip northward, and that the trip by riverboat to St. Louis took the usual six to ten days. According to his naturalization declaration, filed on October 28 of that year, Bandelier had been a resident of Madison County, Illinois, for ten months. It is likely, however, that on making his declaration before the Madison County circuit court clerk, Bandelier simply miscounted and should have said nine rather than ten months. In any event, the naturalization document places A. E. Bandelier's arrival in Madison County at a date earlier than is generally believed to have been the case.

Presumably, Bandelier and Balsiger traveled with their new friend, Adolph Renard, all the way to St. Louis. Indeed, it may be that their acquaintance with Renard influenced them to accompany him to the St. Louis area in their search for new homes. Even more likely, Bandelier had known of Madison County and the community of Highland, twenty-five miles east of St. Louis, through publications about this American Swiss colony even before leaving Europe.

TWO
Early Days in Illinois

Before our eyes extended a prairie landscape, but the level
green was spotted with friendly hills.
                                            —Solomon Koepfli, 1831

T HE TOWN to which the Bandeliers were to become committed
and to whose cultural and business life they would make important contributions was Highland, the "New Switzerland" of Illinois, about thirty
miles east of St. Louis, Missouri.

Two families who lived in the Sursee area of Canton Lucerne,
Switzerland—the Koepflis and the Suppigers—were instrumental in
founding this Swiss colony in America. Both families were unhappy
with the reactionary government imposed on Switzerland by the victorious allies following the collapse of Napoleon's Europe. In 1830, Kasper
Koepfli read an account by a German traveler named Gottfried Duden,
who had spent the years 1824–27 in Montgomery County, eastern
Missouri. Inspired by Duden's enthusiasm, Koepfli and his companions
made a decision to emigrate to the New World.

A small group consisting mainly of Koepflis and Suppigers left
Switzerland in the spring of 1831. The party sailed from Le Havre,
arriving in New York in midsummer. It reached St. Louis in late August,
traveling via the Erie Canal and Lake Erie, then across Ohio waterways,
and finally by steamship from Cincinnati. Using St. Louis as a temporary
base, the group began to investigate possible areas in which to settle.
Dissatisfied with various locations in Missouri and basically opposed to
living in a slave state, the Swiss party soon turned its attention to Illinois,

a state without slavery. Keeping their headquarters in St. Louis, men of the Koepfli and Suppiger families fanned out in small groups on the Illinois side of the Mississippi River. This area along the river was not considered desirable for settlement, but eventually the men discovered the Looking Glass Prairie near Edwardsville, Illinois. Solomon Koepfli was lyrical in his description.

> Here were neither the endless woods of Missouri, nor the monotonous boundless prairie of Illinois. To be sure, here before our eyes extended a prairie landscape, but the level green was spotted with friendly hills. . . . The prairie as far as one could see rested undisturbed in its bounty. Small herds of deer, and at times small horned cattle, grazed in its high grass.

In the fall of 1831, the two families purchased something over 650 acres on Looking Glass Prairie. These inexperienced, well-to-do Swiss immigrants, in spite of their extensive planning and preparation, found life during their first two years on the prairie extremely primitive. Though certain skills were represented in the pioneer party—for example, Kasper Koepfli was an experienced medical doctor—the group quickly recognized that if the settlement were to succeed and grow, blacksmiths, wagon makers, coopers, carpenters, millers, and other craftsmen must be attracted. Publication of Joseph Suppiger's travel journal and of a *Reisenbericht* (travel report) by Suppiger and Solomon Koepfli in Sursee in 1833 led to a second wave of settlers.

One of these newcomers was Moritz Huegy, from the town of Schoetz, Canton Lucerne. On the last day of 1834, Huegy married Maria Josepha Suppiger, who had arrived in the same party as her new husband. Both the Suppiger and Koepfli families were Catholic, and Joseph Suppiger had been trained in Jesuit schools, but the two families were somewhat anticlerical, as might be expected for Swiss liberals of that era. Huegy seems to have been a Protestant; at least his wife and children, later on, were members of one of the Protestant churches. In any event, there was no organized religion, either Catholic or Protestant, in the Highland community in 1834.

On October 11, 1836, the first Swiss-American infant on Looking Glass Prairie was born to Moritz and Maria Josepha Huegy. This baby girl, Josepha (later Anglicized to Josephine) became one of the links that bound the lives and fortunes of the Bandeliers to those of the founders of this Swiss settlement. In 1861, Josephine would become the bride of Adolph F. Bandelier.

The original settlers of Highland had concentrated, by necessity, on farming, and the first nonfarming enterprise was a brick works established by Jacob Eggen on a farm north of the future town. Stimulated by a continuing flow of immigrants, especially from Switzerland, Highland grew steadily. By 1840, a mill, a cooper's shop, a sawmill, and a school had been constructed. By the early 1840s, a cabinetmaker, a glazier, a saddler, a butcher, a shoemaker, and a hostler had settled in Highland, and the same period saw the beginnings of both the German Evangelical and Catholic churches. In the middle years of the decade, a barbershop appeared and there were five general stores in the Highland area. By at least 1843, an orchestra had been formed.

Although most of the early settlers of Highland were German speakers from Switzerland, and later ones came from various German-language cantons and German states to the north, there were also a considerable number of French speakers, mostly from the Protestant Canton of Vaud. The prosperity of the new settlement also attracted a smattering of native-born Anglo-Americans. Accounts of the period speak of the curiosity with which Americans regarded the strange language and customs of the Swiss—and especially their pocket watches. To the Swiss, the Americans' frontier clothing and "free and easy" manners were equally fascinating.

The population of Highland was approximately 120 in 1840. In that year, postal authorities informed the community that there was already a Highland in Illinois, near Chicago. Accordingly, the Swiss reverted to an earlier preference, "Helvetia." In 1843, however, the northern Illinois community changed its name to "Highland Park," and "Helvetia" again became "Highland." Also in 1843, a segment of the national Cumberland Road was completed from Pocahontas, Illinois, through Highland to Troy, where it linked up to Edwardsville, Cahokia, and the rapidly expanding city of St. Louis.

As of the late 1840s, the future of Highland—not yet two decades old—seemed promising. The status of its inhabitants, economically, culturally, and intellectually, was certainly well above that of the average frontier community.

It was to this vital, rapidly growing, and ambitious town that Adolphe E. Bandelier came in the last days of January, 1848. From St. Louis,

Bandelier, with his friend John Balsiger, could travel to Highland by stagecoach, a journey that took six to twelve hours, depending on the condition of the roads, and cost $1.50 per person. Bandelier promptly undertook to acquire land. In late April of 1848, he purchased a forty-acre tract a mile northeast of the eastern outskirts of Highland, as well as a smaller acreage. Bandelier soon built, or perhaps expanded, a house on a small rise of land near the northern edge of the property. This farm was where young Adolph F. Bandelier spent his boyhood, and it remained in the Bandelier family, a focus of family activities, until the tragic events surrounding the failure of the elder Bandelier's banking interests in 1885.

While A. E. Bandelier was busy purchasing a farm and settling into his new home near Highland, his wife, Marie, was also busy arranging matters in Switzerland so that she and young Adolph could join their husband and father. A letter of April 22, 1848, to her brother-in-law, Alphonse Bandelier, and his wife in Corgemont contains the first reference to Marie's plans to take her son to America and reunite the family. Although she was impatient to rejoin her husband, she "did not want to rush off" with her child, as Adolphe was "not yet established." She was waiting for "precise instructions." Three months after this letter, on July 20, 1848, Marie wrote again to her brother-in-law to let him know that she would soon leave for America.

The identity of the ship on which Marie Senn Bandelier crossed the Atlantic is unknown, but it seems most likely that mother and son sailed on August 10 from Le Havre. An August 10 sailing, assuming an average crossing of forty to fifty days to New Orleans and an additional ten days by river steamer from New Orleans to St. Louis, would be in line with an arrival date in early October. It is not absolutely certain that Marie and Adolph used the New Orleans route, but from 1833 on, this had been the recommended way to reach Highland, and A. E. Bandelier had certainly come this way a few months earlier.

Traditional accounts of the Bandelier family have stated that Marie Senn Bandelier and young Adolph traveled with the family maid, Annali Naefiger. Not much is known of Annali, but she was alive as late as January 4, 1881, when Adolph F. Bandelier mentioned visiting her in Highland. Annali probably died soon after this visit. In any case, Marie and her party joined father Bandelier on October 6, 1848. Adolph still remembered this day many years later. In a journal entry of October 6, 1897, a time when he was in South America, Adolph had this to say:

"Forty-nine years today! Since I arrived at Highland and saw Joe [Josephine Huegy] for the first time." It seems likely that the Bandeliers moved without delay to the family farm. There is no record of Adolphe E. Bandelier's purchasing a town house during this period, even though he seems to have spent most of his days in town.

There is no doubt that Highland, at this point in its development, offered a rich field for a man of Bandelier's background and talents. Widely read and especially trained in the law, he came to Highland at a time when a number of French-speaking settlers from both Switzerland and France had joined the German-speaking nucleus of the town. The French-speaking migration was to continue for some years and would lead to heavy settlement of French speakers in the region east and south of Highland, especially around Sevastopol, but also in the vicinity of Highland itself.

On September 6, 1848, "Papa" (as his son usually called him) traveled to St. Louis to welcome an influential French group led by Louis Rilliet de Constant of Geneva and Francis Vulliet from Vaud, a largely French-speaking canton north of Lake Geneva. Vulliet was the pastor of a Protestant sect and probably left Vaud as a result of religious persecution. Within a short time of his arrival in Highland, Reverend Vulliet began organizing a French Evangelical Church in Highland. Among its French-speaking congregation, the elder Bandelier was a founding member. Though he looked after the interests of the French-speaking settlers, Bandelier was also fully integrated into the German-speaking power structure.

Soon after his arrival in Highland in 1848, the elder Bandelier was made Swiss consul, his area embracing the Mississippi Valley to New Orleans and extending eastward to the Carolinas. Highland had experienced steady growth until 1849, but in that year its population, including many of the new arrivals, was severely hit by an epidemic of Asiatic cholera, a disease new to America. In 1848 and the following year, the disease reached virulent proportions, and it took a heavy toll in Highland. Ignorance of the cause of the disease made efforts to control it futile. A second outbreak occurred in July and August of 1852, though it was not as severe as the epidemic three years earlier. The 1850 census gave a population of five hundred for Highland. Had it not been for the epidemic, the number of inhabitants would have been considerably higher.

A French-speaking neighbor of Bandelier's, Susanne Etienette Mange, who in 1850 had settled with her husband and children on a farm about two miles north of the Bandelier property, had a number of dealings with Bandelier *père*. Following the death of her husband in 1852, Susanne turned to Bandelier as a sympathetic neighbor, as a fellow French speaker, and especially as a man of affairs. In a letter to her family in Switzerland, dated January 28, 1853, Susanne wrote, "I feel I should tell you something about Mr. Bandelier. He is a Swiss from Canton Bern, and he is Swiss consul here. He is always very courteous, and we feel free to interview him regarding even minor matters. . . . It is difficult to transact business here, unless one knows both German and French."

Through Susanne Mange's letters, we learn more about the elder Bandelier. He maintained an office in Highland but traveled a great deal. He handled Susanne Mange's will, mailed letters for her to Switzerland, and invested funds she received from Vaud at 10-percent interest. These investments were made by Bandelier personally; the F. Ryhiner and Company bank in which Bandelier was one of three partners was not formed until 1854.

Papa Bandelier, in addition to his farming activities (largely in the capacity of overseer) and his consular service, soon entered the business world in Highland. The Moritz Huegy family, farmers until 1848, moved into Highland that year, and Moritz opened a store. In a short time it became a shared enterprise with F. Ryhiner, Joseph Suppiger, and A. E. Bandelier. The nature and degree of involvement of each of the partners in clerking, providing capital, and so forth, are unknown.

Young Adolph Bandelier spent several years on the family farm. In his autobiographical statements to William G. Ritch, a former territorial governor of New Mexico, in 1882, Adolph spoke of working on the farm until 1854. In another interview, this time with the archaeologist George H. Pepper a quarter of a century later, he remarked that he spent five years in "ploughing, hoeing—and other pleasant work." Among other things, the Bandelier family cultivated grapes, their vineyard being one of the largest in the area.

Young Bandelier also attended public school under the tutelage of Miss Emily Thorp, who taught from 1850 to 1854. Probably he began or extended his knowledge of English there. In the Ritch biography, Bandelier is quoted as having stated that he was in school for only three months. Adolph also recalled private lessons "in 1853 & again at intervals in '55 and '56." It is possible that some of this schooling was given by Julius Hammer, who conducted private lessons in German, using the public school building. Hammer was said to have had more students than Miss Thorp.

Bandelier's major tutelage, however, was surely given by Timothy Gruaz, born in Lyons, France, in 1831, of Swiss parentage. Gruaz was educated at Lausanne and came to the United States in 1849, arriving in Highland after a short stay in Tennessee. He was quickly employed as a private tutor by the Bandelier, Huegy, and Ryhiner families jointly. In addition, Gruaz kept books for Bandelier, as Swiss consul, and generally aided him in his office.

Gruaz tutored not only young Bandelier and Maurice (Morris or Moritz) Huegy, his contemporary in age, but also Frederick Ryhiner, Jr., who was six years younger. He took trips with the youngsters as well. In a drawing book kept by Maurice Huegy, which is now in the historical collections of the Louis Latzer Memorial Library in Highland, there is a whimsical sketch of Gruaz, young Ryhiner, and Maurice Huegy—all in the posture of supplicants, sitting facing a split-rail fence with an audience of pigs. The caption said, "Out of cash and begged." At the bottom of the page was noted, "In Virginia, about 1860," and it was signed, "M. Huegy Artist." Although Adolph F. Bandelier does not seem to have been on this particular trip, he may well have been a part of earlier ones.

In the Ritch interview, Bandelier recalled that from 1854 he was "employed in mercantile pursuits & banking with his father." "Mercantile pursuits" probably had to do with the general store. The store building was eventually taken over by the F. Ryhiner and Company bank, which was founded on July 1, 1854, by father Bandelier with Dr. Frederick C. Ryhiner and Moritz Huegy. It is not clear why the bank carried only the name Ryhiner. Possibly the Ryhiner family had a majority interest, at least in the beginning.

Like the founding fathers of the previous decade, Papa Bandelier was much interested in promoting Highland abroad. In 1850, with three other recent emigrants, at least two of whom were fellow farmers, Bandelier published an informational pamphlet, *Brief aus Highland im Staate Illinois* (Letter from Highland in the State of Illinois). He was also interested in education, serving as school director of the Highland district from 1858 to 1860 and as the first president of the Highland Literary Association, founded in 1859. Father Bandelier was an organizer of the Highland French Evangelical Church, and he followed interests in music and biology. He was a skilled taxidermist and had stuffed and mounted animals in his home.

Although little has been said about it in the literature, there can be no doubt that young Bandelier's mother also had a significant influence on his intellectual development. With her earlier experience as a governess and tutor in Russia, she, too, was admirably equipped to contribute to her son's education in this small frontier community. Until her death in 1855, when Adolph F. was fifteen, the two spent much time together while father Adolphe was hard at work establishing himself in Highland.

Outside the family, there were other influences on young Adolph's intellectual development. The Bandeliers were friends of the highly educated Bernays family, and in the Ritch interview, Adolph mentioned that Dr. Jacob F. Bernays was his private tutor in mineralogy and chemistry. Indeed, young Bandelier had a number of educated and well-read individuals from whom to gather information. The brothers Jacob F. and George Bernays lived in Highland during his youthful years, and George, especially, already had gained a considerable scientific reputation before coming to the United States. Both brothers served as medical doctors, and Jacob was for a time also a druggist. Another brother, Bernard F., or "Lame," Bernays, a well-known art connoisseur, also came to Highland, as did a fourth brother, Charles L. Bernays. The latter was a lawyer, and he also opened a brewery in Highland. In the 1860s, Charles moved to St. Louis, where he became associate editor of Heinrich Boernstein's *Anzeiger des Westens* (Journal of the West), an outlet for some of Adolph F. Bandelier's publications after 1880.

Another intellectually active man who had considerable influence on young Bandelier was the chief owner of the Ryhiner bank. Frederick C. Ryhiner was born in Basel in 1806 and graduated from the University of Basel in 1829 with training in medicine. In Highland, he had a number of intellectual interests, and he joined the elder Bandelier as one of the founders of the Highland Literary Association.

In the fall of 1853, when Adolph was thirteen, a *Turnverein* provided another stimulus for the early physical and intellectual life of Highland. The "turners" were gymnastic organizations modeled after those that had become popular in nineteenth-century Switzerland. As was common in Europe, this *Turnverein* also had a strong intellectual component. In 1859, when Adolphe E. Bandelier, with several other influential members of the community, formed the Highland Library Association, the books were housed in the reading room of the Turner's Hall, with a bust of the great German scientist Alexander von Humboldt looking out over the room. It seems likely that young Adolph was interested in this Highland Gymnastic Society from the first. He was certainly a leading figure in its reorganization in 1866, after the society's inactivity during the Civil War years.

It is clear that young Bandelier had a rich intellectual life animated by urbane parents and family friends and associates who formed an unusually intellectual group, especially for a small frontier town. He clearly was not a disadvantaged youth. He was encouraged to read widely from an early age; in his interview with Governor Ritch, Bandelier said he began reading Humboldt at the age of eleven, three years after his arrival in Highland. Bandelier learned French, German, and English during these formative years; Latin and Spanish were to come somewhat later in life.

In 1854, at the age of fourteen, Adolph Bandelier entered into employment with the F. Ryhiner and Company bank and worked there for several years. He continued his studies, however, obtaining books from St. Louis. His sources included the St. Louis Mercantile Library, which by the 1860s had assembled important holdings in American history, particularly that of western America and Latin America.

A watershed in Bandelier's life was the death of his mother from unknown causes on February 10, 1855, a loss Adolph felt keenly. In later times he seldom mentioned his mother, but he made his feelings clear in a journal entry of December 18, 1881. On learning that his sponsor and mentor, Lewis Henry Morgan, had died the previous day, Bandelier wrote, "It is a stunning blow to me, and fairly the greatest loss since Mama's death."

In 1857, probably to renew his and seventeen-year-old Adolph's acquaintance with Switzerland and with various relatives and friends, Adolphe E. Bandelier took his son to Europe. Unfortunately, little is known of the trip. In 1858, not long after returning from Europe, young Adolph wrote his first published article, "Switzerland and the Swiss," which appeared in the February 23, 1858, issue of the St. Louis

Republican. The piece was a forerunner of an impressive bibliography extending through Bandelier's life and beyond his death in 1914.

The boy Adolph, at the age of eight, had come to a raw frontier town of fewer than five hundred people. By the time he reached young manhood at the beginning of the Civil War, the population stood at perhaps two thousand. Bandelier later spoke slightingly of the town, at one time referring to it as "this awful mudhole . . . physically as well as spiritually. The people, with few exceptions, are mere moles and salamanders."

But this statement was a gross exaggeration produced by some momentary pique. By the time he reached adulthood, Adolph F. Bandelier spoke and wrote several languages. In later life, he was a student of archaeology, ethnology, history, geography, botany, zoology, and meteorology. He knew his way around art galleries, and his tastes in art and literature were sophisticated and worldly. Obviously, his boyhood education had not been neglected. Highland and its people had provided him with an intellectual nurture that helps explain his rise in the next quarter-century to international scientific and scholarly prominence.

THREE
Years of Decision

Out of a sense of honor . . . I have assumed loads which
now almost bear me down.
  —Adolph F. Bandelier to Lewis H. Morgan, April 1877

IN THE YEAR 1860 the people of Highland, like other Americans
around the country, sensed that momentous events were in the making.
The national debate over slavery was coming to fever heat, fueled by the
question of slave policy in the developing West and by continuing re-
pressive, pro-slavery legislation on the part of the southern states.

In 1860, the newly formed Republican party chose for its presidential
candidate a middle-aged Illinois lawyer, Abraham Lincoln, who, although an ardent unionist, was not strongly anti-slavery. Southerners,
however, already considering secession, were profoundly mistrustful of
Lincoln.

One would expect that citizens of Highland, with the example of
such settlers as the visionary and liberal Koepfli and Suppiger families,
would be vigorously against slavery regardless of political affiliation.
Actually, Highland-area people do not seem to have presented an anti-
slavery front, although the presidential election of 1860 did see a majority for Lincoln. After the battle of Fort Sumter in April 1861, President
Lincoln called for volunteers, and a group of Highland citizens launched
an enlistment campaign. The community responded well; according to
later War Department documents, more than 250 Highland-area settlers
were involved in the war.

In the enrollment of males eligible for military service taken at the district provost marshal's headquarters at Alton, Illinois, on November 25, 1863, Adolph F. Bandelier, Moritz Huegy (misspelled Hueggy), and Frederick Ryhiner (misspelled Riehner) were all enrolled in Class 1. Actually, as a Swiss national, Bandelier was exempt from the military. In any event, none of the three sons of the F. Ryhiner and Company bank owners served in the armed forces.

There is no real clue to how the Bandelier family felt about slavery and about service to the United States during the Civil War. Although Papa Bandelier, while in Brazil in 1847, had paid lip service to the evils of slavery—as would have been expected of him by his Swiss correspondents—and although he opted to leave Brazil and move on to the United States, he remained ambivalent regarding slavery. "Select from around you," he once wrote, "anything that included the greatest amount of stupidity, lack of thought and mental activity, assembles the greatest amount of craftiness, and a monkey-like craftiness at that . . . [and] you will have a troop of good Negroes. Their excessive laziness seems to explain Providence's views in tolerating slavery."

With such an attitude, not greatly different from that of southern slaveholders, the elder Bandelier, one might expect, would have been at least indifferent to the moral issue of slavery. Whatever their personal attitudes on slavery and secession, the Bandeliers, father and son, seem to have remained aloof from the Civil War and its philosophical and emotional issues. One gets the feeling that the two Bandeliers, still strongly Europe oriented, wanted to avoid what they saw as a purely American conflict. Young Adolph was a citizen of Switzerland, and though the elder Bandelier had filed a naturalization declaration in 1848, there is no evidence that he ever took further action in the matter.

About the beginning of the Civil War, perhaps in 1860, Paul Emil Bandelier, son of Adolphe E. Bandelier's older brother, Gustave Amedee, with his wife, Rosalie, emigrated to Illinois. The first child of this couple, Elizabeth (Elise, Lizzie) Caroline, was born in Highland on June 23, 1861. A second child, Gustave Adolph, and a second daughter, Emma, arrived after the family moved to nearby Breese, Illinois. The life of Lizzie Bandelier, especially, intertwined with the lives of Adolph F. Bandelier and his wife, Josephine.

It was sometime after the arrival of Emil and Rosalie in Illinois that Adolph F. Bandelier took a bride, Maria Josepha Huegy. At some point, Josepha's name was Anglicized to Josephine, and her husband usually called her "Joe." She was almost four years older than Adolph, and in a community the size of Highland, it would seem that she might have had no difficulty in finding a husband in a more conventional age group. Her marriage to Adolph suggests a "dynastic" union between two prominent families already interlocked in business and commercial affairs.

What kind of person was Josephine Bandelier? Of the women in Bandelier's life, Joe remains the most enigmatic. Her name appears over and over again in Bandelier's journals and letters, and he documented her activities in intimate and loving detail. In spite of such attention, no rounded picture of Joe emerges. For one thing, virtually none of her own writings exist; no diary of Joe's has ever been discovered, and although she wrote many letters, few have been preserved. Unlike the vivacious and opinionated Fanny, Bandelier's second wife, Joe did not flaunt her views and indeed seems to have been a very private person.

The earliest photographs of Joe show an attractive but rather placid young woman, her dark hair severely bound and her face expressionless—even beyond the degree demanded by the "blank stare" fashion of nineteenth-century portrait photography. Joe seems to have been fair of skin with light eyes, and relatively slight in stature. Later photographs show little change other than that of aging.

What did her husband make of Joe? In spite of his numerous statements of affection, there are relatively few revelations of Bandelier's basic view of his wife. In a journal entry of January 5, 1883, while he was in the field in New Mexico, Adolph wrote, "It is our wedding night, the twenty-second, and a memorial [memorable?] one. Oh my God, it is only now that I begin to love her, as should have been the case years ago, and find out how great a treasure she is to me. And so far, far away from her."

Solicitude for Joe formed a strong leitmotif in Bandelier's relations with his wife. Repeatedly he used three adjectives in mentioning Joe: "poor," "dear," and "good," especially the first two, often in combination.

We have only glimpses of Josephine Bandelier through eyes other than her husband's. In 1868, in a letter to an old friend in Switzerland, Albert Haller–von Greyerz, pastor of the cathedral in Bern, Papa Bandelier referred to the cheering and spirit-enriching effect the recent trip to Bern had had on his "shy daughter." In the same letter, he described how Joe was able to hitch up the sleigh after a snowstorm and go out to the family farm. Before leaving, she had directed her father-in-law to say that she would like to send "a couple of Bratworst, a Zurich

Bundle, and some butchered meat to the pastor's wife . . . if it were only possible."

Though the overall impression of Joe is one of docility, she could be firm. Adolph jokingly described to his mentor, Lewis Henry Morgan, Joe's insistence on his attending church on Christmas Day, 1879. The account contained a rare, alas incomplete, description of Joe: "'Now Adolph you must!' and there is a marked impression on the floor by a very small energetic foot, a certain well-known bonnet is put on a particular head with conspicuous and formidable looking little puffs of hair."

In a letter to Morgan about two weeks before the Christmas incident, Bandelier referred to his recent visit to Rochester. He sent special greetings to Annie, the Irish maid, and, tongue in cheek, assured Morgan that Joe was jealous of Annie.

Some years later, we find an interesting, somewhat slanted picture of Joe in comments by Charles Lummis's second wife, Eva, who knew the Bandeliers socially in Santa Fe around 1890. According to Eva, "[Bandelier's] wife was the domestic type, an excellent housekeeper. Dinner at their home in Santa Fe was something to remember. However, Bandelier longed for more intellectual companionship and was easily dazzled by brilliant women."

Adolph and Joe were married on January 5, 1861. In the county court records at Edwardsville, the marriage was listed as "Adolphus Alphonse Bandalier to Josephine Hugy," the registrar managing to misspell both surnames. The two were married in Highland by the local justice of the peace, "Squire"Adolph Glock. It is not clear why Adolph and Josephine were married by a justice of the peace. Perhaps Glock was a close family friend chosen as a compromise because Adolph and Joe belonged to different Protestant churches. It is highly probable that Glock knew both the Bandelier and Huegy families well.

There is no hint that Adolph and Joe took a honeymoon trip. At any rate, a year after their marriage the couple set up housekeeping in a home across from the Ryhiner bank on Troxler Street in Highland. It would remain the Bandelier town house for more than twenty years. There are indications that Papa Bandelier also lived in this house when not on the farm, and there is no doubt that Adolph and Joe spent some of their time at the farm. So the farm and the Troxler Street house formed the axis of Bandelier family life until the dramatic events surrounding the bank failure in May 1885.

With the end of the Civil War, Highland experienced something of a boom. In June 1868, the St. Louis, Vandalia, and Terre Haute Railroad reached the town. Construction of the railroad was accompanied by an extensive building campaign, and the decade following the war represented perhaps the single greatest period in Highland's growth. The Bandeliers entered enthusiastically into this new phase of expansion. Young Adolph was one of the reorganizers of the *Turnverein* in 1866 and was the principal speaker at the dedication of the new Turner's Hall in 1869. The elder Bandelier was the main founder of the Highland Agricultural Society, also in 1869. The two Bandeliers were active in the *Schuetzenbund,* the Shooting Society or Gun Club. The senior Bandelier was national vice-president of this organization for a time just after the Civil War, and young Adolph was secretary of the local rifle club in 1865. At a national *Schuetzenfest* held in Highland in June 1865, A. E. Bandelier gave the welcoming address and A. F. Bandelier offered one of the toasts.

During the same period, Adolph and Joe went to Europe for what amounted to a belated honeymoon, perhaps in relation to the international *Schuetzenbund* movement. The trip may also have been intended to further Adolph's education, but if so, nothing seems to have come of it. From Switzerland has come one of the very few surviving examples of Josephine Bandelier's handwriting, a pressed flower album with notations in German script. It contains very little information, however. By consulting the book, one is able to trace Joe's movements from August 10 through August 23, 1867. Her travels during these two weeks seem mainly to have been visits to ancestral homes. For example, she collected flowers from her maternal grandmother's grave at Sursee in Lucerne on August 18. Her travels on this occasion were to the north-central cantons of Uri, Schwyz, and Lucerne, the last being the home canton of both her father's and mother's families.

In 1868, Bandelier began a series of local meteorological and climatic observations. In 1869 and again in 1871, he was engaged in a series of scholarly lectures at the Turners' Hall in Highland. During this period Bandelier also lectured in St. Louis, and he gradually came into contact with members of the St. Louis scientific community. His interest in meteorology also led to an eleven-year (1860–71) study of the aurora borealis. According to the 1874 annual report of the Smithsonian Institution, Bandelier was a meteorological recorder for the years 1860–64. A

Smithsonian report during the time of Bandelier's observations stated that "Adolphus F. Bandelier used the barometer, thermometer, and psychrometer" in his climatological studies.

Although the 1860s saw Bandelier becoming increasingly interested in science and increasingly less enthusiastic about business, he did begin two business ventures around 1870. In the spring of that year, Adolph and a young friend, Charles H. Seybt, joined in operating the "Confidence Coal and Mining Company," two and a half miles northeast of Collinsville, on the line of the Vandalia Railroad. Around the same time, Bandelier became involved, again with Seybt, in a foundry called the Highland Mechanical Works. In the long run, both ventures proved to be losing propositions.

It is clear that from the late 1860s onward, Adolph, though continuing to be part of the business and financial world of Highland, had decided in his own mind to dedicate his life to scholarly pursuits. According to a statement to ex-governor Ritch of New Mexico in an 1882 interview, Bandelier began a study of Mexican high culture in 1869.

By that time, Bandelier was certainly *au fait* with the collections of scholarly materials in the St. Louis area, especially those in the Mercantile Library with its strong holdings in western Americana, Latin America history, and archival sources. Founded in 1846, this institution continues to the present day as one of the very few subscription libraries in the United States.

In a much later interview with George H. Pepper in the early 1900s, Bandelier mentioned that while at the Mercantile, he had copied parts of the great collection of Mexican codices and early manuscripts published by Lord Edward Kingsborough in nine massive volumes (1830–48). Obviously the young man was expanding his horizons during those years. It was also during this period that Adolph began to study Spanish, a language he was to use a great deal in years to come.

Over the past half-century there has been considerable discussion regarding Bandelier's linguistic abilities. From his boyhood in Switzerland and from his later years in the multilanguage milieu of Highland, Bandelier clearly was conditioned to use several languages. There have been questions, however, about the level of his mastery of them. Two statements by Bandelier himself are helpful. In an 1881 letter to Francis Parkman, Adolph wrote, "My English is poor but I can scarcely avoid its being so. The constant necessity of thinking reading and writing in four

Adolphe Eugene Bandelier, father of Adolph F. Bandelier. (Museum of New Mexico, neg. 9140.)

Adolph F. Bandelier as a young man. (Museum of New Mexico, neg. 9111.)

Bandelier family group, Switzerland, about 1867. Adolph stands at upper left; Josephine Huegy Bandelier, his first wife, is seated in front of him. Others in the group have not been identified. (Museum of New Mexico, neg. 9166.)

Lewis Henry Morgan (1818–1881). Morgan was a major influence in Bandelier's life. (Museum of New Mexico, neg. 9170.)

languages is not conductive to perfection in any single one.—I feel that, while the Spanish naturally rises [improves], the English, French, and German at least remain stationary."

Some years later, in 1887, Bandelier was preparing a long manuscript in French on the early colonization and missionization of the Southwest. He commented in a letter to Charles E. Norton of the Archaeological Institute of America: "In six weeks I shall be through with the Papal work. Then I shall only have to write english, and that is easy. French is a horrid language to write in, owing to grammar and syntax.—I prefer german, spanish, and english—most decidedly to french: notwithstanding the latter is my native tongue."

It is clear that by the early 1880s, Bandelier could use not only his three childhood languages but Spanish as well. He made good use of these abilities in preparing himself for the great intellectual adventures of the decades to come. By the time Bandelier actually went to Latin America—the greater Southwest, Mexico, and western South America—he had already worked through much of the literature in several languages. As his research efforts intensified, he began to seek source materials and interaction with colleagues outside Highland. Important among these associates were Emil Preetorius of the *Westliche Post* in St. Louis, the famous St. Louis botanist and physician George Engelmann and his son, George J., a physician and ethnologist, and Gustav Bruhl of Cincinnati, a physician, writer, and newspaper editor who had a lifelong interest in Latin America and also in American archaeology.

It was the year 1873, however, that saw Bandelier's first contact with the anthropologist who was to have such a powerful influence on his developing career. The circumstances of Bandelier's first meeting with Lewis Henry Morgan are obscure. It happened while Bandelier was on a trip to the East Coast, in the course of which Adolph visited Rochester, New York, Morgan's home town. There, he was introduced to Morgan by the president of the University of Rochester, the Reverend Dr. M. B. Anderson. Morgan's own illustrious career had begun well before 1873. By that time, he had published widely in anthropology, his works including *League of the Ho-de-no-sau-nee or Iroquois* (1851), *Laws of Descent of the Iroquois* (1857), and the world-famous work on comparative kinship, *Systems of Consanguinity and Affinity of the Human Family* (1871).

The acquaintance between Bandelier and Morgan developed into a genuine friendship. The two men corresponded frequently, and numerous letters have survived, dating from 1873 to the time of Morgan's death in 1881. Almost all of them, however, are from Bandelier to Morgan. Bandelier's first letter discussed the literary works of the Spanish conquerors, priests, and chroniclers, as well as the Indian cultures described by these early writers. Although the relationship between the two men was of great benefit to Adolph, it was also of direct interest to Morgan, who could expand his sampling of world ethnology with the help of Bandelier's linguistic abilities, especially in terms of the Mexican tribes and source materials in Spanish.

Morgan had already formulated certain fundamental ideas about the level of development of American Indian, especially Mexican Indian, cultures. He divided governmental systems into two distinct forms. The first, based on individual persons and personal relationships, he designated "societies," whereas the second, founded on territory and property, he termed "states." These divisions are somewhat like the divisions defined by some modern anthropologists as "band," "tribe," and "chiefdom," as against "state." In Morgan's mind, no American Indian culture had ever advanced to being a state.

Around the time he first met Bandelier, Morgan was working on a more general theory of cultural evolution in which the various social groups in the modern world represented way stations—"social fossils," as it were—of a unilinear evolution involving all mankind. Morgan's idea rested on three developmental stages—savagery, barbarism, and civilization. Each stage was more advanced than its predecessor, and more advanced in *every field of human endeavor*—language, religion, political and social organization, technology, art, and so forth. Given the right conditions and enough time, every group of humans would presumably work its way through savagery and barbarism to reach civilization. By the nineteenth century, however, only Europeans and, to a lesser degree, certain Asians had reached this civilized stage. This Social Darwinism made good sense to the colonizing European powers of the time, because it gave an intellectual underpinning to colonialism with its assumption that Europeans were culturally and racially superior to the rest of the world. It made Morgan internationally famous as the champion of the unilinear evolutionary school.

Today, it is clear that Morgan and the other evolutionists could make a valid case only for technology and, to some degree, political organization—things tied to population density and an increase in the "carrying capacity" of a given resource area. Language and religion seem to be about equally evolved in all cultures. Modern social and behavioral scientists have essentially discarded unilinear evolutionism. Indeed, even in Morgan's day a few advanced thinkers were challenging the evolutionary model of human culture and history.

Bandelier was hardly an advanced thinker, but he had been trained in a different school, strangely enough combining a "romantic" approach with a factual approach to history. At first he believed that the advanced cultures of South and Middle America (Incas, Aztecs, Mayas, etc.) were formed into "states" or, in the case of the Incas, an empire (a point that seems self-evident to modern scholars). But for all that, Bandelier yielded to Morgan at almost every point.

The conversion was a gradual one as Adolph sought to learn and Morgan, in turn, sought to teach and persuade his "disciple" (Bandelier's term) to accept the evolutionary interpretations. By degrees, Adolph became a strong champion of Morgan's views before the world, though it seems unlikely that he fully understood these views. Bandelier had a fact-oriented mind; theory was generally beyond his ken. Following Morgan's death, at any rate, very little was heard from Bandelier about evolutionism.

One of Adolph's early interests centered on a manuscript he had found at the Mercantile Library in St. Louis. This was the *Crónica Mexicana,* written by the native Nahuatl- (Aztec-) speaking Hernando de Alvarado Tezozomoc in 1598 and published as part of Lord Kingsborough's *Antiquities of Mexico.* In June 1874, Bandelier had written to Morgan that Tezozomoc's chronicle might prove to be the most valuable document published on the aboriginal institutions of Mexico. By the end of 1874, Bandelier claimed to have finished an English translation of this massive volume. It was never published, however, and the manuscript has never been found.

Bandelier's first letter to the great Mexican historian and bibliographer don Joaquín García Icazbalceta (1825–94), was written in Spanish on September 18, 1875, and it largely concerned the Tezozomoc work. This was the beginning of an extended contact. The two men eventually met in Mexico in 1881, and they became intimately connected, corresponding until 1891.

In 1877, Bandelier published his first major work, "On the Art of War and Mode of Warfare of the Ancient Mexicans." His correspondence with both Morgan and García Icazbalceta was now intense. From the latter man, Bandelier asked guidance in finding new material relating to problems in reconstructing the culture history of Latin America. Around the same time, Adolph made another professional contact in Wendell Phillips Garrison, literary editor of *The Nation* and a friend of Morgan's. In the years after 1877, Garrison requested numerous book reviews from Bandelier for publication in *The Nation*.

On August 31, 1877, Joe's mother, Josephine Suppiger Huegy, died after an agonizing illness. Adolph mentioned the family's loss in a letter to Morgan. Bandelier, considering Mrs. Huegy "a true mother," clearly mourned her death.

It was about this time in 1877, and possibly as a direct consequence of Mrs. Huegy's death, that Maurice Huegy, Jr., her son and Joe's brother, joined the F. Ryhiner and Company bank. Maurice's father, Moritz, Sr., had died in 1862, the first of the three original partners to pass away.

Later, in the fall of 1877, Bandelier sent Morgan a second paper on the ancient Mexicans, "On the Distribution and Tenure of Lands, and the Customs with Respect to Inheritance, among the Ancient Mexicans." With the paper came the request that if Morgan approved of it, he should send it on to F. W. Putnam at the Peabody Museum in Cambridge, Massachusetts. The paper appeared the following year in a Peabody Museum publication. Adolph's final letter for 1877, written on December 28, was a brief note acknowledging that "it has been such a heavy, sorrowful year, but I thank God for every minute of it, nevertheless." Season's greetings were also extended to Morgan and his family from the three Bandeliers—Papa, Josephine, and Adolph.

Just a week later, on January 4, 1878, Bandelier announced to Morgan that "due to actual overexertion, I am compelled to lay aside scientific work in the shape of *production* for a few weeks, and must confine myself exclusively to reading at night." Adolph meant to make abstracts from books he did not own. In addition, he wrote that his partner in the coal business, Charles H. Seybt, was going to Europe accompanied by "one of my partners in the bank." This is a curious statement. Seven years later, the Ryhiner bank was to collapse, with tragic consequences for the Bandelier family, and evidence at that time makes it questionable whether Adolph was ever a partner in the Ryhiner bank. Seemingly, he was using the term "partner" in a very general way.

In late January, Adolph was back to his former full schedule, though his collapse a few weeks before hinted of more serious health problems to come. In the midst of his activities, Bandelier's thoughts moved ahead to the approaching meeting of the American Association for the Advancement of Science, which was to convene in St. Louis in August. He wanted to prepare a paper to present there, and he sought Morgan's advice on a suitable topic, eventually settling on "The Sources of Aboriginal History of Spanish America." This paper appeared later, with a slightly changed title, in the *Proceedings* of the AAAS (1879). Also in 1878, Morgan made a trip to the southwestern United States to look at archaeological ruins, returning in time for the St. Louis AAAS meetings. This trip of Morgan's drew Bandelier's attention to the Southwest and was certainly a factor in Adolph's 1880 contract with the Archaeological Institute of America for southwestern fieldwork. It was during this same time that Bandelier gained access to the important holdings of the Lenox Library in New York City.

The year 1879 saw a continuing stream of letters to Morgan. Matters of health and weather, business affairs and problems, evaluations of early source materials—along with various possible interpretations of these data and progress in the writing of manuscripts—were all discussed. Bandelier sometimes had as many as eight projects at a time that he outlined to Morgan. On December 26, 1879, Adolph wrote to Morgan, "Christmas is over, happily, and I am still alive. We are having it cold out here, with a very light snow on the ground, and much sleet beneath it which of course makes very bad walking. There have been a number of accidents caused by the ice and cold, such as broken and sprained limbs, and yesterday a man was found in the streets frozen to death."

But Bandelier's mind was not really on local events, no matter how calamitous. He discussed scholarly matters, especially the misconceptions (that is, anti-Morgan views) of certain authors about the Aztec empire. It is clear that in these final days of 1879, Adolph Bandelier's mind was still fixed on Aztec society and the ramifications of Morgan's new work, *Ancient Society,* as it applied to Native American high culture. The seeds of Bandelier's long southwestern adventure were planted but had not yet germinated. The next year, 1880, would see their striking and sudden fruition.

FOUR
The AIA Connection

... a gentleman well versed in American antiquities and
thoroughly acquainted with the authors on the subject.
—J. W. Powell, July 1880

I N A LETTER to Morgan dated December 24, 1879, Bandelier
noted that "the year 1880 is close at hand" and added the hope "that the
next ten years may be more propitious than the past decennial period
has been, at least for me." As he penned this letter, Bandelier could
hardly have been aware of stirrings in the Boston area that would, within
the next few months, bear directly on his life.

Perhaps stimulated by recent American centennial observances, a
group of twelve men had come together informally in Boston and
Cambridge in the spring of 1879 to draft a circular designed to tap possible interest in forming a "Society for Archaeological Research." Dated
April 14, 1879, it requested a favorable response "before April 21."

In the course of that week, one hundred and eight people expressed
their readiness to join the proposed society, and a meeting was scheduled
for May 10, 1879. The meeting was presided over by Charles Eliot
Norton, professor of the history of art at Harvard University and one of
the original promoters of the idea.

Norton, the first speaker, concentrated his remarks on the need he saw
for increased activity in Classical studies in Greece, Egypt, and other parts
of the eastern Mediterranean. Francis Parkman, the eminent historian,
spoke next, saying that he "had supposed the main purpose of the Society
would be to promote the study of American Archaeology." He supported

Norton's views but at the same time "hoped the Society would at least at some future time turn its attention to American Archaeology." Another speaker, the anthropologist Frederic Ward Putnam, director of Harvard's Peabody Museum of American Archaeology and Ethnology, seconded Parkman's advocacy of American investigations.

A week later, on May 17, 1879, the Archaeological Institute of America (AIA) was founded. Charles E. Norton was elected president, and a seven-member executive committee included both Norton and Parkman. This guiding committee was given full power to determine the work to be undertaken and the mode of its accomplishment, to employ agents, and to expend funds, but not to incur any debt on behalf of the AIA. The group then allotted money for work in the eastern Mediterranean and began to consider funding a study in American archaeology.

By early 1880, the committee was giving serious thought to the American project. Parkman pointed out that it was important to find the right man for the job and "that it was not desirable to have a new hand." He believed Putnam was the only man in the country able to do the work—could not Putnam be employed? Putnam could not, of course, in view of his position with the Peabody Museum, and the AIA continued its quest for a proper person.

In elaborating on the "right man," Parkman had recommended a "daring young fellow" in his twenties who would "go out alone and live long enough on the spot to study the principles of relationship and inheritance and the communistic institutions of the society still existing." It was an interesting foreshadowing of the participant observer approach that was to be so important to later anthropologists and that, indeed, was being put to use by people like Frank Hamilton Cushing at Zuni Pueblo, New Mexico, at about that very moment.

At this early date, the AIA was still thinking in terms of generalities. For example, it decided that Norton should correspond with the Bureau of Ethnology (later the Bureau of American Ethnology of the Smithsonian Institution) in Washington, D.C., and with officers of the United States Army and others, in order to learn what aid and cooperation might be expected from persons already in the field. Recognizing their lack of familiarity with the general field of North American archaeology, the executive committee also decided to ask Lewis Henry Morgan for a scheme of procedure to follow.

The committee next convened on January 17, 1880, to receive a communication from Morgan, who had responded to Norton's letter of inquiry. Morgan suggested archaeological work that the AIA could carry out in the Southwest during the coming spring and summer, and Norton endorsed Morgan's ideas, adding that "the work indicated by him could be done presently, before railroads have made too many changes in the manners and customs of the native tribes."

This comment by Norton is of particular interest in light of twentieth-century efforts to interrelate archaeological findings with ethnographic data. Both Norton and Morgan, as well as Parkman, were thinking well ahead of their day along these lines. The railroad construction would have an obvious impact on living tribes but virtually none on archaeological remains, except for the few that happened to lie in the roadbeds and rights-of-way.

Another interesting point in these early AIA discussions is that Norton, Morgan, and Parkman all seem to have understood clearly the importance of correlating archaeology and ethnology in an area where modern Indians had roots going back many centuries. Bandelier, too, in later field investigations, embraced the concept of a seamless cloth of culture that extended from the present back through history into prehistory. His eyes may well have been opened by these men.

Meanwhile, in the first weeks of 1880, Bandelier was still unable to decide once and for all whether to leave the business world and commit himself entirely to a scholarly, scientific career. This agonizing indecision only exacerbated his chronic health problems, which may have involved what today would be called clinical depression. Two letters written by Bandelier's young cousin, Lizzie, Emil Bandelier's daughter, have survived from this period. At this time, "Uncle" Adolph and "Aunt" Josephine seem to have been acting in loco parentis to Lizzie, and the teenager wrote Morgan on January 28 that Uncle Adolph was sick with "nervous prostration."

Only four days after Lizzie's note, Bandelier felt strong enough to write Morgan himself. It was a plea for help, and Adolph stressed that he and Joe *must* leave Highland for a year or more. This letter seems to have crossed with one sent by Morgan on January 31. Morgan suggested a period in the field in the Southwest for himself and Bandelier jointly. Unless he was actually replying to Lizzie's letter—which would indicate a faster mail from Highland to Rochester than is usual today—then it appears that Morgan had already given a great deal of thought to Bandelier's leaving Highland.

Whatever the case, Lizzie answered for her ailing kinsman.

Uncle *has received* your favor of the 31st, and he at once thankfully accepts your offer. Our physician, papa, aunt—they are all of the opinion that it is the very best thing for him. He will be glad to go along with you and assist you all he can. Uncle adds that . . . expenses paid ought to be secured and if possible some compansasian [*sic*] for the outfit, but the latter he leaves to you. He would also call your attention to the advisability of taking [a] photographer along.

Lizzie closed on a rather disheartened note: "Uncle has had a relapse since Sunday."

Relapse or not, Bandelier wrote on February 5 full of glowing excitement about the prospect of two years of joint research with Morgan. It is obvious that Bandelier had caught the Southwest fever. He advised Morgan that he was prepared to visit the southwestern pueblos with Morgan during the first portion of the two-year visit. He suggested that "once our work [is] done at the pueblos, I continue the trip . . . to the 'Casas Grandes'—Chihuahua . . . and finally to Michhuacan [*sic*]."

How seriously Morgan took this ambitious field project is unknown, nor is it obvious just what part he planned to play in the venture. Judging from Bandelier's February 5 letter, it would seem that the AIA was to foot the bill for the joint research. Only two or three weeks later, however, Morgan was negotiating with the AIA on Bandelier's behalf while making no mention of himself. Morgan may have considered the dual research project simply as a backup plan, in the event the AIA would not accept Bandelier's working alone. As it happened, Morgan never visited the Southwest again. Four years later, Bandelier, under the auspices of the AIA, did get to Casas Grandes after a horseback trip through northern Sonora, but he never set foot in the western Mexican state of Michoacán.

In the minutes of an AIA executive committee meeting on February 28, 1880, there appears the first mention of Bandelier. Morgan had proposed his name for work in the Southwest, and Norton was cautiously supportive, speaking of Bandelier as a leading student of Spanish America who had already published two highly regarded papers.

In promoting the idea of work in "New Mexico and that vicinity," where Norton foresaw the displacement of the native people by the whites, he made the observation that "if we miss this opportunity now we shall never have it again." This comment had been preceded by the unsophisticated opinion that "no additional sites would probably be found in the Ohio valley and nothing but pottery, of which so much had already been found."

The AIA continued to waffle; some influential members felt that studying the "barbarous" American Indians was a waste of time and money. To complicate things further, a countermove was afoot to arrange for Bandelier to join the Lorillard-Charnay expedition in Mexico. As it turned out, Bandelier did go to Mexico in 1881.

Bandelier wrote a number of letters to Morgan in March 1880. Perhaps the most significant of them again expressed appreciation for Morgan's encouragement and also informed the Rochester scholar that Papa Bandelier had finally realized that business was not Adolph's vocation. In fact, Adolph was very much looking forward to a new career.

The next paragraph revealed Bandelier's long-range goal: "I am . . . strongly in favor of going directly from New Mexico down to the city of Mexico on horseback." He explained that with his experience among the Pueblo Indians of New Mexico, and after becoming familiar with their mode of life, his next task would be to go among the Indians of Mexico, enough of whom were still left, and "do likewise." "It is no pleasant task, but I am ready for it."

Bandelier's final paragraph dramatically suggested his own religious inclinations and foreshadowed some basic decisions in his future life. It also announced his intention

> to make my principal object, the records of the clergy [which] must be carefully searched. It requires particular facilities for that purpose, which I am now securing. Of course, it will be a merely personal matter, and will not involve you nor anybody else into any obligation towards, or [in] connection with, the Catholic church. I shall obtain a letter of introduction to the bishop of Santa Fe, and a circular letter of recommendation from our bishop to all priests, requesting them to facilitate my researches by free communication of books and papers.

This curiously cautious approach was surely because Adolph knew of Morgan's strong anti-Catholicism. Bandelier's own attraction to the

Catholic church remained a close secret for the next two years, as Papa Bandelier was also very much against Catholicism. Morgan, who died in late 1881, was never to know.

AIA planning proceeded slowly. On March 17, 1880, Morgan, perhaps trying to needle the AIA into confirming his protégé, suggested to the executive committee that Bandelier be sent to the Southwest with a salary of $500 a year plus $1,000 for expenses. In the later part of April, the committee met again to discuss various programs. After reporting on his correspondence with Morgan, Norton announced that he was prepared to propose, at the annual meeting in May, an appropriation of $3,500 to $4,000 for an expedition to Colorado and New Mexico—"for this the autumn was the proper time, the summer too hot." The impression that southwestern summers were unbearably hot seems to have been common, especially in the eastern United States, and it is a belief still rather widely held. AIA members who had visited the Southwest apparently made no attempt to explain to Norton that the dry heat of a southwestern summer was much easier to endure than the stifling misery of a moisture-laden heat wave in Boston, New York, or Washington, D.C.

Meanwhile, Bandelier and Morgan had exchanged further correspondence; a letter from Adolph on April 15 closed with these words:

> Lastly, it becomes clearer & clearer to me that if the history of aborigines in Spanish America rests on a frail and unsatisfactory basis, this is not at all due to any lack of material honestly collected and preserved by the Spaniards themselves, but much rather to the careless and superficial study of these Spanish sources by modern compilers [*sic*] or so-called historians. One of the very worst of all is Mr. H. H. Bancroft, as evidenced among others by his notice of Itza in vol. IV, p. 133.

On May 15, 1880, the second annual meeting of the AIA convened, with twenty-six members present. Again, the issue of Old World versus New World research surfaced. Several members questioned the value of gaining knowledge simply to satisfy curiosity. The study of Indians, "barbarians," was admittedly of some interest but was essentially absurd when compared with studies of more advanced cultures. When Parkman replied on behalf of the executive committee, one AIA member, Harvey D. Parker, challenged him from the floor. According to Parker, the very writings of Parkman demonstrated that the Indians were low on the scale of civilization. He concluded with the comment, "If we possessed all the pottery ware, kitchen utensils and tomahawks which they had made, it would be no better for us."

Parkman rebutted this classic bit of know-nothingism, stressing the value of acquiring knowledge, not objects of art. The heavy emphasis already placed on the Eastern Hemisphere made it the AIA's duty to undertake work in America. It was not a matter of the one or the other, but rather of concentrating on "this side of the water." Then Parkman made his crucial point:

> The speaker failed to comprehend the bearing of Ethnological investigation; potteryware, etc. were interesting in themselves and simply that, but the study of tribes involves questions of the greatest importance, the evolution of the human race, its civilization and many questions of the greatest interest—it was by no means a matter of such small interest as had been represented.

This argument shows with great clarity the stranglehold that evolutionism had on the intellectual minds of the late nineteenth century. What Parkman was actually saying was that American Indians, in this case southwesterners, were living fossils whose societies could tell Mr. Parker and the other AIA members something about the evolution of European societies thousands of years ago.

Parkman's evolutionary position also reflected the temporal vacuum in which the antiquarian archaeologists of Bandelier's day operated, at least in situations where they had no historical data to apply. Except for historical documentation, none of today's absolute dating techniques—dendrochronology, carbon 14, and archaeomagnetism, among others—were known in Bandelier's time. When Bandelier approached Pecos, for example, his first archaeological project in the Southwest, he had historical information that told him the pueblo existed in 1540 and was deserted in the early nineteenth century. What he did not have was any means of projecting Pecos's culture into prehistoric times—beyond assumptions that ignored the reality of cultural change.

Bandelier, indeed, was deficient in archaeological methodology even for his own time. In the 1880s, the idea of using pottery types found in stratified archaeological sites as a mechanism for *relative* dating was just coming into vogue. Although this ceramic dating technique became more secure and sophisticated during Bandelier's time, he never really understood or used it. Occasionally he tried to date structures according to their complexity, using evolutionary ideas that often led him to erroneous conclusions. He seems also to have had no clue about the antiquity of various American cultures. Modern concepts like *Archaic* or *Paleoindian* would have meant nothing to Bandelier, who lacked a grasp of historical geology, at least as it applied to the New World. It is not clear even how Bandelier stood on the landmark questions of his day— biological evolution and geological uniformitarianism. One wonders whether Bandelier perhaps had religious objections to these ideas so central to modern biological and geological sciences.

Bandelier did understand the concept of ethnographic analogy. He also understood and searched for evidence of cultural continuity, linking prehistoric remains with existing cultures or associating archaeological data with ethnographic material. *The Delight Makers,* his 1890 novel about the late prehistoric Keresan and Tewa Indians of the Frijoles Canyon area in New Mexico, drew from later, historical data to create a rich cultural description projected back into the past. Still, the lack of chronology meant that Bandelier was never able to sort out the changes that took place even in conservative, traditional Pueblo Indian life. Had he placed *The Delight Makers* at A.D. 450 rather than at A.D. 1450, he likely would have used the same ethnographic data to paint the same picture of Keres and Tewa life, even though most or all of the ceremonialism he described would have lain several hundred years in the future, and Keresan and Tewa speakers did not even live in the Frijoles Canyon region at such an early time.

Bandelier did have a few insights that make him seem rather modern. He was one of the first scholars to use a holistic approach to archaeology, applying botanical, historical, geographical, linguistic, and zoological data to archaeological interpretations; it was the poor quality of such data in his day and the lack of precise dating methods that betrayed him. In addition, Bandelier pioneered the idea that there were important archaeological connections between the Southwest and Mesoamerica.

Francis Parkman was not alone in defending American archaeology against those who advocated Old World studies—"where civilization was superior to ours rather than inferior"—during the annual meeting of the AIA in 1880. Some two weeks earlier, J. W. Powell, director of the Bureau of Ethnology, had been invited to attend the meeting to add his expertise to the deliberations. In a lecture, Powell urged the society to become involved in American archaeology: "There is scarcely a county in the United States which is not of archaeological interest. Besides the 29 [occupied] pueblos there are some 3000 or 4000 ruins yet to be explored, cliff dwellings and communal lodges."

Powell had also been asked about Bandelier's qualifications to undertake the southwestern work. His letter endorsing Bandelier was presented to the society; it became a basic ingredient in Bandelier's ultimate appointment by the AIA.

Meanwhile, Adolph continued to fret and wonder why the AIA was delaying its decision. On May 16 he had written Morgan, assuring him that Papa and Josephine were "fully resigned to part with my precious self. They even express the hope that, after a few years of hardtack, I may come home a wiser and better man."

In another, longer letter, Bandelier proceeded to "unburden his soul" to Morgan. In essence, he begged that the AIA send out an expedition, even one person (ideally, but not necessarily, Bandelier himself) on a very restricted budget. His lengthy commentary revealed a remarkable understanding of the scientific and logistical problems and the potential benefits of such an expedition—remarkable especially when one remembers that as of the early summer of 1880, Adolph had not been farther west than St. Louis, Missouri. But the appointment still was not made at the May meeting, and Adolph, understandably, grew perplexed and impatient.

By mid-June, however, his situation had suddenly moved ahead—"at long last!" Following a visit by Bandelier to Washington, Powell reaffirmed his support for Bandelier in a letter to Norton dated July 8, 1880. According to Powell, "You will find him a gentleman well versed in American antiquities and thoroughly acquainted with the authors on the subject."

While in the East, Bandelier had also visited Norton at his home in Ashfield, near Boston. In the course of their conversation, the two made an arrangement whereby Bandelier would write frequent letters to Norton from the field. These letters would serve as "official reports" in case something should happen to Bandelier's own field records or to Bandelier himself. When Adolph's communications were of a personal nature, he would address Norton as "Mr.," but when they were official, he would use "Professor." Today, this seems a bit like playacting, but it was probably meant to assure Bandelier that truly *private* letters would not become part of the AIA files. Bandelier remained in the Boston area for almost two weeks working out details of his research. Then, after brief stops in New York and Baltimore, he returned to Washington to consult further with Powell. At the Bureau of Ethnology, Powell gave Bandelier copies of schedules he had prepared for his staff. Bandelier wrote, "They are certainly well conceived, practically American, and therefore facilitate work as much as they incite and invite to it." The phrase "practically American" probably meant "with American practicality," suggesting that Bandelier shared the nineteenth-century European view that Americans were unsentimental realists who got things done.

Though excited about the research, Bandelier held no illusions that all his problems were solved. In a rather acerbic letter to Morgan on June 23, he commented that he needed rail passes because of the scanty amount of money he was to receive—$1,200 for both salary and expenses for twelve months, which does seem meager even for that day.

One wonders what had happened to the $3,500 to $4,000 mentioned by Norton in May. The amount allotted to Bandelier, however, did fall near the $500 per year plus $1,000 in expenses suggested by Morgan to the AIA. Obviously, Bandelier did not know his benefactor had recommended such a rock-bottom budget. Still, he closed the letter philosophically: "I believe this is the poorest outfit ever extended, but I trust in the undeniable fact that the most valuable explorations have cost the *least money.*"

In a second section of the letter to Morgan, Bandelier mentioned that Norton had asked him to write a historical introduction to the Pueblo Indians, using documentary sources. This assignment must have been especially pleasing to Bandelier. Over the past decade, he had become familiar with many accounts of the Southwest written by early Spanish chroniclers. This was a great opportunity for him to synthesize his historical knowledge and to show Norton, at the outset, his capabilities.

Taking time to comment on various people he had met during his eastern trip, Adolph came to Professor Norton:

Norton appears to be a man of *large views.* Detail work is not distasteful to him; he is too highly cultivated for not to feel & understand its indispensability, but his training after the historical method has also convinced him of the necessity of guiding principles which stand higher than the in-

ferences drawn from partial dissection, & this he has not so much in-
structed me in what I should do than warned me from what I should
avoid. . . . Lines of thought are superior, in the end, to lines of facts, because fact is dead without the constant action of thought upon it. I shall,
therefore, while going out to gather facts merely [primarily?], have future
thought in view preeminently.

What Bandelier appears to have been saying, in his usual circuitous and
tortured English, was that Norton appeared more interested in underlying theory than in research detail. Bandelier himself believed that *both*
facts and underlying theory were necessary.

On the way back to Highland, Adolph stopped briefly in Cincinnati
to visit Dr. Gustav Bruhl. He reached home on August 5, and in a note
written to Norton that same day, Bandelier said that his good friend
Bruhl had offered him use of an excellent library on the history of
Spanish America, and that he had taken the opportunity to make extracts and abstracts of a number of these early sources. The brief note was
written in response to an "amiable" letter from Norton which Bandelier
founding awaiting him at home.

On the following day, August 6, Adolph Bandelier celebrated his for-
tieth birthday. He had arrived at a significant point in his career and the
beginning of a great adventure. During his first forty years, Bandelier
had been largely an armchair scholar, conducting his research mostly in
libraries. Now he was going into the field—and he would spend much
of his remaining thirty-four years in active field research. On this birthday, however, Adolph could have had no inkling of the toil, hardship,
and turmoil of the years ahead.

A few days later, on August 10, Bandelier finished a long letter to
Morgan. He briefed Morgan on his valuable findings in Dr. Bruhl's library—such as the Gaspar Castaño de Sosa *Memoria* (1590–91) and some
of the Juan de Oñate materials from the early seventeenth century. He
also sent messages for Morgan to relay to Putnam, Powell, Norton, and
others at the upcoming meeting of the American Association for the
Advancement of Science in Boston. "Thank God, I have cast off the foreign garb and am gradually becoming an *American*."

This last remark suggests that Bandelier equated his life in Highland
and the business world with a foreign or European existence, while the
future, in the company of the giants of American anthropology and his-

tory, was the essence of Americanism. This patriotic mood was not to last long, although Bandelier did eventually become a citizen of the United States.

Bandelier next reviewed plans for his work in New Mexico and the Southwest. He intended to begin work at the pueblo of San Ildefonso, a Tewa-speaking town in the Rio Grande valley between Española and Santa Fe. He had selected that pueblo because it was of easy access.

Besides, while its people are *very tractable,* it presents the most complicated features of organization & social arrangement. It is inhabited by a conglomerate of Indians of several linguistical stocks, and thus has suffered a doubly modifying influence: the impinging of several tribes upon each other, & the weight of Spanish government & colonization rule. If I succeed in tracing out the lines of organization of each tribe for itself, under these great disadvantages, the work of observation in a pueblo like Taos or Acoma will be mere child's play afterwards. Besides, it is easier to become "naturalized" there than anywhere else.

It is not clear where Bandelier got this clutter of misinformation about San Ildefonso. Nonetheless, his next comment was absolutely prophetic. "However, all these plans may yet be changed while on the spot. Until I have been at Santa Fe for a week I cannot give you anything positive."

With this flurry of correspondence behind him, Bandelier turned his energy and thoughts to preparing for his departure for the Southwest and his new life in New Mexico Territory.

FIVE
The Great Adventure Begins

My life's work has at last begun.

To CHANGE CAREERS at the age of forty is not something one undertakes lightly. To be sure, Bandelier had been drifting away from business and toward increasing scholarly involvement for several years. By 1880, Joe seems to have accepted and perhaps even welcomed the fact that her husband was unhappy in the business world. The long hours he devoted to study every evening may not have offered a conventional home life, but it was a life Joe could share. Adolph would read Morgan's letters to her, and she would write to Mrs. Morgan, sending photographs and Christmas presents.

Papa Bandelier was less enthusiastic about Adolph's withdrawal from Highland and the business community. Still, he took a certain pride in his son's contacts with the intellectual world and in the AIA appointment, and by the fall of 1880 he was ready to give his blessing to the new enterprise. In any case, Adolph did not make an immediate break with the bank and other business interests in Highland. By 1880, his father was the only survivor of the three original partners in the F. Ryhiner and Company bank, and family loyalty kept Adolph from dissociating himself completely from business concerns until the bank failure in 1885.

On returning home from the East, Adolph quickly wrote the first pages of his "Historical Introduction to Studies among the Sedentary Indians of New Mexico" and mailed them to Norton. Then, like a small boy getting ready for his first camping trip, Bandelier plunged into packing clothes and other living gear, books, and maps. On August 20,

1880, he said good-bye to Joe and Papa and left for St. Louis. At Kansas City, he transferred to the Atchison, Topeka and Santa Fe Railroad for the trip to New Mexico Territory. The railroad in New Mexico was still being built, but by February 1880 it had reached Lamy, seventeen miles south of Santa Fe. As is still the case today, Santa Fe passengers had to detrain at Lamy, and Adolph entered the city by buggy.

On the day of his departure from St. Louis, Bandelier began keeping a journal on loose sheets of heavy, 5-by-8-inch paper. He wrote in his journals virtually every day for the next twenty years, and then sporadically for another eleven. It is remarkable that these journals have survived essentially intact, for Bandelier took them wherever he went. He began nearly every entry with weather observations and then jotted down names of people he met, names of those he received letters from or wrote letters to, and also geological, astronomical, botanical, zoological, and entomological data. He similarly noted items of Indian culture: ruins, house structures, pottery, and other material things. He described the Indians and noted vocabulary items and aspects of social and political organization. In addition, Bandelier sketched Indian artifacts, buildings, ground plans of archaeological sites, and features on the horizon. He wrote on both sides of the sheets in a small, cramped script in any of four languages—English, Spanish, German, or French. In later years, Bandelier turned more and more to a typewriter, often carrying the machine into the field with him. The top and bottom few lines, where he was unable to type, he wrote by hand.

Adolph's first Santa Fe journal entry was made on August 23, 1880. He wrote, "Reached Santa Fe late (7:30 P.M.). Grand Central Hotel." The next day's entry stated succinctly, "Slept until 9:00 A.M. with bedbugs."

Bandelier wasted no time in trying to contact people whom he hoped would be able to help him. Among these were territorial governor Lew Wallace (of *Ben Hur* fame); Samuel Ellison, territorial librarian; Henry M. Atkinson, surveyor-general of the territory; Henry Waldo, lawyer and former chief justice of the New Mexico Territorial Supreme Court; J. C. D. Thurston of the Santa Fe office of the Indian Bureau; and vicar-general Father Peter Eguillon of the Catholic diocese of Santa Fe. On August 25, Bandelier reached an agreement with the local photographic firm of Bennett and Brown to take photos for him, and he met the well-known collector and trading post proprietor, Jake Gold. It was also at this time that Bandelier recorded his first impression of Native Americans.

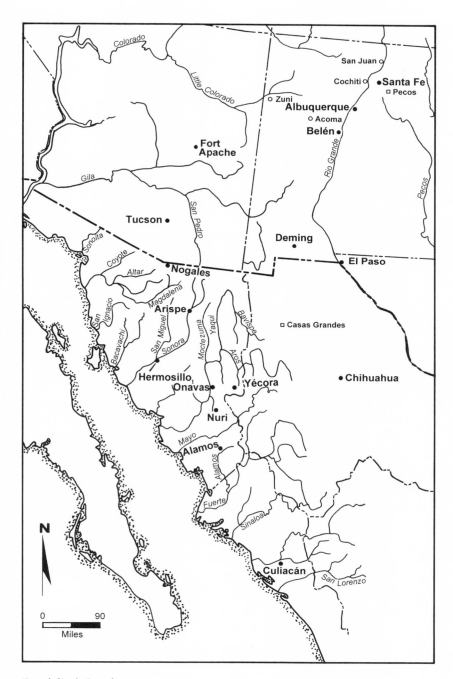

Bandelier's Southwest

"Saw Pueblo Indians on the streets, fine fellows, clad in white with hair tressed behind and hanging down each side. Driving a herd of burros."

Adolph continued with his impressions of Santa Fe.

> Great vice here, gambling—at hotels, at Mr. Gold's, everywhere gambling places, in the form of "clubs." Meat (sheep and beef) hung out on the portales here. Not very inviting. Padre Eguillon very strong concerning the wanton destruction of the archives under Governor [William A.] Pyle, says it was done on purpose to destroy Mexican claims.

Adolph almost immediately made himself known to the Catholic hierarchy in Santa Fe. The powerful, headstrong, and hyperconservative John Baptist Lamy, French by birth and education, had been in office since 1851 as bishop, then archbishop, and had brought numerous French priests to New Mexico. Lamy fought a vigorous and generally successful battle to undercut the Hispanic folk traditions of the New Mexico church. Ruthless, narrow, and totally committed, Lamy bore little resemblance to the benign and saintly father figure, Bishop Jean Marie Latour, of Willa Cather's later book, *Death Comes for the Archbishop.* When Bandelier met Lamy, however, the old warrior was near retirement and only a few years from death. Adolph referred to the archbishop by saying that he had been "charmingly rec'd." Always careful not to impugn the church, Bandelier made no adverse comments and, indeed, showed little interest in the hostility of Lamy and his French clergy toward Hispanic and Indian culture.

Over the next few days, Bandelier enjoyed an orgy of sightseeing in the 270-year-old city of Santa Fe. The city had been officially founded as the capital of Spanish New Mexico in 1610—ten years before the Pilgrims landed at Plymouth Rock. Indeed, this new colonial capital may have been built on the site of a slightly earlier (perhaps 1607) foundation. Santa Fe followed the Spanish colonial pattern, with a central plaza; the seventeenth-century Palace of the Governors (now part of the Museum of New Mexico) formed the plaza's north side. When Adolph arrived in August 1880, Santa Fe was the largest city in New Mexico Territory and had a population of over 6,500. For the first time in its history it was beginning to provide civic conveniences: in late 1880, a municipal gas system was installed; a municipal water system had to wait until 1882.

With the coming of the railroad in early 1880, modernization throughout northern New Mexico had accelerated, though living conditions remained relatively primitive. To the ever-present flat-roofed adobe structures were added gabled and "tin-roofed"buildings like those common in the East and Midwest. Sheep and cattle ranching, mining, and land speculation had brought a sizable Anglo-American population to the territory. Over the next twelve years, Bandelier was to meet and interact with such people, and also with long-time Hispanic and Indian citizens of the Southwest.

After spending a few days getting acquainted with Santa Fe, Bandelier's immediate interest was to begin his fieldwork for the AIA. Oddly enough, his initial investigations were not with the Pueblo Indians but were something more in line with the historical sketch he was writing for Norton. Adolph had already determined that the deserted and ruined pueblo and mission at Pecos had been an important place during the early Spanish period, and the Pecos area seemed a logical site to begin field investigations.

On August 28, 1880, Bandelier, along with J. C. Thurston of the Indian Bureau and a Pennsylvania resident, J. D. Culbertson, arrived by buggy at Baughl's Switch in the Pecos valley, thirty miles southeast of Santa Fe. Adolph took lodging in the boarding house of a Mrs. Root. Baughl's Switch was a railroad spur and also a large storage place for railroad ties; most of its buildings were temporary ones. In a direct line, Baughl's Switch lay about one and a half miles from the ruins of the pueblo and mission of Pecos. The following day, the Bandelier party, with John McRae, an old Canadian trapper who had lived at Pecos for many years, went to measure the ruins. These were the first pueblo ruins that Adolph had examined, and he filled his journals with his initial impressions, including measurements of wall thicknesses and dimensions of buildings—although he did not always precisely identify and locate these buildings in his journal entries.

That night, back at Baughl's Switch, Adolph wrote to Morgan: "[I] have to-day completed the survey of the great pueblo of Pecos, the ancient 'Cicuyé' of Coronado." Pecos Pueblo, situated on a low hill along a small tributary of the nearby Pecos River, was truly an impressive place. A Towa-speaking village founded sometime after A.D. 1300, Pecos was at the height of its power when Coronado invaded New Mexico in 1540–42. One of the easternmost of the pueblos, poised between the

Pueblo world and the High Plains, Pecos stood at the center of a lucrative trade in turquoise, pottery, maize, and shell going out into the plains, and bison hides and meat, flint, and wood for bows coming into the Pueblo area. From a population of more than two thousand souls in 1540, the town declined under Spanish and Mexican rule and was finally abandoned in 1838 when the fewer than twenty survivors moved to Jemez Pueblo, the only other Towa-speaking village and one still in existence today.

Adolph completed his survey of the ruins on September 1. Starting on August 31, he did some haphazard excavations. He noted that the ruin in general had been much vandalized by people who had left a scatter of excavated debris, including broken beer bottles with the inscription "Anheuser-Busch Brewing Co., St. Louis, Mo." Bandelier sketched a plat for Norton and promised to collect "a lot of stuff," including potsherds, stone implements, and "if possible portions of the adobe walls of the old church" for the Peabody Museum at Harvard. A few days later, Bandelier shipped two boxes of material items for the Peabody. It is unclear whether collecting for the Peabody was in his contract with the AIA, but considering that Frederic Ward Putnam, one of the AIA's founders, was the director of the Peabody, this seems likely.

As an archaeologist, Bandelier was painstaking and thorough, especially with ground plans and architectural features. At Pecos, he sensed that the broken pottery was significant but did little about it because he lacked an appreciation of the possibilities these potsherds offered for determining stratigraphy. Ironically, the uses of pottery in establishing time and space relationships in the Southwest did come in large part from Pecos—but not until the early twentieth-century excavations there by Alfred V. Kidder.

Kidder's later research was, of course, much more extensive and sophisticated. Still, Kidder believed that Bandelier, especially given the short time he was at Pecos, had done productive work. He wrote, "Bandelier with his usual thoroughness and accuracy, described the ruins as they were at that time. . . . While his work was not accompanied by excavation, which would, of course, have solved many of the problems that puzzled him, Bandelier arrived at remarkably accurate conclusions."

From September 2 to September 6, Bandelier pursued his investigations in the Pecos area. With Bandelier in tow, George C. Bennett of Bennett and Brown, the Santa Fe photographic firm, took photographs for a projected publication on Pecos. Adolph also talked at considerable length with a number of old-time residents, among them Mariano Ruíz, an elderly Jemez Indian who had been adopted by the Pecos tribe in 1837. From Ruíz, Bandelier gained valuable information about the few surviving Pecos Indians in the 1830s and about their migration to Jemez Pueblo.

On September 5, Adolph wrote to Morgan, giving details of his Pecos work. He concluded the letter with these enthusiastic words: "I am dirty, ragged and sunburnt, but of best cheer. My life's work has at last begun." He returned to Santa Fe by train the next day. Between his return from Pecos and the start of his next field trip, into the Rio Grande valley on September 23, he busied himself in completing the writing of both his Pecos report and the "Historical Introduction." To do this, he located documents pertaining to Pecos in the surveyor-general's office and also used materials from the territorial library. In addition, he began to prepare for coming ethnographic work.

Adolph sent part of the Pecos report to his family in Highland, explaining to Norton in a September 16 letter, "They are anxious to hear from me and to *see* some of my work." Bandelier's father was to forward the manuscript directly to Norton. Adolph ended this letter with the following remarks about Morgan: "Father Morgan has written also.—I say frankly, *he is* the only man who has ever done any work on the "pueblos," and without a perfect knowledge of his views and methods, it is impossible to do any work here."

This statement borders on the inane. Morgan had never done fieldwork among the living Pueblos, but others certainly had. As early as 1850, Lieutenant Joseph C. Ives of the U.S. Army stopped in at Hopi, and he published an account of these Indians in 1861. Major J. W. Powell, one of Bandelier's sponsors, had visited the Hopis in 1870, and his material on Hopi culture was published in 1875. More to the point, the Stevenson party from the Smithsonian Institution's Bureau of Ethnology had been in the field since 1879. This group included Frank Cushing as well as Colonel James Stevenson and his wife, Matilda Coxe Stevenson, later to become famous for her extensive studies of Zuni and Zia pueblos. Adolph was soon to meet both the Stevensons and also J. K. Hillers, photographer for the expedition, and it is impossible to believe that he was unaware of the rush of fieldwork going on around him.

Bandelier left Santa Fe on September 23 to go to the little Spanish town of Peña Blanca on the Rio Grande between the Indian pueblos of

Santo Domingo and Cochiti. The first week in Santa Fe, Adolph had met the resident priest at Peña Blanca, Padre José Rómulo Ribera, and the priest had invited the scientist to stay with him. After spending a night with the padre, Bandelier was taken to nearby Santo Domingo Pueblo, a Keresan-speaking village on the east bank of the Rio Grande. The pueblo he visited, however, was not the present-day village; that Santo Domingo was washed away in the great flood of 1886. The Santo Domingo people then rebuilt their town farther back from the river and on somewhat higher ground—the location of the present-day pueblo. At Santo Domingo, Adolph was housed in the former priest's quarters while tribal leaders conferred over whether he could live there and study them—the decision being in the affirmative.

During his initial days at Santo Domingo, Bandelier collected a surprising amount of ethnographic data on a variety of subjects. He busied himself measuring buildings and rooms, the church, and the fields. He acted as secretary for the tribe, recording the names of some sixty young men going out into the plains to trade with the Comanches. Flushed by his successes in these early ventures, Bandelier became somewhat careless and insensitive to his Indian associates. Within a few days, his activities and his constant questioning had irritated the archconservative Santo Domingo Indians to the point of no return.

The scientist was told about the practice of witchcraft at Santo Domingo and the modes of punishment for it. He was puzzled that no one mentioned the office of cacique (the head ceremonial officer); however, he learned the names of the "Spanish" set of officers, which included the governor, the alguaciles, and the fiscales. Bandelier also noted the Santo Domingos' fine pottery, as well as their use of loosely woven baskets for washing grain (mostly wheat) in the river prior to grinding it on a series of graded metates. He commented on the *pregonero*, or town crier, who often made community announcements from the rooftop at sunrise. Bandelier also noted the presence of men called *principales* (members of a council of present and former holders of major tribal offices) and their roles in community affairs. In terms of clan organization, he counted "eight gentes." Actually, this was a misnomer. As anthropological studies advanced and specialization in social organization developed, "gentes" became the term for patrilineal kinship groups, and "clans," the term for matrilineal kin groups. At Santo Domingo, these groups have been matrilineal for as long as is known.

On September 28, Bandelier wrote Norton that his work was not progressing well because of the reticence of the Indians. But "even if it takes me three months," declared Bandelier, "I shall not leave the post." He had no more than written this letter when his work at Santo Domingo began to fall apart. While in Peña Blanca that same day, he discovered that the Santo Domingo Indians did indeed have a cacique, and on his return to the village he foolishly flaunted this bit of highly sensitive information. Understandably, hostility increased and soon reached new heights when the Indians learned that Bandelier had invited Bennett of Bennett and Brown to come to the pueblo to take photographs. Curiously enough, Bennett was allowed to photograph on October 1 and 2—perhaps mainly because the Santo Domingo Indians did not fully realize what he was doing. He took pictures of the church, one kiva, several street scenes, and a new bridge that the Indians were building across the Rio Grande. A few people even permitted Bennett to take their pictures.

On October 2, Adolph had been asked (ordered?) to stay in his room "and not look out." Instead, he left the room and found a vantage point from which to watch a burial in the cemetery, thinking, incorrectly, that he would not be observed. That same night, Bandelier showed a visitor the old church, which greatly angered the sacristan. Bandelier noted in his journal, "I go to bed late at night, while they are still watching me outside."

Bandelier was suffering the consequences of gross carelessness and insensitivity. Despite his inexperience, he should have read enough of the history of the Pueblo Indians' relationships with Europeans to have used more common sense. These Indians, agricultural and "puebloan," or town dwellers, had been in the Southwest for centuries before the Spaniards missionized the area early in the seventeenth century. The Spanish Franciscan missionaries were ruthless in trying to suppress the native weather-control, fertility, and curing rites that were celebrated with religious dances, often by masked impersonators of the gods. Not only did the Spaniards forbid the all-important ceremonies, but soldiers and missionaries also ransacked and desecrated the kivas, or ceremonial houses, and associated paraphernalia.

After the Pueblos' savage revolt in 1680, Spanish authorities slackened their brutal repression of native religious practices, but the damage had been done. What had once been relatively open now became secret and guarded. When Catholic Christianity eventually took hold in the eastern, or Rio Grande, pueblos, it was blended with native elements, and in any case was practiced side by side with the traditional rites.

In spite of this history, some of the pueblos were reasonably hospitable to outsiders in the nineteenth century, especially to the newly arrived Americans, who were perceived to be friendly with the Indians. Of all the pueblos, however, Santo Domingo was probably the least tolerant and most suspicious of foreign ways, a characteristic that holds to this day. Into this tense situation blundered a totally inexperienced Bandelier. Arrogant in his belief in the superiority of European ways, he ignored the danger signals. It is true that most nineteenth-century ethnologists felt innately superior to the groups they studied, but they generally acted with a certain appreciation and tact, something that, at Santo Domingo at least, seemed to be beyond Bandelier's capabilities. In his defense, we should also note that Padre Ribera had sent the novice ethnographer to this most conservative and least approachable of the Southwestern pueblos. One wonders about the good padre's sense of humor.

At any rate, on October 5 Bandelier walked through the Santo Domingo fields and crossed over to those of neighboring Cochiti Pueblo. There he met his first Cochiti Indian, Teodosio Cordero, a *principal* of that tribe and governor two years before. The Cochitis were also Keresan speakers and proved to be much friendlier than the Santo Domingos. It was easy for Bandelier to take Padre Ribera's advice and move to Cochiti, remaining there for the balance of the fall, 1880. Another Cochiti Indian, Juan José Montoya, who became a close friend, rented Adolph a room in the village, and Bandelier was soon at work. The Santo Domingo experience had taught him a lesson, and he did much better at Cochiti, undoubtedly aided by the fact that these people were considerably more open and cordial. Certain Cochitis were among the few Indians who ever really befriended Bandelier.

In the first few days in his new home, many people, including a number of tribal leaders, cooperated with Bandelier, relating and explaining their customs and beliefs, as well as giving him the locations of many archaeological sites in the area. Juan José told Adolph the "Montezuma" story. Montezuma (Moteuczoma II) was the last Aztec emperor, who was murdered in 1520, perhaps by the conquistador Hernán Cortez. The story of Montezuma was probably brought to the Southwest by Mexican Indians in the entourage of the Spanish conquerors. Whatever the case, a

Bandelier and his father at the de Vargas Street house, Santa Fe, December 31, 1889. Photograph by Charles F. Lummis. (Museum of New Mexico, neg. 9171.)

The Bandelier family at the de Vargas Street house, Santa Fe, 1890. Seated: Josephine Huegy Bandelier (left) and her niece, Fanny Lambelet. Standing: Adolph F. Bandelier and his father, Adolphe E. Bandelier. Photograph by Charles F. Lummis. (Museum of New Mexico, neg. 9167.)

(top right) The Palace, old residence of the governors, restored. Today it houses part of the Museum of New Mexico. (From Bandelier's "Histoire" manuscript, Vat. Lat. 14116-487.)

(bottom right) Lower San Francisco Street, Santa Fe. (Museum of New Mexico, neg. 11337.)

José Hilario Montoya, 1891. Often governor of Cochiti, Montoya was a long-time friend and frequent guide of Bandelier's. Photograph by Charles F. Lummis. (Museum of New Mexico, neg. 923.)

Mission of San Buenaventura, Cochiti Pueblo, about 1890. (Museum of New Mexico, neg. 12286.)

Cochiti Pueblo *tablita,* or corn, dance, July 14, 1889. Dancers are doing the "first round" in front of the mission church on the annual feast day. Photograph by Charles F. Lummis. (Museum of New Mexico, neg. 4831.)

Adolph F. Bandelier and Adelaido Montoya of Cochiti Pueblo at Frijoles
Canyon, December 5, 1880. Photograph by George C. Bennett. (Museum
of New Mexico, neg. 6056.)

(top left) Juan José Montoya and his daughter, Cochiti Pueblo. Montoya
was one of Bandelier's principal informants. This obviously posed picture
was taken by George C. Bennett of Bennett and Brown, Santa Fe, probably
in the early 1880s. (Museum of New Mexico, neg. 4845.)

(bottom left) North wall of Frijoles Canyon, New Mexico. Cavate
dwellings can be seen at the base of the cliff. Known as "Long House" today, this group of ruins sits above the major ruin of Tyuonyi on the canyon
floor. (From Bandelier's "Histoire" manuscript, Vat. Lat. 14115-321.)

The pair of stone lions and the shrine on the Potrero de las Vacas, Bandelier National Monument. Note the entrance to the shrine in the upper left corner. Photograph by Charles F. Lummis, 1890. (Museum of New Mexico, neg. 2279.)

complex legend with southwestern, Mexican, and Catholic elements grew up among the Pueblos. It cast Montezuma as a culture hero, a kind of "once and future king" who would someday return to rescue his people. Bandelier found the tale fascinating and continued to learn additional details of the story throughout his years in the Southwest.

At Cochiti, Bandelier became much more a part of the community than he was able to do at Santo Domingo. He witnessed several religious ceremonies, observed daily behavior in the homes and around the village, and gathered Keresan vocabulary and other linguistic information. Indeed, it was about this time that Bandelier told Norton he "was fast learning the Qqueres [Keres or Keresan] language." There is no evidence, however, that Bandelier—though proficient in several European languages—ever mastered Keresan or any other American Indian tongue. There is not even any particular evidence that he ever realized that American Indian languages were as complex and structured in morphology and syntax as English or Latin or any other language. At Cochiti and with other Pueblo Indians, Bandelier commonly used Spanish, which was more widely spoken by these tribes in the nineteenth century than was English.

While at Cochiti, Bandelier made the delightful discovery that he could draw and paint. This partly eliminated the need for cumbersome photographic equipment or photographers, who often found it difficult to keep up with Adolph and endure field conditions with him. He sketched Cochiti items of material culture and was even given permission to paint ceremonial paraphernalia. He also visited ruins in the area with various Cochiti men. These long trips, either on foot or on horseback, provided great opportunities for Adolph to learn about hunting practices, ethnobotany, and tribal prehistory and traditions, and to ask in greater detail about Cochiti ceremonial, social, and political structures.

On October 23, Bandelier left with his friend Juan José Montoya on an extended horseback trip to the Rito de los Frijoles, a narrow canyon ten miles north of Cochiti, where there were spectacular cliff dwellings, talus remains, and surface ruins that the Cochitis claimed as the homes of their ancestors. In recording their arrival at the south rim of the canyon and their descent into it, which took a half-hour by foot, Bandelier wrote: "The grandest thing I ever saw." The *rito* became a favorite spot of Bandelier's, and he was later to use it as a setting for his novel *The Delight Makers*. In 1916, two years after Bandelier's death,

President Woodrow Wilson officially designated the area embracing Frijoles Canyon as Bandelier National Monument.

Archaeological work in the Frijoles region has continued intermittently to the present day. Bandelier, on this same trip, was shown a set of mountain lions roughly carved from bedrock. This pair of lions was on the fingerlike projection of land known as Potrero de las Vacas, just south of Frijoles Canyon. A separate, single lion, was on the mesa called Potrero de los Idolos in the Cañada de la Cochiti, a short distance to the south. From the time Bandelier first viewed this latter site, there was but one lion and no sign of a companion (two lions together would be more consistent with Puebloan traditions). All the lions and their surrounding circles of large rocks showed signs of disturbance and mutilation. The single lion is of harder volcanic rock and the carving is more readily recognizable as a mountain lion, although none of the carvings is particularly representational. These lions are shrines of ceremonial importance to the Cochitis and other Pueblo peoples as well; the single lion had been lost to the Cochitis until one of us (Lange), with a Cochiti companion, rediscovered it in 1952.

What Bandelier observed in north-central New Mexico, especially at Frijoles Canyon, gave him the naive belief that he had seen a full cross section of Pueblo Indian ruins. He saw no reason to travel to the fabled cliff dwellings of the San Juan River area, just beginning to be discovered, or the better known but still mysterious ruins of Chaco Canyon. Indeed, in all his years in the Southwest, Adolph never visited either the Mesa Verde–Four Corners area or the Chaco area.

During Bandelier's stay in Cochiti, Norton suggested to him the possibility of having a Protestant minister work under him. Adolph firmly rejected this idea. He wrote Norton that his own acceptance at Cochiti was "based upon the pledge of absolute neutrality in religious matters." Later, especially after his conversion to Catholicism in 1881, Bandelier was to react strongly against Protestant missionization of the southwestern Indians.

By mid-November 1880, Bandelier was growing weary of the hard life at Cochiti. On the eighteenth he wrote to Norton from the pueblo, summarizing his activities. He mentioned a communal rabbit hunt, a pueblo dance, and excursions into the mountains. A winter storm had frozen the Rio Grande, a relatively infrequent occurrence, and had made his life in the pueblo miserable.

I cannot tell you what I have suffered in my little Room, open to the East [his window had no panes], impossible to heat up with the miserable firewood which my improvident host has scantily gathered. For 48 hours my fingers were constantly frozen to stiffness. It is better now. . . . The work is progressing splendidly. I have 178 pp. of Journal on the Qqueres.

On November 20, Bandelier added to this letter, complaining of the monotony of a boiled mutton diet with very little coffee. He developed an abscess on his nose, a problem that returned to plague him for the balance of the year. Another letter, completed on November 29, told of Bandelier's satisfaction in his newfound skill in drawing and painting. He also spoke of his enjoyment of the simple Indian life, the weather having ameliorated somewhat.

Bandelier had planned for some time to do additional photography, so the same day he mailed the letter to Norton—Monday, November 29—he met Bennett at Peña Blanca. On December 1, together with Bennett and Cochiti friends, he made a horseback trip to the Frijoles area for photographs. They camped in Frijoles Canyon and explored the mesas for several miles around. The group returned to Cochiti on the afternoon of December 7. It was a tiring trip and often very cold, but Bandelier termed it "glorious." It shows the scholar, now fully acclimatized to southwestern conditions, at his rugged best.

Bandelier was now near the end of this field period. On December 15, Father Ribera drove him to Santa Fe. He left for St. Louis on December 18, and on the twenty-first "reached home safe at 9 A.M. Surprise complete. All well. . . . Everybody overjoyed." He immediately made plans to go east for consultation with Norton and Morgan, and on December 27 he wrote to Norton requesting railroad passes. Meanwhile, Bandelier turned to work on his Keres vocabulary, completing it on the final day of 1880. As his journal entry for that New Year's Eve indicates, he was in an optimistic mood, sore nose and all.

Thus the most important year of my entire life draws to a close. Thank God, thank God, for every blessing, every sore, for weal and woe, which He has been pleased to dispense. So far, so good, and there is hope for better. . . . Have no reflections to record. Future action is all that occupies my thoughts.

SIX
Mexican Interlude

All will pass in secret and in silence. I have forbidden that
it should be spoken of.

SHORTLY AFTER New Year's Day, 1881, Bandelier received a
telegram from Charles Norton of the AIA, instructing him to report to
Francis Parkman on January 7. Adolph's swollen nose had not cleared up,
however, and he also came down with chills and fever. When he finally
did leave for the East, he was forced to purchase his own tickets, the railroad passes requested of Norton having failed to materialize. The archaeologist reached Rochester on the twelfth of January and spent the
evening and night with Morgan. Arriving in the Boston area on January
15, Bandelier heard for the first time about a new project.

The institute planned to send Adolph to Yucatán as part of the
Lorillard-Charnay expedition, a group sponsored by the French government and by the American-French financier Pierre Lorillard. The prime
mover in this AIA plan was Allen Thorndike Rice, editor of the North
American Review. Rice, presumably acting as Lorillard's agent, had requested a backup scholar who could assist and, if necessary, supersede
Charnay. As events were to show, Charnay himself may not have known
about these arrangements.

Bandelier accepted this change in plan without much objection, but
he did stipulate that it not interfere with his long-term work in the
Southwest. The scholar took advantage of his time in Massachusetts to
get pointers in architectural and topographic drawing from the well-

known architect William R. Ware, then of the Massachusetts Institute of Technology but soon to assume a professorship at Columbia University.

On January 26, the final terms for the Mexican work were agreed upon, and a special meeting of the AIA executive committee was held. The committee allotted Bandelier money for travel expenses, and he was to have a salary of $100 per month beginning February 1, 1881, plus monies to purchase books. Expenses in the field were to be paid by Rice. The committee also decided that Bandelier should continue to receive $100 a month in salary and a monthly allowance of $100 for expenses so long as he remained in the service of the AIA.

Adolph left Boston on the morning of January 27 and spent the afternoon in Worcester with Stephen Salisbury, Jr., who had just stepped down from the presidency of the American Antiquarian Society. It was in Worcester that Bandelier wrote the news of his imminent arrival in Mexico to the historian and archivist don Joaquín García Icazbalceta, with whom Adolph had corresponded for several years but whom he had not yet met. From Worcester, Bandelier returned to Rochester, where he spent the next three days with Morgan. It was the last time the Illinois scholar would ever see his older mentor.

Adolph arrived back in Highland on February 3 after a tiring trip. He found his family well and, as the journal for that day stated, "not only reconciled but even enthusiastic" about the trip. During the next few days Adolph shopped with Josephine for clothing, made arrangements for the trip to New Orleans, where he would take a ship to Vera Cruz, and made final rounds of visits with family and friends. Among these visits was one to Father Joseph Meckel, the Catholic priest at Highland, and to Sister Severa, the mother superior of the Hospital Sisters in Highland. Finally, on the twentieth of February, Adolph took leave of his wife at St. Louis's Union Station. As he commented in his journal for that day, "Dear Joe, Poor, dear thing. It is hard, very hard for both of us, but then it cannot be helped." The long trip to Mexico was under way.

Adolph reached New Orleans on February 22, getting his first sight of the city since boyhood. He did some sightseeing and then on February 24 boarded the steamship *City of Mérida;* at 8 A.M., he was on his way to Mexico. The ship skirted the gulf coast, reaching the mouth of the Rio Grande on the morning of the twenty-sixth, when passengers from another vessel were taken aboard. The voyage continued smoothly; and on

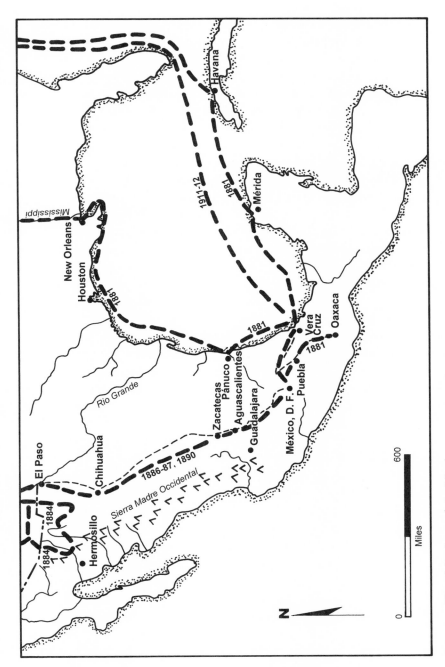

Routes of Bandelier's travels in Mexico

February 27 the ship arrived at Tampico, where Bandelier obtained information on the local Indians from a fellow passenger.

On the morning of March 1, Adolph landed at Vera Cruz and got first-hand information on the Charnay expedition. It was breaking up: Charnay was in Mexico City but planned to return to Europe. Bandelier decided on the spot to go to Mexico City to confer with Charnay. He left by train about midnight, arriving in Mexico City at 7 P.M. on March 2.

It was a trip of breathtaking beauty, especially through the broad Puebla valley with its stunning view of towering mountains. From the top of the pass where the railroad broke into the Valley of Mexico, the majestic volcanoes Popocatepetl and Ixtaccihuatl pierced the southern sky. Below him, Bandelier could see the awesome expanse of the Valley of Mexico, mysterious in the diffuse light of an early March evening. This sight is often denied today's visitors who drive the excellent highway from Puebla to Mexico City. Coming over the pass, above eight thousand feet, they descend into what seems to be a level and featureless pea-soup plain. Such is the air pollution over this great modern city.

Arriving in Mexico City, Bandelier immediately looked up Charnay, who was staying at the Hotel Iturbide, Mexico City's largest hotel of the period. In his journal of March 2, Adolph made this laconic comment: "Called on Charnay. He is in bed already. Had a long talk with him. He is much irritated at Rice & cannot do anything. Am completely dizzy & very tired. Hotel splendid." The following day, March 3, Bandelier wrote Norton in much greater detail.

[Last night] I found out that indeed Mr. Charnay had disbanded his corps, and abandoned all work until 6 months from hence. He has been attacked by fever at Palenque & needs rest. But while it is out of the question to go with him now, it is useless for me to return crying. I have money at least for a month here, and shall therefore go to work at once. . . . Next Sunday I start for La Puebla and then to Tlaxcala and to Cholula, to survey the Ruins; whatever they may be. Do not expect big results, for the destruction of buildings here is much greater than in New Mexico.—In the meantime take care of Mr. Rice and hold him to his contract, while I will take care of myself here and work for the *Archaeological Institute* alone.

It is the most fool's errand that anybody was ever sent upon. Charnay is as mad as a march hare.

Bandelier also commented that he and Charnay had basic disagreements about archaeological interpretations. He was probably referring to Charnay's belief that all native Mesoamericans were Toltec and that the oldest ruins dated no more than eight centuries into the past. Bandelier was certainly correct in scoffing at such a chronology, though he himself had no inkling that in Mexico, massive monuments were being built centuries before the Christian or Common Era.

Assuming AIA support (correctly, as it turned out), Bandelier pushed rapidly ahead. On March 4, he finally met Joaquín García Icazbalceta, who expressed enthusiasm for the Cholula work. During the next two days, Adolph explored ruins around Mexico City before leaving for Puebla on March 6. The Puebla region was important both archaeologically and historically. Although Puebla itself was mainly a Spanish settlement, the Tlaxcalans—Hernán Cortez's first and most important allies in the conquest of the Aztec empire—had their city a few miles north of Puebla. Cholula, just west of Puebla, on the other hand, had been staunchly pro-Aztec, and its citizens were massacred by Cortez and his men.

On March 7 Adolph stayed at Puebla, and on the following day made his first visit to Cholula, whose enormous Aztec pyramid, with a Spanish-built church on top, remains one of the most impressive monuments of ancient Mexico. Indeed, the whole Puebla valley in Bandelier's time, as it is today, was a maze of rich archaeological sites and grandiose, sixteenth-century Spanish buildings, especially churches. At Cholula, Adolph met for the first time the local priest, Father José Vicente Campos, to whom he had brought a letter from García Icazbalceta. Father Campos was to become an important figure to Bandelier in the months ahead as Adolph moved toward conversion to Catholicism.

It is not entirely clear how Bandelier's salary and expenses were handled by the institute during the time of this fieldwork, but the traveler obviously felt money pressures steadily throughout his months in Mexico. The monthly check from the AIA seems to have gone directly to Joe in Highland. The exact amount of money Bandelier received from Rice and the *North American Review*, if any, is unknown.

Adolph remained in the Puebla-Cholula-Tlaxcala region for several months. He accomplished an absolutely prodigious job of mapping, measuring, and describing the various ruins. He also commented on native customs and transcribed material from city and church archives. He found time to do mountain climbing on the slopes of Popocatepetl and Ixtaccihuatl. Not all the work went smoothly; when he visited the Indian town of Cuauhtlancingo a few miles southeast of Cholula, he was met with open hostility. This was one of the very few times that Bandelier had to use the revolver he had purchased in February in St. Louis. According to information that he mailed to Highland, which was written up by the local newspaper, *Die Highland Union,* "the courageous man, thinking only of his mission, remained [at Cuauhtlancingo]. . . . He moved into a room which he had rented from an Indian [and] explained to the Alcalde, while waving his revolver, that he would immediately punish every injury, and continued his investigations regarding architecture, customs, and usages of that tribe of people."

It should be said that Bandelier normally did not resort to such absurd and self-defeating field methods. For the most part he behaved himself and was received hospitably. This hospitality did not, however, greatly change his feelings toward the native Mexican Indians. Writing from Calpan, a town west of Cholula, on May 22, 1881, Adolph commented, "I have here learned to despise deeply the present day 'Nahuatl' Indian and I cannot conceal the fact." Actually, Bandelier—as he often did in such matters—blew hot and cold. At one point he wrote Morgan a long letter from Cholula in which he generally praised the Nahuatl Indians, although he did call them "mulish and bloodthirsty when aroused." Whatever the Mexican Indians' shortcomings in Adolph's eyes, he never described them with the same expressions of hatred and fear, bordering at times on the pathological, that appear in his later writings on the Aymara Indians of Bolivia.

During his three months in the Cholula area, Adolph saw a great deal of Father Campos, and references to him in the journals are uniformly warm. Bandelier occasionally stayed at the curate's house, borrowed church records and material objects for copying and painting, and asked the priest's expert advice on many points of local history.

There were also serious discussions of doctrinal matters, but such topics are only touched on in the journals and are left virtually unmentioned in Bandelier's letters to Norton and Morgan and in articles, or *Reisebriefen,* published by the Highland newspapers. Correspondence from Adolph to his family has been lost, so the extent to which he hinted of his coming conversion is unknown. It is certain that Adolph did not discuss his religious activities in letters to Papa Bandelier. It is likely that he said nothing to Josephine either; Father Bandelier was very much the family patriarch and would naturally have expected to share any letter Joe received from her husband.

As the weeks went by in the Puebla area, Bandelier did a great deal of fieldwork, but he was beginning to be troubled by a series of ailments. By the first of June he was feeling quite ill, although he persevered with previously made plans to visit Oaxaca. Around midnight of the ninth of June, sick and weak, Adolph began his trip, taking the train to Tehuacán in southern Puebla state. He spent the night of June 10 in this provincial town, describing it as "large, neat, and very good looking." In his book on this Mexican research, *Report of an Archaeological Tour in Mexico,* published in 1884, Bandelier talked of ruins of great antiquity on the mountain slopes around Tehuacán, which he had no time to investigate. He did not realize, of course, just how old some of the sites in this area actually were. Many years later, the hills near Tehuacán were to yield evidence of early native agriculture going back six or seven thousand years.

In 1881, the railroad did not reach south of Tehuacán, so Bandelier joined a mule train traveling on to Oaxaca. He became increasingly ill, but pushed on and reached Oaxaca City around noon on June 16. Adolph carried a letter from the governor of Puebla to the governor of Oaxaca and was treated kindly, being provided with the governor's own horse and a dragoon sergeant for escort. The scholar left for the great prehistoric Zapotec center of Mitla, some twenty miles away, on the morning of June 17. En route, he visited the huge *sabino* of Santa María de Tule, a tree that measured about 130 feet in circumference in Bandelier's time and was a tourist attraction then as well as today. The American scholar worked for a number of days at the ruins of Mitla and also collected cultural information from a local Indian.

During this entire period, Bandelier suffered from recurring chills and fever and almost constant diarrhea. He tried a variety of medications—opium, acetate of lead, pepsin, and bismuth—to no avail. He returned to Oaxaca on June 28 a very sick man, the diarrhea controlled only by heavy doses of opium. In spite of his disability and an increasing depression, Adolph continued his work at the local libraries and archives. On July 2, in spite of the "strongest attack of diarrhoe [*sic*] of the whole 'season,'" the scientist left with a guide early in the morning for the enormous site of Monte Albán near Oaxaca City. This vast ruin, occupied by the Mixtecs in late pre-Hispanic times, also held complex structures that archaeologists have now dated to several centuries B.C. Bandelier did not recognize the great age of the site, but he spent about half a day exploring and mapping Monte Albán. Then, still horribly ill and increasingly weak from vomiting and diarrhea, he left Oaxaca for Tehuacán and Puebla, arriving at Puebla on July 8.

By the seventeenth of July, Adolph was finally beginning to shake off the debilitating effects of the diarrhea, though he suffered a relapse on the night of the nineteenth. Two days later he noted in his journal: "Splendid morning, but am very, very ill again. Diarrhoe has set in with great violence. I am weak & hardly able to stand, & very thirsty. What will become of me yet? Shall I die in Mexico? If so, I am ready for it, & better a happy death than an unhappy life."

In spite of these morbid thoughts, Bandelier wrote Norton the same day, giving his reasons for "having been lazy" and relating something of his activities during the preceding week. For one thing, he had made a gift to Father Campos on the occasion of Campos's completion of fifty years as a priest. The curate, according to Bandelier, "rightly deserved it, for he is my mainstay here in everything." Adolph ended this letter to Norton with a criticism of Protestant missionaries in the area.

Bandelier was now rushing toward a great decision, one of the most crucial of his life. It is curious that his activities during the last days of July, as recorded in his journal, barely even hint at it.

> *30th of July, 1881:* Fine day, I ret'd on foot to Cholula & in the afternoon to Puebla, arriving there in time to avoid a drenching. In the night fell sick with most violent pains. Could not sleep. Fierce diarrhoe.
>
> *31st of July, 1881:* D. Joaquín García & his son came. Spent the day quietly and pleasantly. Fine, though at nightfall slight Rain. Very ill at night.
>
> *1st of August, 1881:* Very ill til noon, then began to feel slightly better. Usual Rain in the afternoon. Went to bed very early. Diarrhoe strong again, &, at night, painful.

On July 27, Adolph had written to García Icazbalceta:

> The ceremony has been set for the coming Sunday, the 31st. On Saturday I am going to Puebla, that is to say I will be at the station at 5:00 Sunday morning. If it is at all possible, come personally, for I have to speak to you of strictly confidential matters. Only to you can I attest them.

There will be neither feast nor celebration. All will pass in secret and in silence. I have forbidden that it should be spoken of. After the ceremony they will await us in the parish house.

On Sunday, July 31, 1881, at the parish church of San Pedro, Cholula, Adolph F. Bandelier was baptized into the Roman Catholic faith with the name Agustín Vicente Adolfo Francisco Bandelier, "de Berna Suiza." Father Campos, of course, performed the ceremony, and Joaquín García Icazbalceta stood as *padrino,* or godfather. It was a watershed in Adolph's life, but the baptism took place, as the new convert had requested, in secrecy and silence.

In our tolerant and skeptical age, Bandelier's secretiveness in changing from one form of Christianity to another seems a bit extreme. We must remember, however, that nineteenth-century Americans were more likely to feel strongly about their religion than is the case today. At that time, anti-Catholicism was considerable and often strident. Two men whom Bandelier regarded highly—his own father and Morgan—were both strongly against the Catholic church. The upper-class New Englanders with whom Adolph dealt through the AIA were apt to feel the same way, especially with the continuing immigration of Irish Catholic working-class people into the Northeast. Norton himself was an agnostic, probably an atheist, but he may have been affected by the current *social* attitude toward Catholics, no matter how indifferent he was to religion. Under these circumstances, Bandelier had good reason to keep his conversion secret, at least for the time being.

Adolph continued his research during August and the first days of September, dividing his time between the Cholula region and Mexico City. He worked in various archives in the capital and visited new friends José María Vigil, librarian of the national library, and Alfredo Chavero, the historian and antiquarian. As time went on, he gradually recovered his health and strength. Today, it is not clear from what ailment or ailments Adolph suffered. In letters to Highland, he spoke of getting out of Oaxaca just in time, and of having "the real Vera Cruz color." This would suggest that Bandelier was seriously jaundiced. He may have had amoebic dysentery combined with hepatitis, bacterial dysentery complicated by malaria, or perhaps even yellow fever, which was endemic in the Mexican lowlands at that time. In view of all he endured, it seems clear that Bandelier was endowed with a strong constitution.

On September 11, 1881, Bandelier left Mexico City for the United States, sailing seven days later from Vera Cruz. His ship docked at Mérida in the Yucatán peninsula, the nearest the archaeologist ever came to Maya Indian country. Adolph took the opportunity to visit the Mayan specialist Augustus Le Plongeon, and the two men spent an evening together in Mérida. The American visitor recorded this caustic comment in his journal: "His work is very important but on the whole he is thoroughly crazy." Bandelier probably had in mind Le Plongeon's eccentric beliefs about the Mayas, including the curious idea that ancient Mayas practiced Masonic rites!

From Mérida, the ship journeyed to Havana, Cuba, where Bandelier spent the evening of September 26. The following morning, he did a bit of sightseeing. "Rose early & went to see the Cathedral with the tomb of Colon." Parenthetically, the claim that the Havana cathedral holds the bones of Christopher Columbus is a very shaky one. Most experts are of the opinion that Columbus's grave is to be found on the island of Santo Domingo.

Bandelier arrived in New York harbor on October 1. After a round of visits in New York City, he journeyed on to Boston, where E. G. Greenleaf, secretary of the AIA, met his train with an overcoat—in case a stay "in the tropics" had left Adolph especially sensitive to the cold. Adolph conferred with Parkman, took some of his collections to Norton, and saw Putnam. He also had an "unsatisfactory meeting" with the AIA treasurer, H. H. Higginson. Adolph left Boston on October 10 and reached Rochester the following day. To his great distress, he found Morgan ill. Because any strong emotion was deemed bad for the sick man, the family decided not to tell Morgan about Bandelier's visit. On the twelfth of October, Adolph left Rochester without seeing his benefactor. After a dreary, rainy trip, he reached St. Louis in the early afternoon of October 13 and finally arrived in Highland at 5:00 P.M. Everyone was well, and the homecoming was a happy one.

The Mexican adventure was over, and Bandelier now turned to home affairs. During the late fall of 1881, he worked on the Mexican report, gave lectures in Highland and St. Louis, and sparred in the mails with officials of the AIA. Because of cash flow problems, the institute had temporarily suspended payments to Bandelier, and he complained bitterly. Adolph obviously missed the stimulation of the Mexican research and felt let down and depressed.

On October 18, Adolph wrote a long letter to García Icazbalceta commenting on his recent conversion. He explained to García the necessity of going very slowly. Bit by bit he was letting out the information to his own family. Adolph told Papa and Joe he was going to "assist the Catholic Church," but he seems to have withheld the fact that he had actually joined it. It does seem likely that Joseph Meckel, the priest at Highland whom Bandelier had met with in January 1881, knew of the conversion. At any rate, Adolph informed García Icazbalceta that he was slipping into the habit of visiting the local Highland church "from time to time to accustom people to it."

This circumspection might seem amusing except that Bandelier took it in deadly seriousness, and so, very likely, did Papa Bandelier, who must have realized quickly that something peculiar was going on. Even so, it was quite a few months before Adolph told Joe and Papa about his actual conversion. In a letter dated October 11, 1882, a year after his return from Mexico, Bandelier indicated to Padrino Joaquín that he had finally informed his family of the great event. Papa, predictably, took the news badly.

Probably because of the religious controversy, Adolph's relationship with his father seems to have deteriorated. Journal entries for the late autumn of 1881 are filled with bitter commentaries about Papa Bandelier's bad temper and how his son was becoming more and more unhappy living under the same roof. On top of all this, Josephine became ill, and then on December 18 came the terrible news that Morgan had died the previous day. Enclosing the journal entry of December 18 in a black line to emphasize his mourning, Adolph wrote: "A black, dark day! God be with him, the dear, good, faithful friend. It is a stunning blow to me, & fairly the greatest loss since Mama's death. One tie less to this country. Wrote all day and night, very assiduously. He died 17th."

By New Year's Eve, 1881, even though Joe had now recovered, her husband was in a somber and reflective mood. The year had been an eventful one for Adolph Bandelier, and it changed his life in dramatic ways.

In 1881, Bandelier had done his first fieldwork outside the United States. It was a time in which field decisions had to be made in short order and by the neophyte scholar alone. Bandelier came out of the year more secure and confident in his abilities and more inclined to insist on his own way of doing things. He had lost Morgan, and with Morgan's death, Adolph shifted away from his teacher's extreme evolutionism—of which García Icazbalceta had always been critical. García now became more than just a senior and respected scholar; he was Bandelier's godfather, and his influence on the younger man was strong.

Last, 1881 was the year that saw Bandelier's final decision to join the Catholic church. As shall be seen later, the Bandeliers, father and son, had remained almost untouched by the rationalist movement that influenced many intellectuals in the nineteenth century. Nor, apparently, had they been influenced by the "higher criticism" in biblical studies. Religion was a serious matter to them, and the conversion influenced Adolph's social being and his approach to scholarship for the remainder of his life.

SEVEN

Back to the Southwest

. . . for it is high time to go to New-Mexico.

THE BEGINNING of the year 1882 found Bandelier at home in Highland, Illinois, working on the report of his 1881 Mexican work, reorganizing field notes, and painting watercolors from sketches made in New Mexico in 1880. Within the family, things were not going so smoothly. Joe was unwell much of the time, and "Papa's ill humor" was a constant thread running through the journal entries. On January 6, Adolph and Gustave Bandelier, a much younger second cousin, had a row, and Adolph told Gustave to mend his ways or leave. Papa blamed it all on Adolph, and in his journal Adolph wrote, "It is the old, old Story over and over again. I must be the cause of everything. Better for me to leave for good." But following another fuss on March 3, it was Gustave who departed.

In February, a frustrated and restless Bandelier wrote Norton proposing further research in New Mexico followed by an extensive trip by horseback to Mexico City. The precise route would be determined, when the time came, by the location of raiding Apache Indians and the prevalence of yellow fever. He also requested that the institute allow him to take Joe to Santa Fe to take advantage of the "pure dry atmosphere." Adolph added that after eighteen months "of trial," he felt justified in requesting a salary increase. He urged Norton to respond "at once . . . for it is high time to go to New-Mexico, if such a course be decided upon."

Bandelier assured Norton that the costs would be modest; in any case, the German geographical publication *Das Ausland* was helping with the expenses in return for some popular letters on his travels. The Illinois scholar explained to Norton that ethnological and archaeological facts would be communicated to the public only through AIA publication.

Not having heard from Norton, Bandelier wrote again on March 3, repeating that he and his wife were leaving on March 6. Noting once more his belief that Josephine's own expenses would be minimal, Bandelier stated in the letter, "I therefore draw today on [AIA Treasurer] Higginson $100.— for February, & tomorrow $225.—. for expenses." Norton was not happy with Adolph's high-handedness but did authorize payment of this particular overdraft. In any case, the Bandeliers left Highland on March 6, although they went only as far as St. Louis, where they made final preparations for the trip.

A family friend, Pauline T. Kihlberg, acting as a kind of lady traveling companion for Joe, accompanied the Bandeliers from St. Louis to New Mexico. On March 17, Pauline stopped off to visit relatives in Las Vegas, New Mexico, at this time a growing community on the Santa Fe rail line. Adolph and Joe went on to Santa Fe, reaching there later the same day, and Pauline soon joined them.

Argument over the AIA salary and expenses continued for some time. As it turned out, no additional salary was forthcoming, but Bandelier's expense budget was roughly doubled, from $1,300 to around $2,500 per annum. In addition, Bandelier enjoyed an extraordinary amount of freedom in determining the direction of his research, something a present-day anthropologist or historian might envy.

This was Joe's first visit to Santa Fe, and Adolph was pleased that she adjusted so easily to the seven-thousand-foot elevation. The couple spent many of their evenings walking around the town together, viewing things of interest. Bandelier, impressed with Santa Fe's growth since he had last seen the city in December 1880, wrote in his journal, "New houses have sprung up, some two-story, of stone and brick, some of one-story adobe, with metallic roofs. The latter houses are very fine and good-looking."

During the day, Adolph worked at the territorial library, which brought him into contact with the librarian, Samuel Ellison. He renewed his acquaintance with ex-governor William G. Ritch, who was trying to revive the New Mexico Historical Society, which had become inactive during the Civil War. Bandelier promised Ritch a public lecture for the society. He also visited with Archbishop Lamy and wrote for *Das Ausland.*

With both Joe and Pauline Kihlberg accompanying him, Adolph made his first visit to Tesuque Pueblo, north of Santa Fe. There he continued his observations on Pueblo culture. On March 24, Joe and Pauline left for Albuquerque, where they were to stay with relatives until Bandelier had completed his fieldwork.

Governor L. Bradford Prince invited Bandelier to view his collection of antiquities. Adolph did additional work in the archives and found them "very interesting." There he discovered his first references to witchcraft, a subject that was to fascinate him for the remainder of his years in the Southwest. An outbreak of eczema forced Bandelier to remain indoors, and he used this time to work on his 1880 paintings of Cochiti ceremonial objects. On March 28, Ritch took notes while interviewing Bandelier about his life and career—one of several interviews with prominent people the governor recorded in the 1880s.

On April 1, Adolph left Santa Fe for Santo Domingo and Cochiti. It surprised him to find the Indians at Santo Domingo "exceedingly friendly." A Cochiti Indian came to Peña Blanca on April 3 with a horse to take him to Cochiti. Adolph had his old room again and was given a warm welcome. He picked up his ethnographical queries where he had left them in December 1880, gathering rich ethnographic data, including a description of Cochiti pottery making and of the Easter *tablita,* or corn, dance.

Bandelier inquired into Cochiti dietary habits and sent plant specimens to Dr. George Engelmann, the eminent St. Louis botanist. During this period, according to his own story, Adolph was offered entry into a secret and sacred kachina dance. He refused, telling the Cochitis that he would be duty bound to describe the event in writing and eventual publication if he were actually a witness. This frankness and self-denial gave him a certain stature, in his own mind at any rate, and he fully expected that the Indians would later be more willing to talk with him about esoteric matters.

Bandelier rode on horseback with a Cochiti friend, José Hilario Montoya, to Santa Fe on April 26. He found that the lecture he had promised Ritch was scheduled for two nights later at the Palace of the Governors. Adolph was now becoming something of a public figure, and his lecture, "Kin and Clan," went off well. Bandelier also collected insects that he regularly sent to Amalia, or "Mali," Huegy, Joe's sister in Highland. Mali Huegy was an avid "bug" collector, though she seems never to have raised her arthropodic activities to the level of entomological research.

On April 29, Bandelier left for Albuquerque, meeting Samuel Eldodt at the Lamy depot. Adolph and this trader from San Juan Pueblo were to become close friends in later years. Together with Joe and Annie Borchert, wife of Joe's host in Albuquerque, Adolph visited archaeological sites and pueblos in the region of Albuquerque. Joe seemed to be recovering her health somewhat. On May 6, Bandelier left for Acoma Pueblo by a somewhat circuitous route, going the first leg by train. As he passed Laguna Pueblo, Adolph noted his impressions but did not stop to visit. Laguna, a late-eighteenth-century settlement, was not as interesting to Bandelier in a research sense as the other pueblos with longer traditional heritages.

Both Acoma and Laguna are Keresan-speaking pueblos, although they use a western Keresan language somewhat different from that of the eastern Keresan towns of Santa Ana, Zia, San Felipe, Santo Domingo, and Cochiti. It was logical for Bandelier to go to Acoma because the town was pre-Spanish in origin and had figured heavily in accounts of the Spanish expeditions of the sixteenth century. The scholar was at Acoma Pueblo for nine days. His work was somewhat hampered as he found few people who could speak Spanish, the lingua franca of the Rio Grande Pueblos. Even fewer people spoke English, since Acoma was off the beaten path in 1880. Bandelier described the Acomas as "ruder and coarser" than the Cochitis, a curious evaluation probably meaning only that the Acoma Indians were less acculturated to Hispanic or Anglo-American ways.

Eventually, Bandelier was housed with a young Acoma, Andrés Ortiz, who spoke a little Spanish and had served his tribe as interpreter at one time. While the scholar was in residence, Ortiz's wife died, but Adolph was nonetheless allowed to remain in the house. This afforded him a rare opportunity to observe and record in detail the Acomas' funerary practices.

Using Acoma as a base for area trips, Bandelier struck off in every direction in turn, recording ruins, rock paintings, and petroglyphs and talking to everybody he met about the Acoma Indians and about ruins in the area. One informant was Father John B. Brun, who served as Lamy's priest at Acoma, Laguna, and Zuni. The scientist ventured into the great areas of *malpaís* (badlands), the extensive fields of hardened lava that flank

Acoma to the west. Some of these lava extrusions are very recent, no more than a thousand years old, and the sharp lava makes walking difficult, dangerous, or even impossible. Even today, great areas of the *malpaís* have not been fully explored.

Bandelier's host took him to the water basin at Acoma, and Adolph drew a plat of the village. He was so intrigued by the mesa on which the pueblo was built that he made a detailed sketch of it. He added a number of Acoma words to the Keresan vocabulary he had collected at Santo Domingo and Cochiti. When time permitted, Adolph collected plant specimens for Engelmann and wrote for *Das Ausland.*

During this time, the possibility of attack by either Navajos or Apaches was constantly on Bandelier's mind, and it is true that certain Apache groups were in a chronic state of warfare with both Anglo-American and Mexican authorities. Adolph's fear of warring Indians continued for several years, especially during his trips to southern Arizona and to Sonora and Chihuahua.

The dreamer and romantic in Bandelier rarely comes through in his writings, but his obsession with hostile Indians may have been the inspiration for this lyrical journal entry of May 24, 1882.

Left for Cebollita [Cebolleta Mesa, west of Acoma] about 9 A.M. . . . A gentle descent began into a laughing plain, surrounded by mesas on two sides, by a high ridge on the south-southwest, and an immense dark malpais on the west. Spurs of sandstone wander, so to say, into the llano. The sight is very pretty and realizes that often repeated dream of mine, seated on a horse and galloping across a plain of that kind, with the dread of Indians before me.

In the Acoma area, Adolph also attempted to correlate certain pottery types with two prehistoric architectural classifications he had formulated: large communal houses and scattered small houses. He suspected, as he had at Pecos, that pottery types were significant. With this kind of early insight, it is odd that Bandelier never succeeded in doing much with ceramic classification. To the end of his career, Adolph's main talent lay in the measurement and description of architecture. To that extent, he remained very much Morgan's disciple.

At Cubero, Bandelier was only a two-day horseback ride from the magnificent ruins of Chaco Canyon. He agonized over his earlier decision not to go to Chaco. In the end, however, he decided to leave Chaco to others and "to bury myself in the unknown south." To this decision Adolph added, "As it is, I believe to hold the end of the line: as far as architecture is concerned. This line runs down to Central America, and I am confident of the most important results."

Bandelier was right about the "unknown south," if by that phrase he meant the area of northern Mexico between the American Southwest and the high cultures of central and western Mexico. It was not until after World War II that this region (Sonora, Chihuahua, and portions of Coahuila, Sinaloa, Durango, and Zacatecas) received the serious archaeological attention it deserved. And Bandelier can be given considerable credit for blazing a trail, especially for alerting future generations of archaeologists to such great sites as Casas Grandes in Chihuahua.

On May 30, Adolph returned to Albuquerque to join Joe, who was staying in "Old Town," the original Albuquerque near the Rio Grande. He went from there to Bernalillo to survey the Tiguex ruins, towns formerly occupied by Tiwa-speaking Indians. There he claimed to have found nine of the twelve pueblos described by Coronado in 1540–42. Bandelier then went south from Albuquerque to Socorro and San Marcial, where he explored six ruined pueblos and pronounced them (correctly, it would seem) as being the former homes of the Piro Indians.

The Bandeliers left Albuquerque on June 29 for Santa Fe. A few days later, Joe became extremely ill, and Adolph sent for Dr. William Eggert, the first homeopathic physician in the territory. Eggert prescribed a course of medication and ordered Josephine to stay quietly in Santa Fe. Joe, however, recovered rather quickly and ignored Eggert's instructions, going with her husband to Galisteo south of Santa Fe and then to the Cochiti corn dance on July 14.

On the day the couple left Santa Fe for Highland, Adolph wrote in his journal an indirect tribute to the New Mexico climate: "Homeward bound again. Joe is well and happy." On arriving in Illinois, Adolph again recorded his feelings in the journal. "The country a perfect paradise in the lovely hues of the setting sun. Never saw it so beautiful as now." Usually, people who have lived in the Southwest find an Illinois summer almost intolerably humid, but Bandelier failed to comment on this.

The return to Illinois at this time violated the schedule Adolph had earlier given to the AIA. He was to have continued south to the Casas Grandes ruin in Chihuahua and ultimately to Mexico City, for the most part on horseback. On July 24, Bandelier wrote to Norton explaining his change of plans. It seemed that Joe's weakened condition required his escorting her home. Danger from Apaches and the beginning of the rainy season in the Southwest made it more practical to delay this portion of the fieldwork. In addition, Adolph wanted to complete his "Historical Introduction" in Illinois. It is not entirely clear why. Many of the historical materials would have been available in New Mexico, but perhaps Bandelier wished to consult the holdings of the Mercantile Library in St. Louis.

In any case, the scholar asked for and received permission from Norton to stay in Highland until the end of September. At that time, he planned to return to New Mexico. Meanwhile, Bandelier sent Norton his report for 1882. In it, Adolph stressed that three hundred years of Spanish and American acculturation had dramatically changed the Pueblo Indians. This point perhaps seems obvious, but even today students of the Pueblos sometimes act as if the Indian culture of the twentieth century mirrors that of the fifteenth and sixteenth centuries.

In his report to Norton, Bandelier described the ruins he had seen and measured and gave the linguistic affiliation of the Indians who lived in these ruins in Coronado's time. He discussed tribal government, ceremonial life, and material culture of the Pueblos, sometimes showing—especially when talking about social organization—remnants of Morgan's ideas and influence. But Bandelier was mainly fascinated by two types of architecture he thought existed aboriginally in the Southwest. One of these was the multistoried "communal house" (it is not entirely clear what Bandelier meant by the word "communal"), and the other embraced the numerous, scattered small houses of stone. For some reason, Bandelier failed to see, or at least to mention, the numerous adobe structures in the Southwest.

The communal houses were those of the Pueblo Indians. Adolph believed that the small houses might have been ancestral to the larger pueblos or that they were possibly the dwellings of the Jumanos or Apaches. Probably many of what Bandelier called small houses were no more than the field houses of Pueblo Indians past and present; it is unlikely that any were Apache habitations. Bandelier was also interested in the Apache language and suggested possible ties between it and the Nahuatl of central Mexico, on one hand, and Puebloan languages, on the other. Bandelier's conjectures mainly reflect the embryonic condition of American anthropology in the early 1880s. Apaches and Navajos were relatively late in arriving in the Southwest, and they speak a language of the Na-Dene stock—which is spoken only in western North America and is totally unrelated to the language of any other Indian group in either North or South America. It is generally believed that Na-Dene peoples entered the New World from Asia at a comparatively late date, probably no more than a few thousand years B.C. Hopi, however, and probably the Tanoan languages (spoken by all the modern Rio Grande Pueblos except for the Keresan group) are related to Nahuatl. Keresan and Zuni are not related (except perhaps on a very early "Amerind" time horizon) either to the Tanoans or Hopi or to each other. At the time of Bandelier's initial fieldwork, these linguistic relationships had yet to be worked out.

With his report finished, Bandelier returned to the "Historical Introduction: Part II," dealing with the expeditions to New Mexico of Fray Agustín Rodríguez, Antonio de Espejo, Gaspar Castaño de Sosa, and Juan de Oñate, who had explored (and, in the case of Oñate, settled) New Mexico in the 1580s and 1590s. As Adolph finished each section, he sent it along to Parkman, who in turn sent it to Norton. The AIA never published this manuscript, though it was mentioned in subsequent AIA publications. Bandelier did use the data he had collected in his own later works, the "Histoire" (1887–88) and the *Final Report: Parts I and II* (1890–92).

Even before completing the historical introduction, Adolph began to plan for his return to New Mexico. He wanted to find how far Pueblo architecture had penetrated into Chihuahua. Bandelier still intended to reach Mexico City in his attempt to relate the Pueblo Indians and Mexican cultures. For the field, he requested from Norton a 5-by-8-inch dry-plate process camera with fifty plates, a good pocket compass, and a good pocket level. He also requested a letter from the secretary of war to the southwestern military authorities.

Norton probably honored all of these requests. Bandelier certainly had his own camera a few weeks later, and in the AIA files was a letter from Robert Lincoln, son of the Civil War president. Lincoln, who was secretary of war, wrote on September 22, 1882:

> I have the honor to acknowledge the receipt of your letter of the 20th instant, asking that Mr. A. F. Bandelier, may have such a letter as may suffice

to secure him proper support and protection, in case of need, to the Commanders of the various military posts in the region he is to visit along the frontier of New Mexico. In response it gives me pleasure to enclose to you a letter addressed to Colonel R. S. Mackenzie, 4th U. S. Cavalry, in Command of the District of New Mexico, which will secure for Mr. Bandelier the protection desired, so far as it can properly be given.

Bandelier thanked Norton for his aid in this matter and in the same letter requested additional supplies, including drawing paper and paints. He sent Norton what Adolph called his "pets," seventy-eight sheets of watercolor paintings. These included ground plans, details of architecture, and images of articles of personal use, ornaments, pottery, and so forth. Bandelier also asked Norton's help in securing railroad passes.

Adolph, for all his preparation, did not get off for the Southwest by the end of September. From October 13 to 23, he was in Rochester with Mrs. Morgan. During this time he also wrote to the linguist James C. Pilling, of the Bureau of Ethnology, asking whether Pilling wanted a "vocabulary of the 'Queres' language of New Mexico. . . . It is in the Cochiti dialect."

On returning to Highland, Adolph made his farewell calls and then went on to St. Louis, accompanied by Joe. He left that city on the evening of November 2. In his journal Bandelier wrote, "Leave of Joe very very sad. Poor, dear, little wife. But it must be!" At the time, Bandelier thought he was leaving home for perhaps as long as two years.

After a stopover in Las Vegas to explore ruins in the Gallinas and Tecolote valleys, and after a brief stay at Pecos, Bandelier arrived in Santa Fe late in the afternoon of November 15. He crossed paths with Colonel Stevenson, whom he had first met in September 1880. Stevenson reported to his younger colleague on the cliff houses he had seen in Canyon de Chelly in Arizona Territory. Adolph renewed other earlier acquaintances. W. H. Brown, the photographer, aided in developing and printing photographic plates. Unfortunately for posterity, very few of Bandelier's photographs have survived; but some, at least, were used as illustrations in the later "Histoire," which was compiled as a gift from the Archdiocese of Santa Fe to Pope Leo XIII. Adolph also made a number of regional trips, including ones to the Cochiti and Tesuque areas, taking photographs and recording ethnographic data.

Returning to Santa Fe, Bandelier met José Olivas, who was to accompany him as guide and companion. Olivas was said to have been on one of the early territorial boundary surveys and to have served as a guide for Kit Carson. Of particular interest to Adolph was that Olivas was said to have seen Jumano Indians.

The Jumanos, who lived in the southwestern plains, were in early historic times traders between the eastern Pueblos and the Plains Indians. Bandelier was uncertain what language the Jumanos spoke, though early scholars considered it to be Apache. This now seems unlikely, and recent studies suggest that it was a language similar to Piro, the tongue of the southernmost Pueblos along the Rio Grande and in the Salinas region east of the river and in the Manzano Mountains.

At last "the long journey," as Adolph often referred to it, had begun. The route of the two companions took them from Santa Fe to Galisteo and then through the corridor east of the Sandia Mountains to San Antonito, Chililí, Tajique, and Manzano. The wind, snow, and cold were almost unbearable. At San Antonito, there was nearly a foot of snow. On December 24, the two men reached Manzano; Padre Louis Bourdier, a priest brought by Bishop Lamy to New Mexico Territory, insisted they stay with him. In his journal, Adolph made no mention of Christmas but did mention that he was again suffering from sores on his nose and lip. He saw the old Franciscan apple orchard, which local lore credited with giving the community of Manzano (Spanish for "apple tree") its name. Although Adolph was told of what he thought were small house ruins, he could find no one who recalled the Jumano Indians or the names of the pueblos as recorded by Oñate.

From Manzano, Adolph and José Olivas proceeded to the northern Salinas area, known today for its large, sandstone pueblo ruins and the seventeenth-century missions of Quarai and Abó. Deep snow hampered his collecting much surface pottery. He was impressed, however, as viewers are today, by the standing red sandstone walls that remained at these mission churches. Of Quarai he later wrote: "Cuaray is among the few picturesque sites in New Mexico that deserve the epithet of lovely."

Bandelier was at Abó as the year 1882 ended. On both the thirtieth and thirty-first of December he was taken by a local settler, don Román Cisneros, to Abó Pass and the Cañoncito de la Pintada (the route of present-day U.S. Highway 60) to observe the rock art, pictographs, and petroglyphs there. He copied a number of these figures, likening them to some he had seen in the Cueva Pintada when he was at Cochiti.

Adolph ended his 1882 journal with these remarks: "The night was spent at home (?) And at home [Highland] also are my thoughts! God be thanked for all his blessings. May He bless Joe, Papa, and *all*. May He lead me back again home, in body and in heart. The year is past, and an eventful year it was too. Tomorrow a new period begins. I wish I was at home."

EIGHT
A Hazardous Journey

. . . a journey memorable for archaeological science.

THE SALINAS AREA of New Mexico, where Adolph Bandelier found himself in December 1882, was so named because of the extensive salt deposits in its dry lakes, or *playas*—deposits that were economically important in both prehistoric and historic times. Today, the area is also referred to as the Estancia valley.

For "the long journey," Bandelier had come equipped with only the barest necessities. He packed a dry-plate camera with fifty plates, a wire tripod, a compass and a pocket level, drawing paper, black and white paints, and a few brushes, as well as the ever-present pages with pen and ink for his daily journal entries. He carried only a minimum of clothing and personal possessions.

Adolph and his guide, José Olivas, traveled on horseback. Olivas had been hired to care for the horses and Adolph's "bodily wants." The record is meager as to what the two men ate and how they were housed. On occasion, a resident priest took them in; at other times, they camped under the stars. Mail was at best infrequent. The bitter cold and snow that they had encountered since leaving Santa Fe on December 18 continued unrelentingly into January of 1883. Adolph noted that on this trip, "it snowed 16 days (or nights)."

Bandelier had come to the Salinas area to see the impressive stone ruins of the pueblos and seventeenth-century mission churches of Abó, Quarai, and Gran Quivira. These are now part of the Salinas Pueblo Missions National Monument, formed in 1980 when the New Mexico state monuments of Abó and Quarai were combined with Gran Quivira National Monument. The name Gran Quivira, used by Bandelier for one particular pueblo, is still used today, although it refers to the settlement known in the seventeenth century as Las Humanas.

Bandelier had also come here to test his hypothesis that the scattered ruins of small stone houses and villages in the Pecos, Cochiti, and Acoma-Cubero regions, which he had seen in 1880 and 1882, were actually remains of a widespread Jumano culture. Did small houses exist also in the Salinas? And was there additional evidence for the elusive Jumanos in this Salinas region, where a major pueblo (Las Humanas) seemed to carry the Jumano name?

Bandelier and Olivas spent the last week of 1882 and the first two weeks of 1883 in the Salinas area. Using Father Bourdier's residence at Manzano as their headquarters, they visited the ruined pueblos and Spanish mission churches of Quarai and Abó, taking photographs and measuring architectural features. Throughout this general area, Bandelier asked local residents about the Jumano Indians but could find no one who remembered them. He was, however, told of a number of small house ruins in the surrounding area, as well as near such neighboring pueblo ruins as Tabirá, Tenabó, Pueblo Colorado, and Pueblo Blanco.

On January 4, 1883, Bandelier left Manzano for Gran Quivira in a wagon with don Manuel Luján of Torreón, while José Olivas rode horseback. On January 5, they proceeded through the snow to Monte Alto and then crossed the Cañada de León and the Cañada de Aguaje. They climbed the Aguaje and camped at an elevation of 7,100 feet that night. The next day, Bandelier met a party of travelers and wrote a note to Josephine for them to mail at the nearest post office at Sabinal. His journal entry that night was one of the very few in which he permitted himself to express his deep feelings for Joe.

Bandelier, Olivas, and Luján pushed on in spite of terrible weather that made fieldwork next to impossible. The scientist did manage to describe the broken walls of the ruined pueblos and the great shells of the fallen mission churches. During Spanish exploration and colonization in the late sixteenth and early seventeenth centuries, the Salinas area had been a major population center in New Mexico, with an estimated ten thousand Indian inhabitants. But Spanish missionization there lasted less than one hundred years, and even before the Pueblo Revolt of 1680 the area was virtually abandoned. Besides devoting attention to the ruined architecture, Bandelier was curious about the Indians' water supply but noted that contemporary farmers in the area were growing maize without irrigation.

On January 7, the party discovered its horses missing. When the animals still had not been found by the ninth, Bandelier decided to return to Manzano on foot, leaving Olivas and Luján to continue the search. It was a dreadful trip, the snowpack averaging six inches, and Bandelier "broke through at every step, 35 miles, 11 hours."

Adolph reached Manzano the following day and again stayed at Padre Bourdier's home. At noon on January 11, Olivas and Luján arrived with the horses and wagon. Olivas, however, was ill, "even delirious," and had to be sent back to Santa Fe on horseback. During the next few days, Bandelier examined various ruins including Abó, sketched, and continued his search for small houses. On January 16, the scientist was afflicted with backaches and dizziness, and he stayed indoors to catch up on his sketching.

Several earlier biographies of Bandelier have stated that two of his companions died in a blizzard on an 1882 trip, and that at some point in his travels Bandelier had contracted smallpox. Possibly the illnesses of José Olivas and of Bandelier himself in the first part of January 1883 gave rise to such wild tales. At least, this Salinas trip was the only time Adolph encountered blizzard conditions with two companions.

On the morning of January 17, Adolph and Padre Bourdier left in Bourdier's buggy for Belén, with Bandelier's horse tied behind. The route took the two men through the Abó pass on a good road. The long anticipated trip to the Salinas region was over. By his own count, Bandelier had, since December 1882, traveled "239 miles on horseback and 35 miles on foot, secured the groundplans of 11 ruins, located 26 more, took 21 photographs & made fair collections." It was an impressive month's work by any reasonable standard.

Bandelier stayed in Belén until February 11, resting and recovering from the illness that had overcome him at Abó. On arriving, he found letters from Joe and other Highland family members. Adolph also noted a letter from Frank Bigler, his first known mention of this young railroad man who later was to become so important in the life of Bandelier's second wife, Fanny Ritter. He caught up on his own correspondence and sent his photographic plates to Brown in Santa Fe for developing; he was very pleased with the photographs when they were returned to him. He spent several days painting ground plans of the Salinas area ruins and images of pottery he had seen and meeting locally important people. The last was a habit Bandelier practiced everywhere, and it served him well. His new friends often passed him on to others who had special knowledge of regional Pueblo ruins and Indian history. Much of Bandelier's information in 1883–84 originated with such acquaintances.

In late January, Adolph made a quick excursion to the Tiwa-speaking pueblo of Isleta, where he recorded significant information. Except for his very brief visit to Tesuque Pueblo, this was the scholar's first experience with a non-Keresan-speaking village. After Isleta, he made a side trip to Albuquerque to visit William Borchert, the relative with whom Josephine had stayed in 1882. At this time Bandelier met, for the first time, Franz Huning—an important figure in early Albuquerque history and the builder of "Huning Castle," an ersatz German castle made of adobe and wood that was a landmark in Albuquerque until it was torn down in 1955.

Bandelier made his final departure from Belén on February 11, 1883, with a guide, Francisco (Frank) Rivalé, who went with the scholar as far as the Rito de San José near Laguna Pueblo. At Laguna, Bandelier met Frank Bigler and was the guest of Captain George H. Pradt, husband of a Laguna woman. Pradt had worked with the surveyor-general's office in Santa Fe for a time but had moved to Laguna in 1876 and, after his marriage into the tribe, had served as governor.

Bandelier also became acquainted with one of the Marmon brothers, although his journal entry leaves it unclear just which one. Like Pradt, both Walter and Robert Marmon were surveyors who had settled at Laguna, marrying women from the pueblo and ranching in the general area. Also, like Pradt, each of the Marmons served as governor at Laguna —Walter in 1880 and Robert in 1886. At Laguna, Bandelier met still another famous early New Mexican, Dr. John Menaul, a Presbyterian minister who in 1883 was involved in translating American schoolbooks such as McGuffey's first reader into Keresan. These men were all helpful in providing Adolph with information about the region and travel through it.

With his new friend, Frank Bigler, Bandelier examined ruins in the Laguna area, and the two men rode to Acoma "in a furious blizzard of snow," as Adolph wrote to Mrs. Morgan. The Illinois scholar recorded more ethnographic data at Acoma and then, back again at Laguna, watched a "Chacuan" dance with Bigler. Bandelier's "Chacuan" was probably the *chakwena,* a masked dance representing the kachinas, or ancestral spirits.

Leaving his horse at Laguna, Adolph took the train to Manuelito, a rail stop west of Gallup near the Arizona border. Finding no other transportation available, the scholar walked the thirty miles to Zuni Pueblo, arriving there on the evening of February 21.

Zuni was and is the last of the cluster of towns the sixteenth-century Spaniards called "Cibola," whose people have spoken an isolated language called Zuni. In late prehistoric and early historic times, the Cibola-Zuni Indians were important middlemen in an extensive trade moving from northern and western Mexico and from the Gulf of California into the Southwest. Contacted first by Fray Marcos de Niza in 1539, the Zuni people were missionized in the early seventeenth century. They joined the Pueblo rebellion of 1680, but when the Spaniards returned in 1692, the Zunis made a nominal gesture of submission. The Spaniards held Zuni only loosely, however, during the eighteenth century, and the Zuni people observed their weather-control and fertility ceremonies without much interference from Spanish authorities. The Zunis held themselves aloof from the Mexican authorities after Spain lost control of her colonies but were more or less friendly with the Americans, perhaps in alliance against Navajos who from time to time threatened the pueblo. By Bandelier's day, there were missionaries as well as anthropologists actively working at Zuni.

The original Spanish name, spelled with a tilde (Zuñi, pronounced *zunyi),* was actually a corruption of the Keresan name for the Zuni Indians used at Acoma Pueblo. We followed the old-style usage, Zuñi, in the first volume of *The Southwestern Journals of Adolph F. Bandelier,* published in 1966 when such use was still fairly common. For consistency, we continued to use Zuñi in the subsequent three volumes. Today, however, the word "Zuni" is preferred by Zuni Indians and others, and we use it here.

Arriving at Zuni, Bandelier was welcomed by Frank Hamilton Cushing (1857–1900) who had come with Major J. W. Powell's Smithsonian expedition of 1879. Attracted to the Zuni Indians and their culture, Cushing left the expedition and lived at Zuni Pueblo until the spring of 1884. During his residence there, Cushing worked his way into important ceremonial positions. He learned the Zuni language to some degree, as is demonstrated by letters Cushing wrote in that language to

Zuni friends and tribal elders. These letters can be read by Zuni speakers today, though they are somewhat garbled grammatically.

For Bandelier and Cushing, with their many similar interests, these weeks together must have been mutually influential. Cushing certainly knew and understood Zuni culture better than Bandelier ever knew and understood Cochiti or Santo Domingo. But the older man, with his extensive documentary knowledge and archaeological information, had a broader comprehension of southwestern culture history than did Cushing.

Cushing proved to be well informed about ruins in the Zuni area, and Bandelier visited and drew ground plans of many of them. The two men climbed the Zuni sacred mountain, Dowa Yalanne, just east of the pueblo. Together they witnessed a number of dances, and Cushing told Bandelier many Zuni myths, a particular interest of Cushing's. W. L. Metcalf, the artist for *Scribners* and *Harper's Weekly,* was serving as illustrator for the Cushing party at this time and gave Adolph pointers on his drawing. Christian Barthelemes, a musician in the Thirteenth Infantry stationed at nearby Fort Wingate, was also at Zuni photographing while Bandelier was there and offered to share photographic plates.

Bandelier found the whole experience at Zuni so rewarding and intellectually stimulating that it was difficult for him to break away and resume traveling. In a letter to Mrs. Morgan, Bandelier praised his younger colleague, calling him "the direct successor to Mr. Morgan in the study of Indian life." High praise, that, from Adolph Bandelier!

In a letter to Francis Parkman about the same time, however, Bandelier did offer a mild criticism of Cushing in the course of explaining his own plans.

> There is absolutely no use in making disjointed explorations. The picture must be full or else it will look like a painting without a background. Had I gone to Chihuahua at once, I would have done fragmentary work only, now I go with the current and see the banks well on both sides. And I have felt at Zuñi, that I must do such work *myself,* as even Frank Cushing yet lacks the basis of critical knowledge.

Presumably, Bandelier saw his work for the AIA in American Indian culture history in a bit different light from that in which he saw Morgan's theory building. Perhaps Cushing, like Morgan, might not have been the best person in the world for the kind of historical study that Bandelier chose to pursue.

On March 7, 1883, Bandelier and Cushing left Zuni together for Fort Wingate, an army installation east of Gallup, New Mexico. They traveled in a buckboard with a team of what proved to be two very stubborn mules. En route, they stopped to inspect the ruins of Heshota Ucla (Heshotula), where they camped for the night. The next day, continuing their trip, Bandelier tried to help Cushing whip up the mules, fell overboard, and was dragged several feet, one wheel running over his chest. Although he suffered no broken bones, Adolph was badly bruised.

A Zuni Indian on a mule overtook the two men at Nutria, bringing items that Cushing had forgotten. Cushing rode the mule to Fort Wingate, leaving the Zuni man to accompany Bandelier for the remainder of the trip to the fort. In a journal entry of March 9, 1883, Adolph wrote, "Besides, am very hungry, had nothing to eat, and still have nothing but water and some strong tea. I write this at 4 P.M., and I have now been 30 hours without a morsel." This situation was soon rectified when W. L. Metcalf arrived from Fort Wingate with "a big 4 mule train, laden with choice provisions. . . . Mr. Cushing sent beer and segars, also whisky. I could not help but need stimulants this time, although my bruises are fast waning and disappearing."

On arriving at Fort Wingate, the Illinois scholar first met Dr. Washington Matthews. An army surgeon, Matthews (1843–1905) had studied the Indians near Fort Union in Montana, and since being stationed at Fort Wingate he had become particularly interested in the Navajo Indians in the area.

As he had with Cushing, Bandelier shared numerous common interests with Matthews. Dr. Matthews told Bandelier about Navajo culture, and Adolph used some of his time measuring pueblo ruins and painting ground plans. Having finished his drawings, he packed up and returned to Laguna by train on the twenty-third of March. On this leg of the trip, Bandelier met Dumas Provencher, founder of the town of San Rafael, south of present-day Grants. At this time, we learn the name of Bandelier's horse, as the scholar noted in his journal, "Chico is a splendid animal." And indeed, Chico *was* a splendid animal, faithfully carrying Bandelier during the long days ahead in Arizona, Sonora, and Chihuahua.

While at the fort, Bandelier made plans for a return to Zuni, had his boots resoled and his trousers reinforced, and collected supplies for the onward trip west and south. He left luggage with Dr. Matthews to be sent south at a later date. After leaving Zuni, Adolph was prepared to travel alone with only two saddlebags and two blankets. For the trip back to Zuni Pueblo, however, he was accompanied by an infantry soldier with a horse and a pack mule. It proved to be a cold twelve-hour ride. On arrival, Adolph was pleased to learn that Joe had written to Mrs. Emily Magill Cushing, who had married Frank only a year previously and was now at Zuni.

Bandelier remained at the pueblo the first five days of April. Again he filled his journal with notes relating to Zuni life and to area ruins. He visited the well-known historic pueblo of Hawikuh and also completed an article for *Das Ausland*. Despite his earlier expressed willingness to proceed west from Zuni alone, Adolph tried to persuade a young Zuni Indian to guide him as far as Fort Apache on the White River, a north tributary of the Salt River. Seemingly, the fact that both Chiricahua and White Mountain Apaches were roaming the region north of the fort made Bandelier wish for a guide.

It was probably for the same reason that the Zuni governor forbade the young man to accompany Adolph. Left with no reasonable alternative, Bandelier left Zuni with only Chico as companion and headed west. He was understandably apprehensive about his Arizona travels, especially the first leg of the journey west and south from Zuni, into an area where hostile Apaches had been reported. Leaving San Juan (present-day St. Johns) and the grassy plain, without a tree, Bandelier found himself in a rather dense stand of piñon and juniper and became confused. After trying several "roads" and riding many extra miles, he returned to San Juan, where he finally located the correct road. This was one of the rare times that Adolph recorded in his journal that he had been lost.

Bandelier's route took him on a fifteen-day trip through San Juan, Show-low (modern Show Low), and on to Fort Apache. Once he reached the fort, Bandelier planned to move from army base to army base in southern Arizona. As it turned out, he depended—as he had in New Mexico—on local ranchers and other settlers for shelter. Even today this part of Arizona is sparsely populated, and in 1883 any visitor, especially an urbane sort like Bandelier, was warmly welcomed. Along the way, Adolph made ground plans of ruins and examined potsherds he found on the ruins' surfaces. His mode of travel did not permit his making collections, and after Zuni, there was no mention of his taking photographs either.

On this "journey memorable for archaeological science," Bandelier considered himself something of a trailblazer, adventuring into unknown territory. In truth, he was following an old Apache trading trail between Zuni and the Gila River drainage. This trail, several hundred years old, was one of the branches of the prehistoric trail system from the upper Southwest to Sonora.

Although Bandelier was indeed traveling through a somewhat remote portion of the territory, Arizona as a whole was not all that isolated. It had become part of the United States as a result of the Mexican War of 1846. The gold rush of 1849 and the Gadsden Purchase of 1854 helped draw Anglo-Americans into the region, and Arizona was formed into a separate territory of the United States in 1863. Cities were founded, especially in the rich Gila and Salt river valleys, a railroad was thrust across the southern part of the territory, and stage lines branched out in all directions. The army established a series of military forts with its own network of primitive roads and a military telegraph system to protect settlers and ranchers from the raiding Apaches. Parts of this network employed the use of heliographs placed on mountaintops, which had the advantage of using no connecting wires that could be cut by Indians wanting to interrupt communication.

Moving along his route, Adolph found and examined innumerable ruins. One of these was in the "beautiful valley of San Jose, or 'Las Tusas,'" where Bandelier found a small pueblo, probably one of the old western Pueblo sites that in part were ancestral to Zuni.

At Show-low, he met the town's founder and well-known early Arizonan, Corydon E. Cooley. This former Confederate officer had an Apache wife, a daughter of the White Mountain chief, Pedro. Indeed, Cooley was said to have married this woman and her sister simultaneously, the sister dying soon after the wedding. Also living in Show-low was Henry Huning, brother of Franz Huning of Huning Castle fame, whom Bandelier had met a few weeks before in Albuquerque.

On April 19, Huning and a Mr. H. Celso accompanied Bandelier to Fort Apache, the men traveling by buckboard with Chico led behind. The scenery must have been especially attractive, for the scholar gave an eloquent description in his journal notes. He wrote of "stately forests of pine" and "wild, heavily timbered mountain scenery, with an occasional fillet of water."

Fort Apache was originally founded as Camp Ord in 1870, and it had been expanded and renamed several times by Bandelier's day. It served to control the various Apache bands in the vicinity. At Fort Apache in 1883 was Sergeant Will C. Barnes, post telegrapher. In later years, Barnes became a popular writer on Arizona history and traditions. In memoirs Barnes wrote many years after the event, there is an account of Bandelier's arrival at Fort Apache. In reality, the soberly dressed Bandelier arrived at the fort by buckboard in the company of Huning and Celso on April 19. Barnes, however, gave a rather fanciful account that is worth quoting as an example of the folklore that later grew up around Adolph.

On the 25th [*sic*] of April, 1883, a lone traveler rode into the Post. The Chiricahua Apaches under Geronimo were then busy making life miserable for the people of Arizona, and it was unsafe to move about unless in strong, well-armed parties. For this reason the lone rider caused more or less comment as he came across the paradeground. He was a singular figure. On his head was a genuine Scottish bonnet, the Glengarry, with the two ribbons hanging down behind; he wore a Norfolk jacket, knickerbockers of rough tweed, and heavy English walking shoes—a costume that would have attracted attention almost anywhere west of the Mississippi River, and certainly so on the Indian frontier in Arizona Territory.

He was mounted on a diminutive yellow mule. A vast Spanish saddle almost covered the beast, which was not much bigger than a burro. The rider's long legs just missed the ground. On the pommel of the saddle was a pair of large Spanish *cantinas;* and at the cantle a roll of blankets inside of which were all his earthly possessions.

Although this was pure nonsense, what happened a few days later was very real indeed. According to Barnes, he was listening to the telegraph on Monday, April 28, when

I heard a message from Fort Whipple Arizona Headquarters, to the Commanding Officer at Fort Bowie, a post some two hundred miles to the south east of Apache and quite close to the Mexican line. I caught the name "Bandelier" in the message. Grabbing a pencil, I began to copy. [The message stated] that reports had been received . . . to the effect that Professor Bandelier of the American Archaeological Institute of Boston had been killed by Apaches of Geronimo's band in the region south of Fort Bowie.

Bandelier immediately telegraphed to Papa and Joe in Highland and wrote letters to various friends, including García Icazbalceta, that, in the words of Mark Twain, "reports of my death have been greatly exaggerated."

Adolph's stay at Fort Apache was generally pleasant. He did become sick one evening from eating spoiled canned salmon, but he was able to go out the next day to look at the nearby ruin of Kinishba, the largest of the sites near Fort Apache. This was a western Pueblo site dating from the mid-twelfth to the mid-fourteenth century, later excavated in 1931–39 by the archaeologist Byron Cummings. Bandelier made sketches, mailing them home to Highland along with some fifty pages of his journal. He painted artifacts and interviewed an influential Apache medicine man named U-clemy. One reason for staying on at the fort was that Bandelier's left foot had become infected from abrasions made by strapping his moccasin too tightly.

Finally the foot healed enough so that Adolph could wear his boots, and he departed Fort Apache on May 8. Because of the danger from Apache resistors, the scholar was provided with a military escort to Fort Thomas, located in the Gila River valley about twenty-five miles northwest of present-day Safford. On the way, Bandelier visited the San Carlos Apache agency and reservation and noted the customs of the Indians. The little party reached Fort Thomas on May 11.

The Illinois scientist spent the next few days exploring the region of the middle Gila River. He returned to Fort Thomas, visited the mining settlement of Globe, and examined ruins of the Hohokam culture in the Gila valley. Following that, Bandelier made a trip into the upper Salt River valley and explored ruins in the Tonto Basin, including the cliff dwellings of the present-day Tonto National Monument. These impressive ruins were badly pothunted in the years following Bandelier's visit. Finally, in 1907, they were designated a national monument, and they were partially excavated in the later 1930s. The cliff dwellings belong to the Salado culture and date from the fourteenth century. Many of the ruins Bandelier visited are now under the waters of Lake Roosevelt.

From the Tonto area, Bandelier moved on to Fort McDowell on the Verde River a few miles north of the Salt River, meeting his first Pima

Indians in this region. From Fort McDowell, Bandelier traveled to Tempe and Mesa City (present-day Mesa), noting the Mormon settlements there.

In that area, Bandelier met Charles Trumbull Hayden, an influential Arizona pioneer who owned a gristmill near Mesa in the Salt River valley. At the time of Bandelier's visit, Hayden's son, Carl T. Hayden, was five years old. Carl Hayden later served with distinction in the United States Senate for many years.

Bandelier next rode eastward to investigate the great ruin of Casa Grande in the Gila valley between modern Phoenix and Tucson. This ruin (now a national monument) is still famous for its four-story-high rectangular building of puddled caliche. It was constructed about A.D. 1300 but had been abandoned before the earliest Spaniards came into the region. At Casa Grande, Adolph stayed in the home of Judge John D. Walker, who had been born in Illinois in 1840—the same year Bandelier was born. Walker had settled among the Pimas in the 1860s. He spoke Pima and was able to give Bandelier a considerable amount of information on these Indians.

On June 26, Adolph finally reached Tucson, having traveled, according to him, "a total of 1847 English miles." Whether this exact figure was true or not, there is no doubt that from mid-December 1882 to late June 1883, Bandelier had visited an incredible number of Indian ruins in New Mexico and Arizona—all in the course of traveling many, many miles.

From Tucson, the scholar backtracked by train to Albuquerque on July 4, and then on the sixth of July met with Cushing in Santa Fe. He found the city hosting a "Tertio Millenial Celebration" under the mistaken notion that the city had been founded 333 years previously, in 1550, a bit of misinformation that Bandelier treated with great contempt.

From Santa Fe, Adolph returned to Highland, where Lizzie Bandelier was to be married to a young resident of Breese, Illinois, named Henry Kaune. Adolph and Josephine Bandelier considered Lizzie almost a daughter, although in fact Lizzie was a second cousin to Adolph.

Few details of the wedding are on record. In his journal of September 11, Bandelier commented, "Botheration of the wedding begins. License, etc. etc." The next day, "Much trouble and bustle in the house. Not less than six women in the kitchen. . . . Rehearsal! Tomorrow the 'love-feast' begins." On the thirteenth, the day of the wedding, he wrote, "Had to get up at 5:30 A.M. The trains (freight trains) going west, collided in the bottom of Silver Creek, thus delaying the passengers. The latter came up one hour behind time. . . . Very happy, but also exceedingly busy day." On the fourteenth, "Everybody tired. Rest of the wedding. At 4 P.M. the old folks left all. Evening pleasant, but all very tired."

On the fifteenth, Lizzie and Henry left for their new home, and Adolph wrote, "The house looks quite empty. Joe is tolerably well, but very, very tired. Am slowly returning to a normal state."

Bandelier spent his time catching up on family business, writing for the AIA, and making plans for future research. He also lectured to the Missouri Historical Society in St. Louis in late September.

An event of considerable importance in Adolph's life was his beginning to write a novel, later to be published as *The Delight Makers.* Originally, however, he wrote the book in German with the title *Die Koshare;* it was published serially in the German-language newspaper *Belletristisches Journal* beginning in 1890. The English version also appeared in 1890 as a book.

Saying farewell to loved ones in Highland, Adolph left with Joe on October 15 to spend a few days with family and friends in St. Louis. He bade Joe good-bye on the twenty-second of October, and three days later he reached Santa Fe to resume fieldwork in the Southwest.

During the last weeks of 1883, Adolph Bandelier was involved in his usual medley of activities, among them a trip by train to Isleta Pueblo, Las Cruces, El Paso, Senecu, and Paso del Norte (present-day Juárez, in Chihuahua). At the last three places he inquired about various aboriginal Indian groups of the area: Mansos, Piros, Senecus, and Zumas. At Paso del Norte, Bandelier met Padre Ramón [Román?] Ortiz, curate of the mission church there, who let him work in the church's archives. Ortiz was and is famous as the person who, in 1850, built the first Roman Catholic church within the city limits of El Paso.

Adolph was now thinking ahead to his field trip to Sonora and Chihuahua, but for the time being he paused in Santa Fe. On November 22 he received a telegram from General George Crook, army commander of the territory of Arizona, advising him not to go into the Sierra Madre because of the existing state of Indian hostilities. The same day, Bandelier renewed his acquaintance with Sam Eldodt, the trader at San Juan Pueblo who would become important to Adolph in later years.

On December 11, 1883, Bandelier left Santa Fe for southern New Mexico; he spent the last days of the year in the Mimbres valley, home of the famous Mimbres pottery with its highly unusual naturalistic painted designs.

Early in 1884, the scientist explored the Gila River cliff dwellings, now the site of Gila Cliff Dwellings National Monument. In late January, he was in Silver City, New Mexico, where he found mail from home. On January 26, Bandelier arrived in Tucson. Ahead was the most dangerous period of his North American fieldwork, a trip into remote areas of the Sierra Madre of northern Mexico.

NINE
Into the Sierra Madre

On the whole I am well satisfied with the results of my explorations. But it is decidedly the last trip.

O N JANUARY 26, 1884, Adolph Bandelier arrived in Tucson by train and rented a room from a Mrs. Black, a woman with whom he had stayed the previous year. By February 4, Bandelier had completed a report for Professor Norton. This document, which appeared later in the AIA's fifth annual report, summarized his travels as well as giving his interpretations of the ruins he had seen from late January 1883 to February 4, 1884.

At this stage, certain AIA members were becoming critical of Bandelier's field methods. Stephen Salisbury, Jr., for example, wrote to Norton on April 6, 1884, expressing these misgivings:

> I wish to tell you that a friend of mine who met Mr. Bandelier at Santa Fe [probably in November or December 1882] considers that Mr. Bandelier contents himself with doing what is easiest for himself, and expressed his opinion that we should never get the best results from his labors. You and Mr. Haynes know best as [to] the value of his voluminous communications, but it has always seemed to me that a delicate request to condense the bulk of matter might do some good. I think Mr. Bandelier thinks there is great virtue in many pages of matter.

Salisbury disliked Morgan's theories and also had reservations about Bandelier, whom he considered a devoted Morgan disciple. But Salisbury was not alone in criticizing Bandelier's reports; several other AIA members shared his view. Norton, however, seems to have accepted Parkman's advice in this regard. It was Parkman's opinion that Bandelier would do his best work for the AIA if left on his own.

There is no question that Bandelier was wordy, and although Salisbury failed to mention it, he wrote what might best be called "fractured" English. All his professional life, Bandelier was criticized for both his volume of writing and his insensitivity to English syntax. Still, it is a little difficult to think of Bandelier's months of travel through New Mexico and Arizona, with their deprivations and exposure to real danger from Apaches, as doing "what is easiest for himself."

With his AIA report concluded, Adolph was ready to undertake the long-anticipated trip to Mexico, in spite of the Apache threat. Reclaiming his horse, Chico, who had been cared for by Dr. J. B. Girard, a friend and post surgeon at Fort Lowell, Bandelier left Tucson on February 7, 1884, his route taking him eastward to the San Pedro River valley. He then rode up the valley, stopping off at Fort Huachuca and crossing into Mexico in the vicinity of the small Arizona town of Palominas on February 20. Ahead lay the most difficult and dangerous part of his reconnaissance.

The hazard from Apaches in northern Mexico was very real. The previous year, General Crook had led an expedition of 193 Apache scouts and one company of the U.S. Sixth Cavalry through Sonora and Chihuahua into the Sierra Madre. Their target had been a group of Chiricahua Apaches who, with members of other bands, had fled from the San Carlos agency under the leadership of Geronimo, Juh, Nané, and other headmen.

Between May 18 and May 29, 1883, the expedition had persuaded Geronimo, Nané, and most of the others to surrender, leaving only Juh and his band still at large. Crook and his troops escorted 374 men, women, and children back to Arizona. According to one account, Juh died, or was killed, near Casas Grandes sometime later that year. Bandelier, however, believed Juh was still alive and roaming with his band in Chihuahua. The possibility of an encounter with the Apache leader caused Adolph real concern. Not only had he been refused assistance by the military, but he also had been specifically warned by General Crook not to go into the Sierra Madre.

Virtually no correspondence exists from this Mexican trip, and one must rely on Bandelier's journals, along with a short printed summary in his later *Final Report: Part I,* to interpret and fully appreciate his work in northern Mexico. The journals give a considerable amount of information, however, and they also reflect Humboldt's continuing influence on the younger scholar. Bandelier made detailed comments on geographical features, flora, and fauna, as well as on the human condition in the sierra. Because of travel risks, Adolph and Chico joined other travelers whenever possible. On short trips between villages, this might involve only one or two men, but on longer segments of the route, there might be virtual convoys.

It was a rigorous trip, and a lonelier one than Bandelier had previously experienced. His major interests continued to be recording ruins and drawing ground plans, describing associated material culture, and recording the ethnography, language, and history of the north Mexican tribes.

At first Bandelier thought the comparatively advanced deterioration of many ruins meant that they were very old, but then he decided that climatic factors were largely responsible. For the most part, the ruins were small pueblos and scattered small houses built of local materials. Some were undoubtedly pre-Hispanic, because the northeast section of Sonora, especially parts of the Sonora, Montezuma, and Yaqui-Bavispe valleys, was heavily occupied by the late fourteenth century. Bandelier was unable to sort out the various cultural periods involved, though in fairness to him, it should be stressed that almost nothing was known of Sonoran archaeology at that time. Indeed, only since World War II have archaeologists achieved any real understanding of the prehistory of Sonora and Chihuahua.

Once in Mexico, Bandelier rode south into the Rio Sonora drainage and followed that stream via Arizpe and Sinoquipe to Banámichi. Using that town as headquarters, the scholar explored this section of the Sonora valley, visiting Huepac and Aconchi and reaching as far south as Babiácora, some twenty miles north of the Ures Gorge.

Bandelier was then in the heart of historic Opata Indian country, and he was extremely interested in the Opatas, their language (by his time spoken only sporadically), and their culture. Opata is a language related to the Tarahumar and Cáhitan tongues and, at a greater distance, to Tepiman. It is part of the great Azteco-Tanoan family of native American languages. It has completely died out today, but there are, fortunately, extensive Jesuit vocabularies and grammars of various Opata dialects.

The Opatas were living in the Sonora valley when Coronado's parties came through in 1539 and 1540–42. At that time, they were town-dwelling Indians who occupied large settlements and had small, warlike "statelets" along the Sonora and Yaqui rivers. Bandelier knew little of this, for the major account of early contact with the Opatas—a journal kept by Baltasar de Obregón during the Ibarra expedition of the early 1560s—was unknown to him. Obregón's work, the primary account of the Ibarra entrada into Sonora and Chihuahua, was discovered by Mariano Cuevas in the Archivo General de las Indias in Seville and was published in 1924, long after Bandelier's death. Detailed archaeology in the Sonora River valley, which uncovered the large Opata settlements, was not begun until after 1970.

From Babiácora, Bandelier turned east, crossing the rugged Sierra de la Palma to Oposura (present-day Moctezuma) in the Moctezuma valley, then made for Casas Grandes. Had he continued south through the Ures Gorge, he would have been within easy reach of Hermosillo and the major west coast route to Guadalajara and eventually Mexico City.

The eastward turn at Babiácora did not mean—at that point—that Bandelier had decided against going to the capital. He may well have wished to go down the *east* side of the Sierra Madre and to see the important site of Casas Grandes before he continued south. If that were the case, his crossing the sierra in these northern parts made good sense. Not only did he reach the Chihuahua basin country reasonably near Casas Grandes, but he also avoided the trails farther south, which were difficult to traverse. However, that still leaves the question of why Bandelier turned back at Casas Grandes as he did, eventually returning to Santa Fe instead of forging on to Mexico City.

Earlier, Bandelier had considered the horseback trip to Mexico City crucial to his understanding of southwestern Pueblo culture history. It is possible, of course, that after his work in New Mexico and Arizona, Adolph had come to believe that the trip through northern Mexico would give him sufficient data to determine the southern boundary of Pueblo Indian culture. If so, he must have made the decision sometime in the early months of 1884. As of the time he left Santa Fe in December 1883, Bandelier still wrote of reaching Mexico City. In any case, neither Norton nor Parkman seems to have been disturbed by this change of plan—at least, no AIA correspondence ever mentioned it. Nor did Adolph himself ever express any disappointment over it or even acknowledge that there *was* a change in plan.

Continuing east from Oposura, Bandelier and Chico reached the Río Yaqui on April 3. At times, the scholar traveled at night for safety or to escape the daytime heat and dust. In his journal entry of April 6, Bandelier described one such night trip from Bacadehuachi to Nacori as involving "seven men, six of them with rifles, one horse, two machos [stallions], and ten burros about." For much of the distance between Babiácora and Nacori, Adolph apparently walked. He had bought a new pair of boots en route, and already at Nacori they needed new soles. It is common, even today, in the more remote and rugged parts of the Sierra Madre, to walk over steep and broken trails, for safety's sake and to spare the horses. Having a horse fall on the slippery slopes is a constant danger to both horse and rider.

From Nacori, Bandelier went on to Huassavas (present-day Huasabas) and spent a few days examining Jesuit church archives. By the first decades of the seventeenth century, the Jesuit order had gradually pushed its line of missions up the west coast and highlands of Mexico. At Huasabas, Adolph also measured "the abundant remains of ancient garden beds and dwellings."

From there he joined a convoy to Huachinera, commenting, "It would have been, to say the least, imprudent to undertake the trip of fifty miles alone; and in a mountain wilderness, where the presumption was that Apaches might be encountered at any moment." From Huachinera and Baserac on the Yaqui River, Bandelier went to Bavispe, the final stop in Sonora. There he turned east and entered Chihuahua on May 1 on a daytime trip with a cortege of seventy-eight horses, mules, and donkeys and twenty-four men. They were using the approximate route General Crook had taken through the Sierra Madre in 1883 from Bavispe to Janos.

Adolph described the ruins at Janos as similar to those at Casas Grandes. From Janos, the scientist turned south and arrived at Casas Grandes on May 8. He spent nearly the entire month at this large and important site, measuring it and drawing ground plans in his journal.

There is nothing in Bandelier's journals to indicate that he was aware that this was one of the points he had been seeking for so long—the area where Pueblo Indian culture and Mexican culture merged. Although his field notes were extremely valuable to Charles C. Di Peso, who in 1958–61 excavated a portion of Casas Grandes, Bandelier himself was not at all clear about what the town represented. He tramped over the

large site, drawing and commenting on the multistoried adobe buildings. He located and traced one of the main acequias, or canals, that
brought water into Casas Grandes. He commented on turquoise that he
said was "found abundantly in the ruins after heavy rains; they call them
chalchihuites." He mentioned finds of worked copper at the ruins and
effigy pottery in human and bird shapes, though he did not see examples
of either metal or effigy pottery. In part II of his *Final Report,* Bandelier
commented that the pottery was like that of New Mexico, but he gave
no details. In fact, polychrome pottery similar to the Salado poly-
chromes of southern Arizona appears in considerable amounts at Casas
Grandes.

Casas Grandes was well known and much visited (and looted) even in
Bandelier's day. The great site was the subject of speculation for many
years, until Di Peso's extensive excavations finally produced a basic understanding of the town and its environs. Casas Grandes is indeed a mix-
ture of southwestern and Mesoamerican traits. The site developed out of
an early Mogollon culture but began to show influence from farther
south in Mexico by perhaps A.D. 700. Its period of greatest expansion
was the Medio period, now dated from about A.D. 1150 to 1450, when
Casas Grandes itself had a population of some five thousand people and
the Casas Grandes valley was also heavily occupied. At that time, Casas
Grandes supplied the upper Southwest with luxury goods including the
much-prized scarlet macaw (*Ara macao*), copper bells, and shells from the
Gulf of Cortez. In return, the Casas Grandes people imported turquoise
and other highly desired trade items.

Di Peso, the excavator of Casas Grandes, believed the site had actually
been taken over by central or west Mexican traders, forerunners of the
later Aztec *pochteca,* a class of organized traders. This seemed to have ush-
ered in the climax period of Casas Grandes culture—the Paquimé phase
of the Medio period, beginning about A.D. 1300. Not all specialists on
the lower Southwest accept the *pochteca* hypotheses, and there is dis-
agreement over what actually went on at Casas Grandes. Most archaeologists, however, concede that it was a major trading center during
Medio times.

Before leaving Casas Grandes, Bandelier made an extremely demanding six-day side trip by foot with two local guides westward into the
Sierra Madre. They explored parts of the Arroyo Nombre de Dios and the
valley of the Piedras Verdes, finding numerous ruins and well-preserved

cave houses. Recent work by archaeologists Paul E. Minnis and Michael E. Whalen have focused to a large degree on these sierra sites.

On June 3, Bandelier rode to Corralitos, north of Casas Grandes, where he received "a bundle of letters . . . from Joe, Mr. Parkman, Greenleaf, Meysenburg, and from Lt. C. P. Elliott," whom Bandelier had known at both Fort Cummings and Fort Lowell. He also received word of the death at age 39 of Charles Lambelet, husband of Joe's sister Bertha Huegy Lambelet, in a shredding machine accident on his Highland farm. Adolph promptly wrote to Joe and to Parkman.

Knowing that Bandelier received letters from both Parkman and Greenleaf of the AIA, one cannot help wondering whether one of them, if not both, carried word of the institute's decision to terminate Bandelier's salary as of January 1, 1885. This action does not seem to have been prompted by criticism of Bandelier, however, for the minutes of the meeting at which the decision was reached also indicate that the AIA had severe financial problems and was cutting back on both its American and Mediterranean research programs. The letters perhaps also contained the more cheerful news of Adolph's election, at the annual meeting in May 1884, as a "Life Member" of the AIA, in recognition of his valuable services. Parkman or Greenleaf, or both, may also have mentioned that three members of the executive committee were willing to provide the necessary funds to print Bandelier's Mexican report. In his journal, Bandelier had no comment to make on any of these matters.

In Corralitos, Adolph seems to have been staying with a Mr. Adolph Muenzenberger, who had moved to Mexico with his family from Belleville, Illinois. Bandelier had first met Muenzenberger on May 5 and arranged for mail to be sent in care of him. When Bandelier turned up on June 3, there was some sort of misunderstanding, and Muenzenberger was quite unfriendly—"but I do not mind it for the ladies are so much the kinder for all that."

Finally, on the night on June 6, Bandelier left for Janos, reaching that town the next morning. He spent a few days examining ruins in the Janos area, and then on the night of June 10 rode north, reaching Deming, New Mexico, on June 14. Regarding his work in northern Mexico, Bandelier had already summed up his feelings in a journal entry of June 5:

> On the whole I am well satisfied with the results of my explorations. But it is decidedly the last trip. These protracted absences from home, the

anxious suspense, etc., they are worrying and wearing [me] out far too much, and Charles' terrible death is a warning from God, not to abuse His leniency and clemency. It is certain that, once at home, other trials will expect me, but He will also grant me the power to go through these.

In Deming, Bandelier learned that the railroad bed between there and Santa Fe had been washed out in a flood that had extended as far north as Santo Domingo and Cochiti. Telegraph wires soon became inoperable as well, so that after nearly a five-month absence, Adolph could not communicate with Joe and Papa. Although the long "journey memorable for archaeological science" was at last at an end, Bandelier was so distraught over the delays ahead that he did not record a final tab of the miles traveled on this leg of his journey or the number of ruins he had examined. He did not even enter the usual few lines of praise for his faithful mount, Chico. Indeed, he made no mention whatsoever of Chico's future upon their arrival in Deming.

As there were still railroad connections to Tucson, Adolph decided to go there and wait until the trains could get through to Santa Fe. He used these days in typical fashion—examining ruins, taking notes on a manuscript, visiting Fort Lowell, and exploring Tucson.

On June 28, Adolph returned to Deming and the next day traveled by rail to Albuquerque. He stopped there long enough to visit the Borcherts and Joe's brother, Eddy Huegy. Moving on, he spent eleven days in Santa Fe, and for most of that time was "unwell." Perhaps the most important thing Bandelier did was to arrange with H. Hartmann to draw a map of Sonora and Chihuahua based on Bandelier's geographical notes. Adolph later used this map in his *Final Report*. He then visited Samuel Ellison, the territorial librarian, in whose collections he found a copy of Vargas's journal and made notes from it.

Bandelier then made a round of calls to say good-bye, and in a journal entry combining the days of July 9 to 12, he wrote, "Shall I ever return? It is impossible to tell. God alone Knows! At all events I believe it will not be very soon, if ever. I leave Santa Fe as quietly as I came into it, four years ago, without fussing at all, no state dinners nor banquets, hardly noticed by the papers."

On July 13, Bandelier and a young companion left for Pecos in a buckboard supplied by General Luther P. Bradley of Fort Marcy. The following day, Adolph went on to Las Vegas, stopping off for three days

to say good-bye to friends there. The July 16 entry in his journal included this statement: "This is my last day in New Mexico, perhaps
forever. How many memories, good and bad! May God bring it to a favorable end."

The Mexico trip was over. Bandelier's feeling of finality about New
Mexico was, as it turned out, premature, since the Bandelier family
would live there for another seven years. But never again would Adolph
visit the Sierra Madre. To some extent, his research in northern Mexico
might even be called a setback to science, because Bandelier never really
understood the archaeological richness and the tremendous archaeological importance of northern Sonora and Chihuahua. By this failure,
Bandelier helped, in his own small way, to foster the myth that northern
Mexico was a cultural vacuum. Within a decade or so after his work in
the Southwest, the feeling was beginning to grow among scholars that
only the American Southwest was worthy of interest. That myopic view
was to dominate southwestern archaeology—with a few notable exceptions—for the next three-quarters of a century.

TEN
A Crisis in Highland

About 4 P.M. came a letter from Papa stating that he
would never return!! Hereafter, he ceases to exist for us.

BANDELIER ARRIVED in Highland on July 20, 1884, noting in
his journal that Joe and Papa were well. On July 28, a journal entry ended
with the words, "Papa had, of course, disagreeable business news"—a
harbinger of the bank crisis ahead.

The F. Ryhiner and Company bank was in deep trouble. Southern
Illinois had suffered a major depression in 1884, one of the economic
swings that had afflicted the United States since the Civil War. Money
was in short supply, and the bank, it would seem, had been in difficulty
for some time. Its primary financial backer was a Swiss banking establishment named Gruner-Haller, whose main offices were in Bern. As the
year 1884 wore on, the fate of the Highland bank lay increasingly in the
hands of the Swiss managers of Gruner-Haller.

Although illness and mounting anxiety about business affairs took their
toll, Bandelier went about much his usual routine for the next two weeks.
On August 4, he journeyed to St. Louis, visiting relatives, friends, and library; he returned home on August 5, "My 44th birthday!" (Actually, his
birthday was the next day, the sixth.)

On August 27, Adolph noted that he had gone to see "Mr. Rod
Graffenried," a wealthy Highland farmer and a long-time friend, about
his business worries. Graffenried urged him "not to give up yet." The
next day, Bandelier went to St. Louis, where the banker Richard Hospes
told him, "Do not give up." After talking with several others, he returned

to Highland, "tired and worn out." On the following day, Graffenried called and gave the Bandeliers fifteen thousand Swiss francs. "Good, noble friend." It is not clear what this money was intended to do; it would hardly have been sufficient to alleviate the bank's shortfall. Possibly Bandelier father and son were having cash flow difficulties.

Combining family business and research, Adolph left for the East on August 30. He spent the first week of September in negotiations regarding bonds and financial aid for the Ryhiner bank. But he also managed some work on his southwestern researches. He met with a number of people including Wendell Phillips Garrison, literary editor of *The Nation,* and an editor of the German language newspaper *New Yorker Staatszeitung* named Rittig. Both of these men encouraged Bandelier in his plans to write a novel about southwestern Indians. In the following weeks, Bandelier was in the Boston-Cambridge area, conferring with officers of the Archaeological Institute of America and checking on his "poor Mexican book," which was in press, to be released later that year. He also visited Francis Parkman at his home in Jamaica Plain. Parkman encouraged Bandelier about his paintings and drawings, suggesting that they were very salable.

Returning to New York City, Adolph visited Princeton briefly and then returned to work at the Lenox Library in New York. He visited the Geographical Society, where he found the earliest map containing data about New Mexico to be *"Ptolomeo, la Geografía by Messr. Pietro Mattioló Senese Medico, 1548."*

The weakness of the Ryhiner bank, however, continued to weigh on Bandelier. On September 30, he returned home to Highland. A week later, he indicated in a letter to García Icazbalceta that he was leaving shortly for Europe.

The bank officials had kept silent about the serious monetary shortfalls that threatened the Ryhiner bank. This was an obvious precaution, since a run on the bank would spell financial disaster for its proprietors. Thus, the upcoming trip was made known as an attempt to find a buyer in Europe for Adolph's southwestern sketches and watercolors. This was true as far as it went, but in fact Bandelier's main goal was to meet with officials of Gruner-Haller, the Ryhiner bank's major creditor.

Adolph left Highland on November 10, and on the fifteenth boarded the SS *Lessing,* bound for Cherbourg. He reached that port on November 23 and the next day traveled through Normandy, arriving in Paris late in the afternoon. From there, he went on to Bern, reaching that city on November 26. The next day, November 27, Bandelier wrote in his journal: "With the most discouraging prospects, I went to [Gruner-Haller and Company] and told everything. No reply, of course."

The final days of November 1884 were spent in conferences with businessmen, scientists, and relatives. The month of December passed with business matters of the ailing bank, the printing of Adolph's watercolors and drawings, and visits with relatives and friends.

The early days of 1885 found Bandelier working at Bern, then shifting southeastward to Geneva and its sister city, Carouge. He occupied himself largely with business negotiations related to the Ryhiner bank, but also found time for exploratory conferences on the printing of his paintings. He visited relatives, spending much time with his Bern cousin, Alphonse Bandelier. Adolph noted several times that he was "unwell" with a variety of ailments including colds and perhaps influenza that sometimes caused him to retire early or even spend a day or so in bed.

Beginning with his journal entry of December 28, 1884, Adolph made some cryptic comments, all similar, for which there is little, if any, explanation. When writing about his scholarly, business, family, and social acquaintances, Bandelier had always referred to them by name. These cryptic new references, however, used simply the initials "N" and "C." On January 2, for example, he called on "N," who seems to have lived in Carouge, "quarreled and left." On January 9, Bandelier met "C," and in Geneva on January 12 "spent a delicious time with C—then returned [to Carouge]. N has left." A few days later he "spent the evening with Moisé Vautier [a Carouge cousin], afterwards with C. Quarreled, as usual." Nothing more is known of these two persons, not even their sex.

On January 27, Bandelier left Switzerland, beginning his journey homeward. On this leisurely trip into France and western and central Germany, Adolph seems to have put his business cares temporarily behind him. He went by way of Colmar, then north to Frankfurt am Main, where he visited for a day. Next he turned south, via Heidelberg and Karlsruhe, to Stuttgart, where he arrived on January 31.

One reason for going to Stuttgart was to visit the offices of *Das Ausland,* where a number of Bandelier's articles on the Southwest had been published the previous year. The editor of *Das Ausland* had been the famous German anthropologist Friedrich Ratzel, but when Bandelier arrived in early 1885, Dr. Karl Muller had taken over the editorship. Bandelier would continue the relationship with *Das Ausland,* publishing papers later in 1885 and in 1886.

In Stuttgart, Adolph visited family friends. On February 4, he left for Munich, where he contacted Professor Ratzel at the Ethnographic Museum and received authorization to use the Royal Bavarian Archives —a source for manuscripts and books pertaining to early New Mexico. Adolph also spent time at the Alte Pinakothek, where he delighted in the "overwhelming collection" of German, Italian, and Dutch masters. "It is simply stupendous."

On February 11, while still in Munich and amid a busy schedule of professional calls, social visits ("lay calls," Bandelier labeled them), and futile efforts to sell at least some of his watercolors, Bandelier presented a public lecture for Professor Ratzel. This talk "began at 7:30 P.M. Prince Louis of Bavaria was present, and was exceedingly kind and pleasant. The drawings appeared splendid. Result of lecture was beyond all description. After the lecture we went to the 'Achatz,' and spent a pleasant half hour. . . . I had to read a chapter of my so-called novel."

Five days later, Bandelier left Munich in the morning, arriving at Leipzig in the early evening. Over the following days, he made a number of calls on people he termed "molish," "greedy," "obsolete," and "tedious." Leipzig itself he characterized as "a poor city." Presumably Bandelier was having no success in selling his paintings and drawings.

Proceeding on to Berlin, Bandelier met with a prominent anthropologist of the day, Adolf Bastian, and with other leading scientists. He visited several museums, art galleries, and libraries. At the Geographical Society, Bandelier was able to examine early maps of the greater Southwest, including a 1703 map showing Casas Grandes.

In Berlin, another cryptic friend, "E," turned up. On February 28, Adolph noted, "night spent pleasantly with E"; on March 6, "a few hours with E pleasantly"; and on March 8, "Night pleasant also. E."

The following day, March 9, Adolph returned to Professor Bastian, "who gave me a long lecture on Ethnology. He is an excellent old man, but very much exalted and therefore extravagant in his views." That evening, Bandelier met with Professor Rudolph L. K. Virchow, the scientist, teacher, and political leader. Virchow's most important contributions came in the study of diseases, but he also wrote on archaeology and anthropology. A journal entry for this period suggests that Bandelier was trying to make arrangements for the time when, of necessity, he would be cut loose from the family business.

[To Virchow] I made a clear statement of everything as far as prudence allowed. I did not want to bore him with private affairs, but still had to tell him enough to explain my position at all events. He would desire me to travel in the cause of American Ethnology, but there is [sic] always Highland [business and family] concerns between me and the future.

Meanwhile, Bandelier continued to have no luck in selling his drawings. He finally arranged for a Berlin agent to take them on consignment and then left for Hamburg. After a day of exploration, he took a small steamer down the Elbe, meeting the ocean-going ship at Stade. Adolph joined ten other cabin passengers, several of whom he found pleasant traveling companions.

Bandelier's ship entered New York harbor on March 29. He paid a number of calls, including one to Dr. G. H. Moore of the Lenox Library, and then left New York City on April 1. Arriving in St. Louis two days later, Adolph was met at the station by Josephine. After visiting relatives, the two reached Highland that same evening. On the following day, J. U. Burckhardt of Bern, Switzerland, the agent for Gruner-Haller, appeared in Highland. Bandelier noted in his journal that Burckhardt "stopped with us until the 3:40 train. Pleasant, but Papa has not changed one bit at all. Always suspicious, ill-tempered, and occasionally cross."

On April 5, Easter Sunday, there was an enjoyable visit to the farm. That evening found Adolph with Morris Huegy, his brother-in-law. "He is lazy and sullen as usual, but grew more lively after an hour or so." In the course of the next few days, Bandelier was busy with correspondence, visits, and work on the paper "Cibola." Economic concerns weighed constantly on his mind.

The catastrophe coming rapidly to a head confronted not only the F. Ryhiner and Company bank but also the other Bandelier family investments—the Confidence Coal Mine and the foundry. A letter on April 8 to Joaquín García Icazbalceta told of Bandelier's fears of a business collapse and of his determination to seek a new life in Mexico.

On the same day that he wrote to García, Adolph noted that "Fritz R. called; he is wild with talk and gab. Evidently his mind is turning." Fritz was the son of the elder Ryhiner, for whom the bank was named. It is important to stress that the bank crisis came at a time when two of the three original partners, Frederick C. Ryhiner and Moritz Huegy, were dead, leaving the elder Bandelier as the surviving original owner. Sons of the deceased partners, Fritz Ryhiner and Morris Huegy, directed their families' one-third shares. Curiously enough, Adolph Bandelier was not officially involved in the bank, although he led the attempts to save it and shouldered much of the blame when the organization collapsed.

On April 9, Bandelier wrote:

> About 1 A.M. was aroused by fire-alarm. The foundry had burnt down completely. Warehouses saved. The flames must have caught very rapidly, as none of the neighbors noticed anything until it was all ablaze. . . . I saw nothing particularly terrible about it. It was an accident for which we are not responsible, and which we must therefore take coolly. I took medicine this morning and then went out to the ruins. Everything of the machinery is gone. There is evidence of incendiarism visible, as the fire caught on the southeast side.

This almost nonchalant attitude toward the loss of the Highland Mechanical Works is curious. Did Bandelier expect insurance to cover the loss of the foundry? It may be that he was simply indifferent to property that, in any case, would disappear in the coming bank disaster.

The following day, Adolph went to Edwardsville, the county seat, with his brother-in-law, Morris Huegy. They left early in the morning and spent the day conferring. Andrew W. Metcalf, an attorney, "strongly advised to take a change of venue." Judge Michael G. Dale, "when I explained everything to him, was of the same opinion. He offers to mediate if possible."

It is not entirely clear just what legal maneuvering was going on, but it probably had to do with the evaluation of the entire holdings of the partnership. On April 12, William Ellison of the William Ellison and Son Foundry of St. Louis conferred with Adolph, Morris, and perhaps the elder Bandelier. They agreed that Ellison would make an inventory of what remained of the Highland Mechanical Works, as well as a proposal in writing, probably an offer to purchase whatever remained that could be used.

On April 16, Adolph left early in the morning for St. Louis, where he had several business meetings. J. U. Burckhardt had visited Highland a few days earlier, while Bandelier was in Edwardsville. Now the two met by arrangement at the Main Street depot. "He was very pale, and communicated to me the fatal Dispatch. I wandered about the city half-idiotic, notwithstanding a severe thunderstorm." Burckhardt had officially informed Bandelier of what must have been expected for some time: the Gruner-Haller officials had withdrawn their financial support.

Adolph returned to Highland, where followed several days of alternating gloom and hope, desultory work on several southwestern projects, and irrational behavior on the part of the elder Bandelier. Papa refused to accept the situation, raging against Burckhardt, whom he accused of trying to take advantage of the whole affair. Then, on April 27, Papa suddenly left Highland, his whereabouts unknown. Two days later, a run on the bank began as panic-stricken depositors finally realized its precarious position. On the last day of April, Adolph's entry was brief: "Thursday. [Bank] closed today. This is the last of F. Ryhiner & Company and the last period of my sufferings at Highland begins finally."

During May, the Bandelier family's financial tragedy became increasingly a personal one. Bandelier finally faced up to the fact that his father had deserted, leaving the younger bank owners and his own son to face angry creditors alone. Adolph's reaction was furious:

About 4 P.M. came a letter from Papa stating that he would never return!! This is infamous, and settles him with us. Hereafter, he ceases to exist for us. We have sacrificed ourselves for him in every way, and now he betrays and forsakes us. This is the result of 25 years of slavery! Now I am ready for anything to come. . . . The Assigners are at work again at the office. This was a terrible day all around.

But matters became even worse. On May 13, young Fritz Ryhiner slipped away, leaving Adolph and Morris Huegy holding the bag. The leading St. Louis newspaper, the *Globe Democrat,* blamed Adolph for the bank's collapse. On May 19, Bandelier wrote that Dr. Werner Schmidt, a local physician and chemist with the Highland Milk Condensing Company, came with a challenge to a duel from Dr. John B. Knoebel, head of the company. According to Bandelier: "I declined; he came back and I declined again. It is, of course, exceedingly mean and silly. We are, however, going to prosecute him [Dr. Knoebel] now. How infamous and vile."

Apparently Adolph, speaking for his father, had assured the milk company officials that if no run on the bank was made, F. Ryhiner and Company would be able to weather the storm. Dr. Knoebel and other Highland businessmen had accepted these words in good faith. When the bank collapsed and the elder Bandelier fled the scene, it created financial hardship and understandable outrage in the business community. Still, this astonishing challenge to a duel seems to have been a highly personal reaction.

May 21 saw Adolph and Morris Huegy arrested, then released on bond. Josephine, as might be expected given her personality and physical frailty, became ill, and the Bandelier house and yard were vandalized—the house splattered with mud and a prized cactus in the front yard slashed. People in Highland were beginning to display a mob spirit.

All this was too much for the bewildered and sensitive Morris Huegy. Bandelier's journal entry for May 28 began, "Early in the morning, about 7:20 A.M., the children came over crying. *Morris had committed suicide!!* Terrible! Everything upside down."

That same day, Adolph was arrested again and taken to jail at the county seat at Edwardsville. This arrest was the low ebb, although Bandelier was treated kindly, even (according to one account) being allowed to spend the night in the jailer's own living quarters. The following day, May 29, several friends in the Edwardsville area provided bail, and Adolph left immediately for St. Louis. On May 30, a cousin, Henry Kaune, visited Bandelier there with the latest news about the family. As Adolph commented in the journal, "Joe is better, thank God! The hounds at Highland appear quieter, and somewhat surprised at my giving Bond so easily." Then he ended the day's entry with the laconic statement, "Left for the West, 8:45 P.M."

Though it might appear that Adolph was deserting "poor dear" Joe, in fact her staying behind made good sense, for some responsible person was needed to look after what remained of the Bandelier properties in Highland.

On June 1, Bandelier detrained at Lamy, where he met several friends, and he arrived in Santa Fe at 1:30 A.M. on June 2, 1885. This return to Santa Fe marked a watershed in Bandelier's life. It is true that his plans were fluid and the question of how he was to earn a living loomed all too seriously. But Adolph had now broken the chains that linked him to Highland and Father Bandelier. From this time on and for the rest of his life, scholarly research would be his primary goal. The future could only appear brighter than the past.

ELEVEN
Return to Santa Fe

My creditors! Let them have it all . . .

IN A VERY REAL SENSE, Bandelier's return to Santa Fe early in
June 1885 marked a new phase in his life. After the trauma of the recent
weeks in Highland, Adolph rejoiced in his kindly reception. The first
night, June 2, he "slept well" at Herlot's Hotel on San Francisco Street.
Further lodging was offered by several friends, and Bandelier accepted
the invitation of Mr. and Mrs. Gerard D. Koch, moving to their home
on the fourth to stay with them until the sixth of June. Koch was a lum-
ber and hardware dealer, and his wife taught music, an art form popular
at the Koch home.

On June 3, while Adolph was busy compiling a catalog of archaeological specimens for Bishop Salpointe, he was called to the cathedral. This
new stone edifice, begun in 1869 by Archbishop Lamy, was now nearing
completion. It actually enclosed the old adobe structure referred to as the
"Parroquia," which had functioned as the archdiocesan seat in earlier
days, and the adobe of the earlier building was now being cleared away.
While opening the north wall of the choir, fathers Michael Rolly and
Francis Gatignol had just discovered a cyst made of brick and coated with
a thin layer of cement. On this coating were two inscriptions, which
Adolph copied; in the cyst were the remains of two seventeenth-century
Franciscans, the Venerable Gerónimo de la Llana and the Venerable
Asencio Zarate, originally buried at Quarai and Picurís pueblos, respec-
tively. These two Franciscans, reburied in the Santa Fe Parroquia in 1759,

have since been moved to La Conquistadora Chapel within the present-day cathedral.

On Saturday, June 6, Bandelier joined a party going to San Juan Pueblo. His companions included Koch, Dr. William Eggert, the Santa Fe physician who had treated Joe in 1882, and John C. Pearce, a local assayer and amateur historian. At San Juan, the Swiss scholar settled down for a long stay, moving in with Samuel Eldodt. The latter man, whom Bandelier had met when he first came to Santa Fe, was a local store owner, trader, and collector of Indian artifacts. Other members of the party seem to have returned to Santa Fe within a day or so.

Adolph spent several weeks writing on various projects, painting specimens from Eldodt's collection, and catching up on correspondence. It is interesting that while in San Juan, Bandelier wrote his initial letters to Joe in care of Charles Boeschenstein in Edwardsville and George Hoffman in St. Louis. Both were old friends who had helped the Bandeliers in the past. In addition, Hoffman's wife, Celia, was a cousin of Josephine's. Thanks to the extended kinship structure among the German communities of Missouri and Illinois, the Hoffmans could be considered "family." Adolph continued writing through these men until, assured that the situation in Highland had calmed somewhat, he felt he could safely write to his wife directly. Exactly what Bandelier feared is unclear. Possibly he thought the postman in Highland might intercept the mail. More likely, he was simply trying to avoid drawing attention to Josephine.

Bandelier also contacted informants, especially "Chino," a San Juan Indian whose real name was José Dolores Ortiz and who was the son of a Pueblo Indian mother and a local priest, one Father Castro. Bandelier had a long talk with Chino and commented that he was "a very intelligent man and well disposed." In conversations with Chino and other informants, Bandelier obtained a number of terms for ceremonial and political officers at San Juan, as well as details on the structure of the town's religious and political organizations. These data he correlated with earlier material he had collected at Cochiti.

Adolph also made a rather superficial effort to compile a ceremonial calendar, with sketchy details on particular dances. These varied activities continued through the first days of July. In addition, a steady stream of visitors passed through, including Archbishop Salpointe and Judge L. Bradford Prince.

On July 12, Bandelier left San Juan by horse and buggy for the Tewa pueblo of Pojoaque, and then moved on to Peña Blanca, where he stayed with Father Agustín Navet, Father Ribera's successor at that post. Early on July 14, San Buenaventura's Day—a "fine day, but very hot"—Adolph left to attend the annual feast at Cochiti and found "reception kindest imaginable. Everybody flocked to embrace the newcomer." There were visitors from a number of nearby pueblos. Having been at Cochiti feast days in years past, Bandelier scarcely mentioned the dancing or the dancers; his journal entries concentrated on the names of pueblo ruins in the nearby Galisteo Basin and the names of medicine men, religious leaders, and officers.

The following day, Bandelier rode downriver in the direction of Santo Domingo Pueblo. The church there was very near the river, and Adolph noted in his journal that the Rio Grande "will wash it away unless it is protected very solidly." This prophecy came true sooner rather than later, for during the very next year, 1886, the Rio Grande indeed flooded, destroying the Santo Domingo church. When the church was rebuilt, the new structure was placed farther from the river and on higher ground to the east, its present-day site.

Over the next few days, Bandelier explored ruins in the La Bajada region, the Ortiz Mountains, and the region around Golden, east of the Sandia Mountains. On July 22, he departed the Golden area about 5:00 A.M. and headed westward to the Rio Grande, where he came to the ranches opposite San Felipe Pueblo. He commented on the neatness and comfort of the houses and on the peach, apple, pear, and apricot trees and the rather coarse fruit they bore.

Father Navet, who had joined Adolph in the Golden area a few days earlier, now caught up with him again at San Felipe. Although the sacristan there was away, Bandelier was "received" in a most pleasant manner by that official's family. The scholar was able to gather bits of tribal lore and vocabulary, and he made observations on the village itself: "San Felipe . . . is a clean and well-built pueblo, built around a large and clean plaza, perfectly square. All the houses around the plaza are uniformly of two stories, only the outlying houses toward the river are sometimes one-story high, and present a less dilapidated appearance. The church is on the south end."

On July 24, with a San Felipe boy as guide, Bandelier climbed the mesa above the pueblo on the west and reached the ruins of the old pueblo and church. He found the pueblo walls well preserved, made of large blocks of lava and filled with well-laid rubble. The walls of the church were of adobe. The following day, Bandelier and Father Navet examined the San Felipe archives, finding nothing prior to 1726. The Swiss researcher took along a number of documents to look over more carefully and possibly to copy when he reached Peña Blanca.

At San Felipe, Bandelier was told that the Keres tribes had separated when they were at the Cañada de Cochiti, or Kuapa, rather than at the Rito de los Frijoles, or Tyu-o-nyi, as he had been told by the Cochitis. He collected additional information concerning the migrations of the San Felipe Indians, locating five different places in their perambulations. He also obtained descriptions of the tribal officers, their duties, titles, and succession procedures.

Just after noon on July 25, Adolph left for Santo Domingo Pueblo, which he reached after a walk of two and a half hours. There, in spite of the weather—hot with a violent sandstorm that lasted for about an hour—he recorded additional names for various ruined pueblos in the vicinity. He reached Peña Blanca about six in the afternoon.

From Peña Blanca, Adolph left on August 1 in the company of his Cochiti friend, José Hilario Montoya, for the Rito de los Frijoles. Starting around 10:00 A.M., the two men first had to cross the Rio Grande to pack for their trip. They had something of a problem in crossing the river but eventually arrived at Cochiti and departed for the *rito* around noon, in a blazing sun with thunderheads threatening in the north and northwest. As they rode along, Adolph noted site names, terms, phrases, and other bits of vocabulary. They reached the *rito* about 5:00 P.M. and were cordially received by a local rancher, Pacífico Baca. As always, Bandelier was awed by the beauty of the place and pleased with his recollections of the surroundings. "My description of the Rito in the novel [*Die Koshare*] is so far correct, only the southern declivity is steeper, more craggy, and more wooded than I had remembered."

Bandelier now turned back toward the Rio Grande, crossing several of the rugged canyons of the Pajarito Plateau. He and Montoya arrived at the river about five miles south of San Ildefonso Pueblo. There, Bandelier parted from his friend and went on alone to Pojoaque. He arrived back at San Juan on August 3, having completed an elongated loop of some 150 miles, traveling by various modes, including a fair distance afoot.

At San Juan, Adolph opened boxes of books that had arrived from Highland while he had been away. He found that "they are somewhat damaged by rain (probably at St. Louis) but not much." He spent the next few days working on articles including his "Cibola" paper, which was published serially that year by *New Yorker Staatszeitung*. August 12 was noted as the feast of Santa Clara, along with the observation that all of San Juan had gone to Santa Clara Pueblo to take part in dancing the *tablita,* or corn, dance, as well as in racing, drinking, and fighting. One participant, a boy from San Juan, was badly hurt.

Adolph stayed in San Juan for a number of days, painting at Eldodt's collection and writing letters. One was a lengthy dispatch to Norton summarizing his recent activities. The scholar also worked with informants, finished the "Cibola" paper, and hosted travelers. Among them were a Dr. Theodore Williams and his wife. Bandelier showed them around the area and took them to a mass presided over by Father Camilo Seux, who had been priest at San Juan since 1868 and who would remain there for over a half century until his death in 1922. According to Bandelier, "Father Seux preached very well. His organ is beautiful, and the whole ceremony was very impressive. The [six-member] little choir did not sing so very badly." We mention the Williamses because Bandelier often met future friends, assistants, or colleagues in just such a casual way. In the case of Dr. Williams and his wife, however, it appears that Adolph never met or heard from them again.

On Monday, August 17, Bandelier began to write in French on the "Discovery of New Mexico, by Fray Marcos de Niza in 1539." He received several letters in the mail. There was a disturbing one from his young Highland cousin, Henry Kaune, who apparently proposed a scheme for keeping family property away from the bank's creditors. Adolph remarked, "His proposition is well intended but I cannot, from a standpoint of honor and morality, accept it. I cannot withhold my property from those to whom it justly belongs. My creditors! Let them have it all, and if then I am unable to support myself and dear Joe out here, may I be justly and duly punished for it."

The following day, August 18, Adolph wrote Henry refusing his proposal. He was annoyed not only with Henry but about something that had happened the night before—one of the very few instances, throughout all his travels, of burglary. He had made a call on the vicar-general, Peter Eguillon, who was visiting from Santa Fe. On returning to his quarters, the scholar discovered that two blankets, one a beautiful Navajo *tilma,* had been stolen. The robber or robbers had entered through an open window. Calling Eldodt to help, Bandelier searched through the night, looking for clues without success.

He continued working at various projects for another week. Then, on August 25, he left for Ojo Caliente with Antonio Joseph, a businessman from that village. With them was one of the Springer brothers of Cimarron, New Mexico, whom Bandelier seems to have met for the first time. The Springers were lawyers who came to New Mexico in the 1870s. Charles later became important in Republican politics in the state, while Frank turned to paleontology, settling in Las Vegas, New Mexico. Considering Adolph's commonality of interests with the Springer brothers, especially with Frank, it is a bit odd that he had little, if any, contact with either man after this initial meeting.

At any rate, with help from Springer and from members of the Joseph family, Bandelier explored ruins, collected pottery, and examined burials in the Ojo Caliente region. On August 28 he departed, leaving his pottery collection to be forwarded by Joseph. Adolph headed southward, stopping at El Rito and then reaching Abiquiu in the lower Chama valley. He made extensive notes on features of the terrain, archaeological sites, and local history, commenting that Abiquiu was an old pueblo of *genízaros,* the enslaved Plains Indians who were resettled among the Pueblos of New Mexico during the eighteenth and early nineteenth centuries. Bandelier also noted the local ruined mission of Santa Rosa de Abiquiu or, as it is sometimes called, Santa Rosa de Lima.

Returning to San Juan on the last day of August, Adolph took care of correspondence that had accumulated during his absence. He saw visitors and painted items from Eldodt's collection. All this time, he had a terrible toothache—"my last upper molar, right-hand side, is decaying, and I suffer considerably from it. At night, had some relief at last." Adolph suffered a great deal from tooth decay, and a few years later, in South America, was fitted out with false teeth.

On September 10, Bandelier found time to write at some length to don Joaquín García Icazbalceta. He was trying to bring his Mexican friend up to date on happenings of recent months, both in Highland, Illinois, and in New Mexico. He gave a rather extravagant portrait of the troubles that led to his arrest. "My wife became ill from pain and fear because of the conduct of people reminiscent of the most loathsome moments of the French Revolution." Adolph went on to say that he was working on articles in English, French, and German. In three months, he had received some two hundred dollars for his articles. He hoped the Prussian government would buy his collection of drawings and plans of ruins, but was not optimistic.

He expressed the hope that Joe, "my loyal companion, the only love that remains to me in my life," would be coming to New Mexico in a few days. He closed by asking García to write to him in care of Father Navet at Peña Blanca. At this point, Adolph was planning to move Joe to a house in Peña Blanca, and the couple's furniture, shipped from Illinois, was being directed there.

In the days that followed, Bandelier continued to work at San Juan, with side trips to Española and Santa Clara. Finally, on the afternoon of September 24, the researcher left San Juan, traveling by wagon. He journeyed to San Ildefonso Pueblo for an overnight stay and then went on to Ciénega, southwest of Santa Fe, reaching there the following evening. On the twenty-sixth, Adolph pushed on, down the valley of the Santa Fe River, finally arriving at Peña Blanca at sunset. There, he found letters and the furniture.

For the next three weeks, Bandelier investigated pueblo ruins in the vicinity of Peña Blanca. He was at Cochiti Pueblo on October 3, noting that the Cochiti bridge had been repaired and made much more solid, with "caissons" sunk in the river as bases for the bridge timbers. On October 7, Adolph walked down to Santo Domingo. The situation there had not changed greatly since the fiasco of his first visit some years back:

> The people of Santo Domingo are as obstinate, suspicious, and superstitious as usual, and the fact that I was introduced by the priest [Father Ribera in 1880] had certainly a very bad effect. The governor told me to leave the pueblo today, and come back tomorrow, for the purpose of drawing, that today nothing could be done. So I left at once.
>
> The river is threatening the church badly, and, if not speedily stopped, its current will cause the bank (now about 30 feet high and vertical, and only 20 feet from the church) to fall, which will entail the fall of the edifice itself.

Padre Ribera had left the church at Peña Blanca in 1883, probably as a result of having broken his chastity vows. Bandelier in late September remarked on the baptismal record of Ribera's two children at Peña Blanca, which included the notation "father unknown." The Catholic church was unlucky in its choice of priests at Peña Blanca in the later part of the nineteenth century; Father Navet, who replaced Ribera in 1884, was to be involved in a sex scandal a few years later.

October 11, 1885, was Joe's forty-ninth birthday, and her husband wrote in his journal, "God be with her and consent to a speedy reunion." He wrote her a letter, taking it to the railroad station at Wallace (present-day Domingo Station), a few miles southeast of Peña Blanca. At the station he found a number of letters including two from Josephine that indicated she might be able to leave Illinois shortly. On the morning of October 19, Bandelier decided to return to Santa Fe to await developments. Unfortunately, his wagon broke down on the way, and he was forced to finish the trip on foot, reaching the Kochs' residence in the evening. He found a telegram there alerting him that he must go in person to the Midwest.

After a busy round of calling on friends, Adolph left Santa Fe on the morning of October 22. Two days later he was in St. Louis, staying with George and Celia Hoffman, where Joe joined him on October 26. Five days later, he went to Edwardsville to handle property transfers and attend to other business affairs.

Bandelier returned to Edwardsville on November 6, then again on the tenth. After considerable legal maneuvering, he seems to have concluded his affairs satisfactorily, and he was released by the court. At the last minute, however, Adolph Ruegger ("that s— o- a b——") came forth with a new indictment. Ruegger, a local businessman and former county treasurer, had been made an assignee of the failed Ryhiner bank. As such, his action is understandable, especially if Henry Kaune's scheme for shielding the family property had leaked to the public.

Apparently there was an immediate hearing on this indictment, and Bandelier was again discharged by the court. The action, however, seems to have completed Bandelier's alienation from Highland. Future visits to his boyhood home would be infrequent, furtive, and brief.

On August 14, four days after the final court appearance, Adolph and Joe left for the west, taking with them young Hubert Hoffman, son of their St. Louis host, George Hoffman. This time they traveled a new route, angling southwestward through Missouri and Arkansas to Texarkana, then across Texas to El Paso. They reached that town early in the morning of November 17 and checked into a hotel for several hours of sleep. The three travelers arrived at Albuquerque late that same night and reached Santa Fe on November 18.

The Bandelier party was cordially met by Gerard Koch, presumably at the station at Lamy. While planning their imminent move to Peña Blanca, Adolph and Joe stayed with the Kochs. A boarding house was located for young Hubert Hoffman. John Pearce, who had accompanied Adolph on the trip to San Juan five months before, now offered the scholar office space. During the next few days, Bandelier worked at Pearce's place, and at night the Kochs gave musical entertainments for their guests.

Finally, on November 24, Bandelier went to Peña Blanca to see about the quarters into which the couple was to move. He found Father Navet away and the rooms not ready for habitation. For the first time, it seems to have occurred to Adolph that the isolation of Peña Blanca would make the gregarious Josephine lonely and unhappy. On the spot, he decided to move their furniture back to Santa Fe. The Bandeliers quickly rented part of a house in Santa Fe from a local merchant, John G. Schumann. The Bandeliers lived in this house, which still stands, at 352 East de Vargas Street for more than five years. Originally they rented only three rooms in the structure at a cost of $15 per month. In 1885, Santa Fe was obviously not the high-rent mecca it has become in modern times.

The Bandeliers settled gratefully into their new home. On Christmas Eve, Adolph made a number of calls and then spent the evening with Joe. He commented in his journal that it was the "first Christmas with Joe for four years. Very quiet but still alone with *her,* and that is a blessing."

Christmas Day was spent pleasantly, though Joe had a severe headache. The following day, Bandelier was again on the move, riding to a dance at Cochiti Pueblo. Returning to Santa Fe on the twenty-seventh, he found Joe better. On the next day, a stormy one with hail and snow, Father Navet braved the weather and visited from Peña Blanca. Adolph also worked on chapter 3 of *Die Koshare* and noted that his first article had appeared in the St. Louis *Globe Democrat* the day after Christmas. Inspired by this, he began to work on still another article for that newspaper.

The year 1885 saw the Bandeliers slip from comfortable, upper-middle-class status to hand-to-mouth uncertainty. For Adolph and

Joe—as indeed for Adolph's second wife, Fanny—this would be the norm for the rest of their lives. The bank failure did more than wipe out the assets of both the Bandelier and the Huegy families. It was also a crippling blow to many of the bank's depositors, who, in the end, received less than thirty cents on every dollar invested. As late as the 1960s, there was still a strong residue of bitterness toward Bandelier on the part of some Highland citizens.

As Bandelier had told García Icazbalceta, his articles were bringing in some money. Still, he desperately needed more income. On December 30, Adolph launched a series of Spanish lessons in which he enrolled the Episcopal minister, E. W. Meany, and two other students—the first of several attempts to teach one or another foreign language. None of these projects lasted very long. One suspects that Bandelier had no real flare for pedagogy.

But for the moment, life was looking up for the Bandeliers. Adolph and Joe spent the evening of December 31 at the Kochs' and had a good time, the party in fact lasting until 2:00 A.M. In his journal, Bandelier wrote simply, "Goodby 1885. God grant that '86 be different."

TWELVE
Histoire and Hemenway

Thank God a thousand times for the good news from
Cushing.

N EW YEAR'S DAY and the year 1886 started with the usual social calls. But on January 2, when the weather brought a fierce snowstorm, the Bandeliers remained at home, partly because of Joe's being
unwell. Adolph continued the Spanish lessons though his already scanty
enrollment had dropped to two. He also worked on his novel and began
an article for the *New York World*.

On January 5 the scholar wrote, "It is our Silver Wedding. What may
be in store for us we don't know, but at all events Joe is better. We got
some very kind presents, but this does not compensate for the bitterness
of the day. God is very cruel."

This diatribe continued the next day. "Everything is useless. We are absolutely doomed, and with all this, Highland, that nest of infidelity,
treachery, and coarseness, prospers! God is very unjust or at least partial. He flatters those who despise him and tramps down those who bend
their knees." These journal entries foreshadowed Bandelier's ragings
against the deity in the future, during his South American years. There are
passages in the South American journals that sound downright insane.

The following weeks were routine. Both Joe's and Adolph's health
waxed and waned from day to day. Friends paid social calls, and Adolph
continued to give Spanish lessons. He worked on his novel, painted, and
wrote articles in English and in German for several journals. Small
checks, for the most part ranging from $5 to $10, arrived from time to

time. Correspondence continued to occupy a great deal of Bandelier's time and thought. Adolph renewed his interest in the Nambe Pueblo witch trials of some years earlier and became intrigued by a newly found "campaign document" that related to the Montezuma legend. It had been concocted in Mexico in 1846 in an effort to win support among the Pueblos in the fight against the United States. Bandelier borrowed the manuscript from a friend at the historical society and made a copy of it.

By early February 1886, Bandelier had completed a considerable portion of the novel *Die Koshare*. On the sixth of that month, the Bandeliers received a plaintive letter from Eddy Huegy, Joe's brother. Adolph remarked sadly in his journals, "Poor boy. We are ourselves as poor as Job and should help him! It is impossible—much as we would like to do it."

On February 9, a letter from Parkman with $100 brought a brief moment of relief, but it soon disappeared as most of the money went to pay existing bills. Adolph promptly acknowledged Parkman's letter with "a thousand thanks." The rest of the month was routine, broken only by a trip to the large ruined pueblo on the Arroyo Hondo south of Santa Fe.

April brought no real change in the Bandeliers' life-style. The weather was unusually disruptive—snow storms, hail, and violent dust storms—and Joe's health ranged from a few good days to spells of nausea, vomiting, and headaches, with extended periods in bed. Adolph began to have cramps and lameness in his right hand. In spite of this, work on the novel progressed, and on May 3 Bandelier wrote a surprisingly long letter to García Icazbalceta. He was responding to a letter dated April 16 in which García told of the sudden loss of a little granddaughter. Typically for Bandelier, he sandwiched a short paragraph of condolence between complaints of chronic "writer's cramps" and a request for help in his research on Casas Grandes.

On May 12, Adolph recorded in his journal, "Today at 7 P.M., I finished my novel! Thank God! I began it in 1883 and until the 28th of December, 1885, had only written two chapters, of 56 pages, about. The other 20 chapters of 420 pages, I consequently wrote in four months and fifteen days. If only the result justifies the work and time spent on it! That God alone can determine."

Ten days later, Adolph wrote that he was turning to painting ground plans because he was "tired of writing." Several callers came that afternoon, and then Adolph and Josephine paid a visit to Fischer's beer garden, a popular place on East Palace Avenue in Santa Fe. Such outings usually took their toll on Joe, and the next day she was in bed with a severe headache, but she was "better at night."

The month continued uneventfully until the twenty-third, when a startling letter arrived from Papa Bandelier—in Venezuela. Although it had been little more than a year since Bandelier had written Papa off completely, he was now ecstatic:

Got a letter from Papa! He is safe and well, thank God a thousand times for it. Replied at once and communicated the news to Bertha, Clotilde, and to Mr. Balsiger.

We are all so happy over it. He is alive and not in need at all. . . . Our friends here are most happy at the news about Papa; they are as glad as we are, almost. It is a glorious day.

Money was, as always, a problem. On the seventh of June, Adolph went to the archbishop "in despair" and was promptly advanced $100, much to his satisfaction. Again, most of the money was gone as soon as outstanding bills were paid. Ever searching for new ways to make a living, Bandelier decided in June to read law with Eugene Allen Fiske, a local attorney. This plan came to nothing, however, and in July Bandelier was traveling again, this time with Joe to San Juan Pueblo with side trips to the Santa Clara region.

August 1886 brought a couple of letters from Papa, and Adolph presented a lecture on the significance of decoration on Pueblo Indian pottery at the Post Hall at Fort Marcy. He was introduced by President L. Bradford Prince of the New Mexico Historical Society as one of a series of speakers for that fall and winter. Bandelier noted that the lecture was a success, though he spoke for only forty minutes, and the hall was hot and provided insufficient light for his drawings. This lecture has not survived, but it would be fascinating to read it, knowing that Bandelier never fully understood the role of pottery in archaeological analysis.

A few days after the lecture, Bandelier walked down to Peña Blanca, most of the way in the rain. The following day, he went over to Cochiti Pueblo to attend a funeral mass for Juan José Montoya, one of Adolph's first and best friends at Cochiti. Home again on August 24, the researcher had another visit with Archbishop Salpointe, who had been given a series of Bandelier's paintings and sketches for presentation to the Vatican.

Donation of the paintings to the archbishop was not really an altruistic gesture; something far bigger than mere paintings was in the works. On the twenty-sixth, Adolph recorded that he "began to write at the first chapter of the big book suggested by Archbishop Salpointe. In French." This was his "Histoire de la colonisation et des missions de Sonora, Chihuahua, Nouveau-Mexique et Arizona jusqu'a l'annee 1700" (History of the colonization and of the missions of Sonora, Chihuahua, New Mexico, and Arizona to the year 1700). The manuscript was to be the archdiocese of New Mexico's contribution to Pope Leo XIII's Golden Jubilee, celebrating the fiftieth anniversary of his first mass on December 31, 1837. Dioceses around the world were vying in presenting rich gifts to the pope. Because New Mexico was a relatively poor diocese, Salpointe decided that a literary gift for the Vatican library would be most appropriate, and Bandelier, a proven scholar and a devout—if only recently converted—Catholic was the obvious choice as the author.

Adolph worked on the "Histoire" manuscript for the remainder of the year. A journal entry for October 4 noted, "Began on my work for Pope Leo XIII! May God help me. . . . Suffer from rheumatism in my back. Can hardly sit up."

But another job, even more promising than the "Histoire" project, was now on the horizon. Earlier in 1886, a well-known Boston philanthropist, Mary Hemenway, had inaugurated a large research program in the Southwest to be known as the Hemenway Southwestern Archaeological Expedition. Frank H. Cushing was chosen as head of the expedition, with Sylvester Baxter, formerly of the Archaeological Institute of America, as secretary. Probably on Cushing's recommendation, Bandelier was named "historiographer" at a monthly salary of $116.

On October 7, a letter came from Cushing with the good news of the Hemenway appointment. "[Cushing] is more than good. I am even in a quandry what to do, the work is almost too much for me at once. Still Joe says I shall take it." That same afternoon, Father Julius Deraches, chaplain of St. Vincent Hospital in Santa Fe, agreed to correct the French in the work for the pope. Later in 1886, however, this task was taken over by Father Navet. Apparently Deraches's duties were such that he could not continue with the added burden.

While he worked on the "Histoire" manuscript, Bandelier was also translating *Die Koshare* into English, reading the chapters to friends as they were completed. Reverend Meany and probably others helped Adolph with English grammar and syntax, a lifelong problem in the Swiss scholar's writings.

The fall of 1886 was a relatively peaceful period in Bandelier's life. In October he heard that the Highland financial matters were at last settled. In November he bought a typewriter, the first of several he was to own over the years. Sadly, however, Hubert Hoffman, the young man who had come to New Mexico with the Bandeliers in 1885, now returned to St. Louis at the beginning of December to be with his mother, who was seriously ill and soon died.

Cushing and Bandelier met at Lamy, New Mexico, on December 16, and Bandelier continued with Cushing to Albuquerque, where they made plans for the expedition. With Cushing was a young archaeologist, Frederick Webb Hodge, who would play a large part in the life of the Bandelier family as well as in the general field of anthropology. At this Albuquerque meeting, it was decided that Bandelier would go to Mexico for archival research. At Cushing's request, Secretary Baxter sent $450 in expense money, and Bandelier and Joe boarded a train for Mexico City, arriving the last day of December 1886. Adolph ended his 1886 journal with a note of high good feeling and unusually kind words for the deity: "God is favoring us, but let Him also preserve us from falling into excesses, temptation, and sin. He is good, very good, even when he strikes. God bless Papa, all our good friends, and all mankind."

For the next several months Bandelier worked at the archives on both the Hemenway and the "Histoire" projects, the two overlapping in subject matter so much that research on one could often be used for the other. García Icazbalceta was always helpful, and Father Agustín Fischer, former confessor to Emperor Maximilian and an ardent bibliophile, also provided considerable help. In March, Louis Huning and his wife from Los Lunas, New Mexico, visited Mexico City, and Joe returned to New Mexico with them. Bandelier had perhaps met Louis Huning in 1883; at least, he had become acquainted with other members of the Huning family that year. The scholar himself returned to Santa Fe in late May and went back to work on the "Histoire" project. By the end of June he had finished seven chapters of this large work.

The final days of June were taken up with preparing plates for the Vatican manuscript. In early July, Josephine left with friends for a short trip to San Juan Pueblo. In her absence, Henry Kaune arrived, and

Bandelier showed Lizzie's husband around Santa Fe, a new and strange environment for the young midwesterner. "The country does not suit him. He is green yet and looks at everything with eastern eyes and ideas."

On August 3, Bandelier received his monthly stipend from Baxter of the Hemenway expedition and, at the same time, a letter from García Icazbalceta. "Both are good! I went down town and paid Mr. Schumann $35. and then home in very good spirits. God is very good to me; much more than I deserve it; because I am a very great offender as towards Him! Well, I presume he does it on account of Joe, and so I take it as a gift, or present." Bandelier's attitude toward God was often rather like that of Tevya in *Fiddler on the Roof.*

Adolph's good spirits continued through the sixth of August, when he described his birthday in upbeat terms. There was a little gathering of friends, and a number of people brought him presents. Ever the loyal husband, Bandelier commented, "The nicest is from Joe, a beautiful cup and saucer." Adolph continued to write on the "Histoire," and with occasional help from Henry Kaune, worked on his house, which seems to have been falling into some disrepair. On August 21, he made extended notes on a meteorite that had exploded the previous evening over the Pajarito Plateau, some forty miles west of Santa Fe.

September and the first weeks of October saw steady work on the "Histoire" manuscript. On October 18 Bandelier wrote, *"Finished the work for the Pope today!* Thank God for it a thousand times! He is very good! I have now finished the manuscript in eight months at most." Actually, this was not quite true, for the work still needed to be copied and edited. But at least Bandelier had finished his part.

This project out of the way, Bandelier left on October 21 for an extended trip to Peña Blanca and Cochiti, Jemez, Zia, and Sandia pueblos. The scholar then retraced his steps to Peña Blanca, where he found the German anthropologist Edward Seler and his wife. They had been visiting Santa Fe and the region on their way to Mexico. Adolph finally arrived back in Santa Fe on the afternoon of November 1. He noted rather fretfully that in the mass of letters awaiting him, there was no check from Baxter (it finally arrived on November 7).

Though the Hemenway expedition continued to pay him, Adolph began to worry again about cash flow. While on his recent trip, Bandelier had met Father J. O. Stephan of the Bureau of Catholic Indians Missions,

Woven and embroidered manta, worn by a Cochiti Malinche dancer. Surprisingly, Bandelier was allowed to copy this sacred object—a task that took many hours and caused him to turn down an invitation to witness a secret kachina dance. (From Bandelier's "Histoire" manuscript, Vat. Lat. 14115-494.)

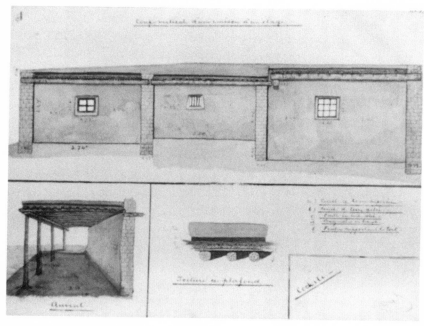

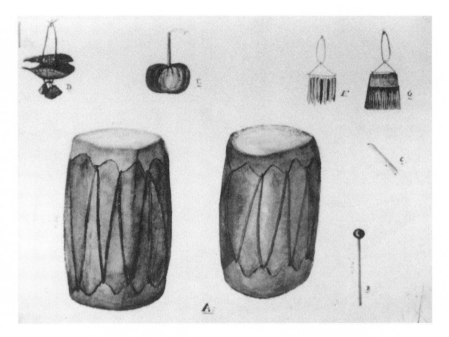

Ceremonial items from Cochiti Pueblo: two drums with stick; whistle; and rattles. (From Bandelier's "Histoire" manuscript, Vat. Lat. 14112-72.)

(top left) Decorated shield, one of several that the Cochiti allowed Bandelier to copy. (From Bandelier's "Histoire" manuscript, Vat. Lat. 14112-56.)

(bottom left) Architectural details, Cochiti Pueblo: cross section of a three-room, single-story house; portal; and cross section of the roof. Bandelier often painted watercolors such as this one and those shown in the following illustrations, in preference to carrying a bulky camera and film. (From Bandelier's "Histoire" manuscript, Vat. Lat. 14112-32.)

 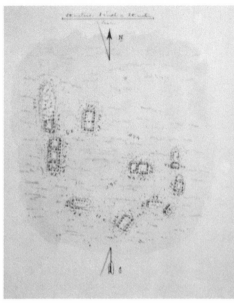

(left) A Cochiti olla. (From Bandelier's "Histoire" manuscript, Vat. Lat. 14112-46.)

(right) "Ruins Thirteen Kilometers East of Fort Thomas, Arizona (1 inch = 20 meters)." This is a good example of Bandelier's use of the north arrow with shadows to indicate the steepness of the terrain—a unique but effective device.

who seems to have had an office at Bernalillo. Now he arranged with Stephan for employment for one year at $25 per month plus travel expenses. This work for the BCIM involved visiting the pueblos and conferring with tribal leaders about educational programs and other school matters.

At this time, Bandelier was also writing the monograph *An Outline of the Documentary History of the Zuni Tribe* (eventually published in 1892), on which he worked during November and December. He also began to write the long-delayed report for the Archaeological Institute of America, the work that would be published in two volumes in 1890 and 1892 as the *Final Report*. At the end of December, Bandelier heard that Father Fischer in Mexico City had died. In a long reminiscence written on December 31, Bandelier spoke of his sadness and loss at the death of the old priest. He remarked, however, that 1887 had been "a prosperous year, blessed and happy!"

The year 1888 began with much the same routine that characterized the closing weeks of 1887. There were social calls, family problems, Joe's ailments, Adolph's hand troubles, and from time to time brief attempts to copy documents. On January 5 Bandelier observed, "Quietly at home for it is the 27th anniversary of marriage. How time flies! God is good to us; we are happier now than we ever were before."

The old problem, a pain in the right hand, flared up again, and Bandelier, who was trying to work on the second part of the final report to the AIA, became discouraged. The new typewriter broke down, and Adolph turned to painting, "since I am prohibited from writing." Eventually he borrowed another typewriter.

Meanwhile, the editing of the "Histoire" was finally completed. Bandelier and Salpointe packed it and sent it to Rome by express, the illustrations having already been shipped overseas. Bandelier could now turn his whole attention to the Hemenway work. He left on the night of January 31 to join Cushing at the Hemenway camp in the vicinity of the large Hohokam ruin of Los Muertos near Phoenix, Arizona. His stay was short; on the fourth of February he departed for a quick visit to friends in Tucson and was back in Santa Fe on February 9. The next two weeks saw trips to Tesuque and to Taos. While Adolph was away, word came that the Italian vessel *Estrella,* on which the plates for the Vatican manuscript had been shipped, was overdue and feared lost. Adolph shrugged off the bad news, merely saying cryptically that Joe had bought a sewing machine during his absence in Arizona and "that is better than all the plates in the world."

As it turned out, the *Estrella* did arrive safely into port, but the plates seem to have miscarried; at least, this was the information from Rome. It was not until March 7 that a telegram arrived saying that the plates had arrived safely at the Vatican. That same day there were two letters from Papa Bandelier indicating that the old gentleman was coming to Santa Fe. "Thank God! He is well and will sail from La Guayra [Venezuela] on the 9th inst."

The remainder of March saw intermittent work on the major projects—the Hemenway expedition, the novel, and the final report for the AIA. Josephine had dropped into a pattern of entertaining a circle, or *kränzchen,* of ladies, probably German-American women for the most part. It is not clear from the journal entries just how often these gatherings were held, but they likely were more or less regular, perhaps monthly.

Bandelier's work periods were interspersed with illnesses: lumbago and a painful sciatica that made sleep difficult lying down. Finally, late in March, after several days of treatment by a local doctor, he felt better and was able to go back to his travels.

On March 31, Bandelier was off to El Paso, primarily to meet Papa Bandelier but also to get in some archival work. The scholar settled in at the Hotel Vendome, but in spite of the warmer weather his sciatica flared up again. Bandelier was disheartened to hear that his old friend, the photographer W. H. Brown, who had moved from Santa Fe to El Paso, had died a year and a half before. This seems to have come as news to Bandelier, which is surprising considering the researcher's penchant for keeping in touch with people by mail.

Adolph was in poor physical shape during this El Paso trip. Not only did his sciatica flare up, but he also developed chills and fever, perhaps a form of influenza. Nevertheless, and rather typically for Bandelier, he made several trips between El Paso and El Paso del Norte (present-day Juárez, Mexico), meeting people and copying documents from local church archives. Finally, on April 6, Papa Bandelier arrived. "Thank God, after three long, sad years. The rest I need not write down. Felt well at once."

The next day Adolph and his father headed back to Santa Fe. "Arrived home with Papa! How happy we are united again. Joe is well. Papa slept well." For the remainder of April and into the first few days of May, life in the Bandelier household moved along happily—with considerable socializing both at home and at the brewery. The younger Bandelier managed some copying as well, and his father occasionally helped with the work. But Adolph's hand worsened, and to add to his woes, the typewriter broke down again, this time a main spring. In addition, Bandelier was at odds with Henry Kaune, Lizzie's husband (whom Adolph referred to as "Baby-Henry!!"), and his long friendship with Gerard D. Koch also deteriorated. According to Bandelier, Koch was "a veritable bore, bloated, pompous, and yet scheming."

The Koch family had hosted Bandelier when he came west after the bank crash. Koch had driven to Lamy to meet Adolph and Joe in late 1885, allowing them to live in the Koch home until rental arrangements could be made. Koch was a proven friend, and although Bandelier wrote cutting criticisms of Koch in his journal entries for several months, he seems never to have reached the level of verbal abuse. Indeed, the Kochs continued to interact with the Bandeliers in the friendliest fashion for the next several years. Bandelier eventually treated Koch more kindly in his journal comments, although he continued to make occasional snide comments about Mrs. Koch.

Perhaps living with Papa Bandelier was again having its effect on Adolph's sometimes mercurial personality. Bandelier's willingness to vilify people in his journal is an interesting commentary on the man himself. Joe, and later Fanny, escaped this pen-lashing, but few of his other long-time acquaintances, friends, and family could say the same. It seems to have been a way for Bandelier to let off steam without actually confronting his miscreant-of-the-moment. It is perfectly clear that Bandelier never intended his journals to be published or made public.

Understandably, given the personalities involved, the euphoria that had accompanied Papa's return soon evaporated. (One might suggest that Josephine never *was* euphoric about it.) The Bandelier couple fell back into their old pattern of angry feelings toward Papa. Only a month after the old man's return, Adolph noted in his journal that "all had a bad night owing to Papa's conduct." And a day later, "Papa a little less ugly, but Joe [because of Papa?], in bed all day with very severe headache."

Bandelier next turned to his work with Father Stephan. On May 18, he went on foot to San Ildefonso Pueblo, and in a meeting with the tribal authorities he explained his ideas, perceiving no particular opposition.

From San Ildefonso, Bandelier went on to Santa Clara Pueblo, on the west side of the Rio Grande. There he found a politically divided tribe, and it is not clear to what extent this factionalism adversely affected Bandelier's educational plans. He visited and apparently stayed with a friend named Alejandro E. Campbell. Very little is known of Campbell, but at the time of Bandelier's visit he was about thirty-eight and seems to have been running some sort of school in the pueblo. At any rate, Bandelier noted that "Alejandro is well liked. He now has thirteen pupils." Campbell also played the guitar and performed at dances in the nearby Hispanic town of Española.

Bandelier spent a considerable amount of time copying from the local church archives, including documents from the months just before the Pueblo Revolt of 1680. After several days of archival work, he returned to Santa Fe on June 2, taking the new Denver and Rio Grande rail line that had been extended from Española to Santa Fe only two years previously. June and July he spent working on the Hemenway project.

Early in July, Bandelier received permission from Edward L. Bartlett, executor of the papers of David J. Miller, long-time chief clerk and translator in the U.S. surveyor-general's office in Santa Fe, to examine Miller's papers. Bandelier copied a number of them for the Hemenway collection.

Later in the month, Bandelier, with Father Luciano Rémuzon, the priest at Española, set out on an extraordinary trip on horseback, with a burro to carry camp supplies. The two went over the eastern slope of the Jemez Mountains, near where Los Alamos is located today, eventually reaching the "Valles," the great volcanic caldera of Valle Grande. Bandelier was justifiably impressed. "On the whole it is the most beautiful country I have as yet seen in New Mexico."

From the Valle Grande, the scientist rode on alone across the wild mountain country to the upper drainage of the Jemez, following that river to Jemez Hot Springs. There he found a number of friends, some with their families, including Koch, Louis Huning, John Schumann, and Mariano Otero, a member of the influential Otero family. The Jemez Springs region, even in those days, seems to have been a popular picnic and vacation spot.

Bandelier went on to Jemez Pueblo the next day, where he received letters, including one from Joe. He stayed with the local priest, J. B. Mariller, while other members of the party returned to Santa Fe. Adolph examined the local ruins and looked over the pueblo, visiting with Agustín Cota, the local Jemez governor whose ancestry was Pecos. Pecos Pueblo, where Bandelier had done his first southwestern field-work in 1880, had been abandoned in 1838, its handful of survivors moving to join linguistic kin in Jemez. Besides Cota, Bandelier interviewed several other Pecos Indians living at Jemez.

On July 25, Bandelier went on down the Jemez drainage to Zia and Santa Ana pueblos, attending the feast day dance for Saint Ann at the latter pueblo on the following day. He then walked to Bernalillo, where he spent the evening with the local priest, Father Etienne Parisis. The researcher recorded several stories of large rattlesnakes kept in caves and fed rabbits and other game by various Pueblo Indians. Leaving Bernalillo on the morning of July 28, Bandelier arrived in Peña Blanca that afternoon, where he found Papa Bandelier settled in. It is not clear where Papa was living—possibly in the house that Bandelier had intended for himself and Joe.

From Peña Blanca, Bandelier returned to Santa Fe, but a couple of days later he was traveling again, this time to Santo Domingo and Cochiti with Father José Rómulo Ribera. This priest seems to have been in retirement, presumably owing to his violation of chastity vows, and was living at Wallace. Bandelier continued a friendship with the errant priest, and Ribera occasionally visited the Bandelier family in Santa Fe until the couple left for South America in 1892.

In August Bandelier returned to Cochiti, trying to work out educational arrangements for Father Stephan, but seemingly with no great success. The next month, the ever-restless Papa Bandelier returned to Santa Fe, immediately creating much tension.

September saw a continuation of the Hemenway work. A Taos resident, Harry S. Budd, who was interested in the northern Tiwa language and who had done vocabularies of Taos and Picuris for the Bureau of American Ethnology, came to Santa Fe with word that Cushing had authorized a trip for Bandelier to Taos. Budd and Bandelier spent a week in the Taos-Picuris area, after which Adolph went on to San Juan Pueblo, where he met Josephine.

After a return to Santa Fe, Bandelier was off again, this time to Zuni to meet Cushing, who was now working on another aspect of the Hemenway research. After ten days of exploring the region around Zuni Pueblo and copying archives from the local mission church, Bandelier left for his first visit to El Morro.

About thirty miles east of Zuni, and now a national monument, El Morro (the headland) is a massive butte of Mesozoic sandstones perhaps two miles in circumference that rises from the flat valley floor. On the northeast side of the headland is a twelve-foot-deep pool of water (about 200,000 gallons) collected from the eastern cliff face. Because of this water source, El Morro has been a favorite stopping place on trails and roads that from prehistoric times connected Zuni Pueblo to Acoma Pueblo and the Rio Grande region. The early Spaniards used the area as a camping station, and as early as 1605 the Spanish governor Juan de Oñate left a carving in the soft sandstone, giving his name and information about his trip. Other Spaniards in the seventeenth and eighteenth centuries did the same, as did pioneers from the early American exploration of the Southwest. Bandelier was fascinated by these graffiti and used five pages of his notebook in copying the inscriptions, an early and important record of this historically rich site.

Returning to Santa Fe by wagon, Bandelier stopped at the new railroad town of Grants, where he spent the night with Emil Bibo, a member of the influential Bibo family that had established ranching and merchandising interests in the Grants and Acoma-Laguna area as early as the 1860s. A member of the Bibo family was at one time governor at Acoma Pueblo.

On October 18, Bandelier met a man with whom he would interact for the rest of his life: Charles F. Lummis, the newspaperman, author, and ethnologist whose writings on the West were to make him as well known as Bandelier himself. Bandelier, unaware of the historicity of the situation, noted in his journal simply that he had met a C. F. Lummis in Grants. Many years later, after Bandelier's death, in an introduction to a reissue of *The Delight Makers*. Lummis gave his own colorful, if somewhat inaccurate, account of this meeting:

> One day of August [*sic*], 1888, in the teeth of a particular New Mexico sandstorm that whipped pebbles the size of a bean straight to your face, a ruddy, bronzed, middle-aged man, dusty but unweary with his sixty mile tramp from Zuñi, walked into my solitary camp at Los Alamitos. Within that afternoon I knew that here was the most extraordinary mind I had met. There and then began the uncommon friendship which lasted until his death, a quarter of century later; and a love and admiration which will be of my dearest memories so long as I shall live.

After exploring the Grants area for a few days, Bandelier rode a freight train to Albuquerque and returned to Santa Fe on October 25. The remainder of the year was relatively uneventful. Bandelier continued to work on the Hemenway and AIA projects. He copied at the surveyor-general's office, spent evenings at Fischer's Brewery, and quarreled again and again with Papa. The Pueblo educational project for Father Stephan ended at the beginning of December, and there was no mention of its being renewed. All in all, it seems to have been a failure.

A relatively prosperous and happy period in Bandelier's life was now coming to a close. The financial security furnished by the Vatican and Hemenway projects was slipping away. The "Histoire" manuscript had been sent, though there is no evidence that the pope ever consulted or even looked at it. The written manuscript, separated from the plates, paintings, and sketches, disappeared into the vast Vatican archives, not to be rediscovered until the 1960s. More important to Bandelier at the moment, fees paid for production of the "Histoire" had by now dried up.

Although Bandelier was still on the Hemenway payroll, his position would last for only another few months, and by the end of 1888 the scholar must have had some inkling that the expedition was in trouble. It had been mismanaged, apparently from the first, and drastic cutbacks and reorientation of its goals were now in order. One of these cutbacks was to drop the position of historiographer held by Bandelier.

Adolph and Joe would remain in the Southwest for an additional two and a half years. Although their situation was not so bleak as it had been during the first months after the bank failure, when lack of money was a daily worry, from 1889 on they again faced a hand-to-mouth plight. And now they faced it with the addition to their household of an irascible, demanding, and financially irresponsible Papa Bandelier.

Adolph's journal entry for December 31, 1888, ended with these comments: "This is the last day of another so far fortunate year. We have succeeded in bringing Papa back, but with him we have secured a cloud in our otherwise happy sky. Well, God has so disposed, and we must take it as it comes. We staid [*sic*] up till 10 P.M. and then retired very quietly. God be thanked for all He has done for us this year also."

THIRTEEN
An End and a Beginning

Thus the greatest undertaking of my life is done, and, so far, successfully.

BANDELIER'S LAST YEARS in the Southwest saw a shift in his scholarly interests. He placed less emphasis on visiting either the antiquities of the region or its living tribes and more on examining whatever documents or manuscripts he could find on the early Spanish period. Even his studies of native institutions seem to have been aimed at revealing the impact of Spanish culture.

With the "Histoire" manuscript finished and employment with Father Stephan terminated, Bandelier's attention next centered on his continuing duties as historiographer for the Hemenway expedition and the reports he still owed to the Archaeological Institute of America. He also worked on expanding and translating from German to English his novel *Die Koshare,* which was to become *The Delight Makers.*

From the second of January, 1889, until the nineteenth, Bandelier did not keep his journal. On the second of the month he had written, "Papa cross, of course; he had a pleasant day yesterday, and it is his manner of showing his gratitude to God and to us. Well, he is old and weak in every way." In a summary written on January 19, it is clear that some things had not changed, except that Adolph had grown less tolerant.

Week before last, Papa grew so ugly and mean that Joe had to give him a very serious talking to. Since then, he was, of course, sick at first, but then he became mild. How long this mildness will last I don't know and don't trust much either. He has been spoiled by everybody, and the poor man cannot realize that his realm is past, and that we will not any longer submit to his despotism. We are *of age*—at last—it is high time at that.

Adolph was now forty-eight, and Josephine, fifty-two. It is interesting that Joe, usually so self-effacing, was the one to stand up to Papa. Whether this tells us something about the dynamic of nineteenth-century Swiss-American households or was simply idiosyncratic of the Bandelier family is anyone's guess.

At least the elder Bandelier was helping with some of his son's projects. On January 23, Adolph noted the completion of an index to documents for the Hemenway expedition. There were fifty-four of these, mostly copies of documents from the Spanish reconquest following the Pueblo Revolt of 1680–92. Father Bandelier had copied three of these manuscripts.

Meanwhile, trouble was brewing at Peña Blanca, where the priest Agustín Navet had been serving since the resignation of Father José Rómulo Ribera. Navet was a friend of Bandelier's and had helped with the "Histoire" manuscript. As early as 1888, Navet had had some sort of liaison with a young woman named Teresa, who was probably a local Peña Blanca resident. Indeed, the two, along with Ophelia, perhaps a sister or cousin of Teresa's, had visited Bandelier in Santa Fe on November 26 of that year. On January 21, 1889, Adolph noted in his journal, "Bad news about *Navet,* if they are true." The next day he remarked, "It is certain now that Navet has left, actually deserted his post! Poor fellow." On the twenty-third, however, Bandelier was less charitable. "The *Navet* business looks very ugly. He has eloped with the girl—*Teresa!* He is simply a scoundrel who has betrayed everybody."

Unlike the rather casual attitude the archdiocese took when Father Ribera's affair with a local girl was discovered, Archbishop Salpointe's attitude in his treatment of Navet was vindictive. In his book *Soldiers of the Cross,* published in 1898, Salpointe actually omitted Navet's name from the list of priests who had served in New Mexico.

The remainder of January passed in a routine and relatively calm manner. Family problems, illnesses, business and scholarly correspondence, social and scholarly visits took up much of the time. On February 3, Bandelier remarked in his journal that he had not felt like going to mass and added, "This life of a Heathen won't do in the long run." Adolph's resolve to mend his ways did not prevent his spending a "pleasant afternoon" with several friends at the brewery later that day. On the seventh of February, Bandelier took the train from Santa Fe to Española and on to Santa Clara Pueblo, where he was welcomed by Alejandro Campbell and Felix Velverde (or Velarde), who was the keeper of the Santa Clara archives. The scholar spent the remainder of the month copying archival materials.

The calm prevailed throughout March, April, and the better part of May. Adolph continued to work on his report for the AIA, mailing off materials on May 15. From time to time he wrote articles for magazines and newspapers in return for small fees. His typewriter failed him periodically—dry ribbons, broken parts, and replacement parts that did not fit. (Adolph customarily sent his ribbons back East to be reinked, and mechanical repairs were usually done at the blacksmith shop!) Fights with Papa Bandelier were virtually everyday events.

There was a trip to San Juan Pueblo in late May, but at the end of the month Bandelier returned to Santa Fe because of problems with the Hemenway expedition. There, he met for the first time Dr. Jesse Walter Fewkes, a young archaeologist who in later years became well known for his work at Mesa Verde and around the Hopi pueblos. Fewkes had been sent from Boston by Mrs. Hemenway to investigate matters concerning the expedition. Bandelier's assessment of the situation was overly optimistic: "Fieldwork is to be stopped, but I am to continue with mine. Everything looks well for me, so far. Thanks to God for it! He is good to us." The next day, Bandelier had further talks with Fewkes before the latter man continued on to Zuni Pueblo.

In fact, the Hemenway expedition was rapidly breaking down. On July 4, Adolph learned from the young troubleshooter, Fewkes, that Cushing had been dismissed as director. He heard additional details from a rancher friend from the Cebolla region east of Zuni: "The news he told me was indeed sickening, Cushing unveiled. The whole troupe appearing as a band of adventurers who have simply abused of Mrs. Hemenway's kindness. Wine cellars found at Zuni, etc. It is abominable."

On another front, Bandelier complained during most of June about the weather—the heat and especially the complete lack of rain. Finally, on July 1, he gave full vent to his feelings: "Let anybody speak to me of the '*Climate of Santa Fe*'! It is the meanest, the most abject, the dryest, the most abjectly windy spot on earth. Not fit for people to honor it with their presence." In fairness to Santa Feans past and present, let it be said that Bandelier generally was fond of his adopted home and often praised its climate.

In August, Bandelier made another trip south to the El Paso area, where he worked with church documents, returning to Santa Fe near the end of the month. Then, as autumn wore on, he wrote on Hemenway materials even though he was beginning to realize that his part in what remained of the Hemenway expedition was nearly over. On the ninth of August there finally came a letter from Fewkes with the unwelcome news. "Everything is given up. So I am on the street again. Well, I must make the most of it I can. It is ignominious on the part of the Boston people. Foolish and very, very SMALL. But Joe shall go east [to St. Louis and Highland] anyhow. One good thing is, that my salary runs until January 1st, 1890."

Although *The Delight Makers* had not yet found a publisher, Bandelier launched a second novel at this time. On October 28, he wrote to his friend, the novelist and travel writer Thomas A. Janvier, that he had completed "three chapters of a second book entitled: 'Fray Luis the Lay-brother. A Reminiscence of Coronado's March.'" This was to be a fictionalized account of the Franciscan lay-brother Luis de Ubeda, who had remained at Pecos Pueblo in 1542 when the Coronado expedition left the Southwest and who was never heard of again. Neither has Bandelier's Fray Luis manuscript ever come to light. It is not even certain whether the author completed it or whether he dropped the subject after three chapters. Another project, however, a report on Bandelier's archaeological work in Arizona and New Mexico in 1888–89, was published in November 1889 as an appendix to the Archaeological Institute of America's tenth annual report. This pleased the scientist, especially because Norton had written a comment "very complimentary to me" concerning the imminent appearance of part I of the *Final Report*.

While Bandelier was busy with the Hemenway and AIA people in Boston, he was also negotiating for a position in California, with Lummis's help, and also for a position at the University of Pennsylvania, with the assistance of Professor Daniel Garrison Brinton. Bandelier telegraphed "final acceptance" of the latter position to Brinton on December 16. However, as will shortly become clear, neither possibility materialized.

On December 10, Joe returned from the Illinois trip—much to Adolph's delight. A week later, Bandelier began to prepare *Die Koshare,* the German version of his novel, for publication in the *Belletristisches Journal* of New York. On December 21, he received word that the publisher Dodd, Mead and Company wished to look at the English version of his novel, and he immediately wrote to Parkman to send it to them. The year ended quietly, and Adolph's first journal entry for 1890 began with a conventionally optimistic message: "New Year's Day. Happy New Year to all!!! God be with us again, and help us through."

Apparently, any prospects of help from the deity quickly faded. By February, Bandelier was in a mental state reminiscent of the bad times of early 1886. On February 11, after several days of not writing in his journal, Adolph committed his frustrations to writing:

> Philadelphia ha[d] been heard of last Sunday morning, in a note from Brinton in which he states that there is nothing! So I am fooled also. The English novel also is accepted, but most likely, I will be robbed of all profits in time. From the *Belletristisches Journal* a few letters, but nothing positive yet. So we are again on the street, so-to-say, cheated and beaten out of the most legitimate efforts to make a humble living. [Thomas B.] Catron talked of sending me to Mexico, and I shall go tomorrow, provided it is not a hoax like everything else. If I go, it will bring no money, but costs none either.

Thomas B. Catron was a prominent lawyer and land speculator in territorial New Mexico and later a senator from that state. He was interested in purchasing the library of Bandelier's Mexican friend, the late Father Agustín Fischer. The Fischer library, an important collection on Mexican history, was intended—at least according to an affidavit Catron gave to U.S. Customs—for the use of the New Mexico Historical Society. Bandelier went to Mexico City on February 12 and quickly made arrangements for the purchase. He was back in Santa Fe on March 6.

The next few months saw Bandelier engaged in mopping-up operations, mailing the last group of manuscript copies to Fewkes, and rewriting portions of *Die Koshare,* which had begun running serially in the *Belletristisches Journal* on January 1. The scholar also worked out an agreement with Max Frost, publisher of the Santa Fe *Daily New Mexican,* for a series of articles. The first of these concerned purchase of the Fischer library, and later ones, the history of Spanish New Mexico. Bandelier was paid $15 per month for eight monthly columns.

Another source of income also appeared at this time. Part I of Bandelier's massive *Final Report* had just been published, and the AIA was willing to subsidize the scholar while he prepared part II. Adolph thought and hoped that this might be a long-term appointment, but that did not prove to be the case. In any event, it offered some immediate financial relief. Bandelier also hoped to be appointed territorial librarian. Certainly he would have been a capable person for the post, but like so many of Bandelier's projects during this period, nothing came of it.

Beginning on May 28, 1890, Bandelier decided to keep his journal in Spanish, and he did so faithfully for some ten months. On April 3, 1891, he switched to German, and then on April 24, he switched again—this time to French. For the next three months, individual journal entries were written in one or another of the three continental European languages. Adolph returned to English for his journal entries on July 28.

A reason for the original switch to Spanish was that Bandelier had hopes of relocating to Mexico and wished to practice the language more. Little is known of his plans for Mexico, but they were probably made as a result of conversations with García Icazbalceta in January or February 1890. Adolph switched to German and French without any explanation, and it may simply have been that he wanted to keep in practice. Working in the Ryhiner and Company bank in Highland, Adolph probably wrote and spoke both languages daily. In New Mexico, he occasionally spoke at least German, but he may have had less opportunity to write in either language.

There is another possibility, too. At the time he switched from Spanish to German, Bandelier had a young woman assistant, Anita Chapman, who was bilingual in English and Spanish but, so far as we know, did not read German or French. Conceivably, he wanted to keep his journal entries private from Anita's eyes, especially since he often wrote outrageous comments about friends and family members.

In July, the Norwegian explorer Carl Lumholtz appeared in Santa Fe, visiting briefly before he went on into northwestern Mexico, the exploration of which was part of his distinguished career. Bandelier was favorably impressed with Lumholtz in spite of the latter's obvious lack of experience and of competence in Spanish.

The later part of 1890 was spent on projects including the writing of part II of the *Final Report* and the copying of documents, especially a long poem by Gaspar Pérez de Villagrá celebrating the Oñate occupation of New Mexico.

On November 2, Bandelier received, at long last, a contract for *The Delight Makers* from Dodd, Mead and Company (actually dated November 3). The contract was not a particularly generous one. The author was to receive a 10-percent royalty on the retail price after the first one thousand copies had been sold. He was also to get twelve free copies. The book had obviously been in production for some time, since Bandelier received his free copies the day after the contract arrived. He was pleased with the book and immediately gave out several copies. By now Adolph nursed the idea of writing a series of novels and making a living income from the royalties. He was still hopeful of this six weeks later, remarking on December 10 that a letter from Dodd, Mead was "Very favorable! What luck!" But as the months went on, he gradually gave up the idea that riches or even a living wage would come from writing novels.

The Delight Makers, unfortunately—though it is today a minor classic of American literature—did not sell well in its first Dodd, Mead edition, and its success remained small throughout Bandelier's lifetime. During our editing of *The Southwestern Journals of Adolph F. Bandelier,* however, we received a letter from Dodd, Mead revealing that *The Delight Makers* was the longest-running title the company had ever had in its inventory.

December 1890 brought domestic distractions: Joe injured her right hand and forearm in a fall, and Papa Bandelier, after still another quarrel, went off to Wallace to stay with Father Ribera. The end of December and the first weeks of January 1891 were cold and blustery, with a great deal of snow. Papa remained at Wallace, keeping his hand in by writing insulting letters to the Bandeliers in Santa Fe. Adolph seems to have been thoroughly fed up, for after noting one of these letters on January 7, he made no further mention of the elder Bandelier until the final entry of his southwestern journals on May 20, 1892.

In March 1891, Bandelier signed a contract for $1,200 with territorial governor L. Bradford Prince to catalog and translate the Spanish and Mexican archives in the state capital. Apparently the contract had been delayed several times, and Bandelier, in his journal entry, was at his sarcastic best: "Three times I had to go to the plaza before, finally, the celebrated, very most excellent Mr. Governor signed the contract. At seven at night the thing was done. What a man! Thank God. The matter is to extend for a year, but who knows? For the following year, the scoundrel will have to nominate me again."

In this work, Adolph was to have the assistant mentioned earlier—Anita Johnson Chapman, a young woman whose husband had deserted his family and who was living with her parents, James Johnson, a wealthy merchant, and his Mexican-born wife, Jesusa. The Johnsons lived on Canyon Road in an architectural gem of a house called El Zaguán (the hall). Today, El Zaguán encompasses a garden named in Bandelier's honor and houses the offices of the Old Santa Fe Foundation, which holds title to the property.

Josephine's injury the previous December was such that she could no longer do ordinary housework; accordingly, Adolph decided to move to another location where others could take care of such chores. On March 16, Joe left for a visit to Highland, and on April 3, Adolph moved into the Johnson home. Joe returned from Illinois in early July and joined her husband there. The hand and arm were still somewhat crippled, but Anita and her sister, Margarita Johnson, were available to help Joe with the housework.

It is not clear what happened to the John C. Schumann house on East de Vargas Street. On June 7, 1891, Bandelier mentioned his attempts to sell a property for Schumann, probably the same house. "Last Sunday [Matt?] Nagel came and I had every hope of selling, at last, the property of Schumann." Events surrounding this proposed sale are not very clear. On the day Adolph mentioned the sale, he also commented that he, Schumann, and Henry Kaune met at the house and then went to the brewery together. Whether this was to finalize the sale to Nagel is simply not clear. In any case, Bandelier's younger cousin and her husband—Lizzie and Henry Kaune—later became associated with the house, and it may be that they actually replaced the Bandeliers. The couple eventually purchased the property from Schumann, but not until 1919.

Bandelier still had hopes for the Hemenway expedition, and it would seem that Fewkes continued to make promises of additional work. On April 20, Adolph finally finished the last section of the *Final Report: Part II,* and mailed it off to William C. Lawton, secretary of the Archaeological Institute of America. This ended Bandelier's obligation to the AIA but again left him without an institutional sponsor. A little earlier that month, Fewkes had given him hope that he might be retained in some fashion or other. According to Bandelier,

On Saturday, the 11th [of April], I had a very important and interesting day with Fewkes. He arrived here Friday night. It appears that all is better. He has written Boston that they should again send me the books and documents, and he has hopes that this will happen. He also has well-founded hope for an appointment for me at $75.66 per month. He says nothing very good about Lumholtz. He is of the opinion that the affair will be a failure.

Later on, Bandelier accused Fewkes of lying to him and to others connected to the Hemenway project, especially the Dutch anthropologist H. F. C. ten Kate, who had worked for a time with the expedition. There is no question that the Hemenway expedition was riddled with politics, inefficiency, and lack of focus. To what extent Fewkes exploited or manipulated this situation is unclear.

One enjoyable aspect of Bandelier's life at this time was his work with Anita Johnson Chapman, whom Adolph often referred to as "the dear [or good] girl" or "the good child" (Anita was twenty-eight at the time). Anita, who spoke and read both English and Spanish, was very useful to the scholar in the indexing and cataloging of the New Mexico archives. She seems to have been a dedicated and tireless worker, able to spend the day with Bandelier in addition to taking care of her two young children and helping Josephine with household duties.

Bandelier always seemed to be attracted to intelligent and educated women. Perhaps because of his own vigor and drive, he seems to have had a preference for younger, more vigorous women. At any rate, Anita, the "loving, good and faithful creature," was a most satisfactory co-worker.

In May, Bandelier went to Isleta for Santa Cruz Day ceremonies. In July and August, he was again at Cochiti and explored the wild and rugged country west of the Rio Grande and north of the pueblo, eventually reaching Española and then San Juan Pueblo, where he examined church records, a project carried out in part for Thomas B. Catron.

Indeed, about this time Bandelier seems to have been representing Catron, and he had a conference with the attorney on returning to Santa Fe. Catron owned large tracts of land in northern New Mexico, including the Tierra Amarilla land grant—580,000 acres west of the Rio Grande in northern New Mexico—which Catron wished to sell at $2.50 per acre. For a time, Bandelier dealt with Reginald Oestrom, an agent for a British syndicate, for sale of this vast property.

Bandelier's role, however, is not very clear, since Catron's regular agent in the matter was Wilmot E. Broad from Chama. Adolph, in a letter to Catron dated October 2, 1891, mentioned that Oestrom planned to send him to London "at Oestrom's own expense," to help further the matter. Broad, however, in a letter to Catron written the previous day, was critical of Bandelier, apparently for suggesting a higher price for the property and unsettling Oestrom. In any case, nothing came of the projected sale. Although Bandelier also acted for Catron in other land matters and seems to have been involved with Catron and Archbishop Salpointe in some unidentified project, there is no indication that Catron ever paid Adolph any great amount of money.

Another project involved Mr. and Mrs. Edward L. Bartlett of Santa Fe, who were interested in organizing a territorial exhibit for the Columbian Exposition held in Chicago in 1893. Adolph assisted in gathering and preparing Indian materials for this exhibit; his efforts included compiling a catalog of Sam Eldodt's large collection of Indian artifacts. Like his efforts for Catron, this was piece work. As Bandelier dejectedly wrote in his journal, "It is hard, very hard, to eke out a living in the manner in which I have to do it."

During the late summer and autumn of 1891, the scholar did a variety of fieldwork, visiting San Juan, Santa Clara, Cochiti, Santo Domingo, Santa Ana, Jemez, and Zia pueblos. On a walking trip to various of the pueblos in late October, Bandelier became ill with diarrhea, which he attributed to a meal of watermelon and grapes. It was probably a bacterial or viral infection, however, for he grew worse over a period of days. After tramping from Jemez to Zia and Santa Ana, Adolph became so sick that he found it necessary to stop over with the Catholic priests in Bernalillo for a day or so before finally reaching Santa Fe. Perhaps as a side effect of the diarrhea, Bandelier became depressed:

> I stopped my journal, owing to depression and a misanthropic feeling of despondency which seized and grew on me powerfully. For weeks, no letters. Had not the heart to hope for anything at all. Joe went to Los Lunas and got into trouble there, owing to [Louis] Huning's drunkenness. I spent most of the time on the road.
>
> At last, I went to San Juan, to nurse S. Eldodt. Then back to Isleta, where I spent the last days of the year and New Year's. With all that, a very cold winter and much snow, all trains much delayed and obstructed.

It is the most dismal time I can recollect, except in Highland in 1885. . . .
I am going to try and get East after New Year's with [Charles F.] Lummis if
I can raise the money at all. Perhaps I may succeed.
Good-bye 1891!!!

Josephine was probably visiting the Huning family in Los Lunas when
she got into "trouble." It does not seem to have been serious, however,
and the couple was reunited at Isleta Pueblo.

The plan to go east with Lummis was the first phase of an ambitious
program in which the two men would switch their research endeavors
to an entirely new field—South America, concentrating on the antiquities of Bolivia. The new project increased in importance for Bandelier
when, on January 8, Catron wrote a letter expressing his displeasure over
the negotiations with Oestrom (and, by implication, with Bandelier's
handling of those negotiations). Catron was blowing cold on the land
deal, in the belief that New Mexico was soon to be admitted as a state
and that land values would then rise. In reality, statehood for New
Mexico was still two decades away.

On January 11, 1892, Bandelier left for Albuquerque to meet Lummis.
Three days later, the two men left for the East, traveling by train to
Chicago and then along a somewhat circuitous route across southern
Canada, finally reaching New York City on the eighteenth.

Busy days followed. Calls were made at Dodd, Mead and at *The
Nation,* where Bandelier and Lummis discussed plans for South American
work with Garrison. The principal reason for their visit to New York,
however, was to meet with the German-American railroad financier,
Henry Villard. The financier, who also owned the *New York Evening Post,*
was interested in collecting antiquities. Some of the initial contact with
Villard seems to have been made by Lummis. It is also likely that
Bandelier was recommended by William Lawton, secretary of the AIA. In
February, when negotiations were going on with Villard, Lawton sent a
circular to the AIA members proposing that the institute join Villard in
funding the South American expedition. Norton, Parkman, and
Salisbury all supported this plan, but other members objected and the
funding never materialized.

Though Lummis had been in on much of the early planning for the
expedition, once they were in New York, Bandelier seems to have been
in charge. He and Villard had both been born in central Europe and had

spoken German from childhood. They seem to have had considerable rapport. The two men met for breakfast (at 1:00 P.M., as Bandelier wryly noted) on January 20. Two days later, the researcher received a letter from Villard offering to assume one-half of the expense of the South American expedition. The financier also gave Bandelier a letter of introduction to R. W. Gilder of *Century* magazine, who, Villard believed, would contribute the other half. The next few days were a whirl of activity; Bandelier met the Villard family and got together with his old friend from Mexico days, Thomas A. Janvier. On January 25, Bandelier and Lummis met Gilder and returned hopeful that something would be worked out.

During that February in New York, Bandelier worked at the Lenox Library, copied manuscripts, visited friends, went to the theater, and courted several potential allies in the new project. Among those he attempted to see was the famous financier and philanthropist Andrew Carnegie. Bandelier called on him on February 11, but unfortunately, Carnegie was leaving for California early the next morning, and Adolph was not able to meet with him.

About this time, Bandelier began to criticize Lummis. "He is extremely ambitious, vain, and begins to be very conceited." This seems a bit hard on poor Lummis, who evidently was the original moving force behind the South America project. The two colleagues may have been feeling some friction over a publishing agreement that Lummis was trying to reach with Charles Scribner's Sons for a series of articles written by himself. The publishing house turned the proposal down because Lummis would not be able to include any material that might go into Bandelier's final report.

R. W. Gilder of *Century* magazine did respond favorably to Lummis and Bandelier in a March 1 letter to the latter man:

> Referring to the subject of our consultation, the Century Magazine would be glad to have from you and your associate, say, five articles at the rate of $400 each, on subjects connected with your intended trip to South America.
>
> Those should be as different in subject from each other as possible, and popular in point of interest. It is understood that each is to have an introduction by yourself, and Mr. Lummis is to furnish a part of the letterpress. It is further understood that these articles shall be about 12,000

words, letter-press with sufficient pictorial material to make them double that length, if desirable.

In other words, both Bandelier and Lummis were to furnish text, though Bandelier, as expedition leader, was expected to write the introductions. Gilder went on to say that *Century* should have the right of first refusal on any resulting book at a 10-percent royalty. He stressed that no one accompanying the expedition should send letters to any other publication and that none of the material published by the magazine (with the exception of scientific reports) should appear elsewhere.

At last, on March 12, Bandelier and Lummis reached a final agreement with Villard. "Oh, how I felt!!" wrote Adolph. "God knows that I have suffered long and terribly and waited patiently withal. Now there is at least hope before me, for Joe and for myself. Also for Lummis, if he is careful and not too conceited."

It was another ten days before the three parties finally signed the contract. In the meantime, Bandelier visited the consulates of Ecuador and Bolivia and did some shopping. Peru did not seem all that important to him at the time, since he planned to do nothing more than traverse Peruvian territory to reach Bolivia. Yet by the time Adolph reached Peru, he was obviously planning a considerable stay there. Neither his journals nor his letters indicate when or why he changed plans.

The researcher left New York City in April, dropping in on the Highland family. He arrived back in New Mexico on May 12. By this time, Papa Bandelier was back in Santa Fe, and there he remained for several years. He acted to some degree as his son's agent and was empowered to open and forward the Bandeliers' mail to South America. It may be that he moved back into the Bandelier house on East de Vargas Street, perhaps sharing it with the Kaune family—at least, he was living with them in the mid-1890s. Papa was, after all, Lizzie's granduncle.

Now the rather fluid plan was for Adolph and Joe to take a ship to Lima, then go by rail to Puno and across Lake Titicaca to La Paz, Bolivia. This city was to be the headquarters for Bandelier's archaeological work. Lummis, whose wife was pregnant, would stay in New Mexico until after the birth, then join the Bandeliers in Bolivia.

It was an end and a beginning. In his last entry in the southwestern portion of his journals, from Santa Fe on May 20, 1892, Bandelier remarked,

Now begins a new period. God give me the power to comply with duty to the fullest extent. It will be difficult frequently, but I hope that I may be equal to the task. . . . Next Monday or Tuesday, we are to leave to San Francisco at last. Thence to Bolivia. The weather here is beautiful, cloudless mostly, a splendid air and sky. A little windy at times but nothing especially aggravating. All are well, and I found and answered a number of letters. Papa is here also. With this, I close this Journal.

South America lay ahead, and it would bring changes beyond anything Bandelier dreamed. Never again would he see the Southwest, and never again Papa. Josephine would die within the year, but that terrible loss would open the door to personal and professional relationships deeper and perhaps more rewarding than any Adolph had ever known before.

FOURTEEN
Two Fateful Years

A new life begins, a new leaf is turned over.

Bandelier STARTED his new journal on Friday, May 20, 1892. By that date, all arrangements with Villard, with *Century* magazine, with the Santa Fe family, and with Lummis had been made. Adolph and Josephine set about the serious business of packing for their extended trip, saying good-bye to friends and relatives, arranging their financial affairs, and generally closing down the Santa Fe segment of their lives. On Tuesday, May 24, Bandelier wrote in his new journal:

> Took leave of everybody in town and that night we left, Henry & Papa accompanying us as far as Lamy. Night dark, shower at Wallace. Goodby to Santa Fé and to all our loved ones. —God bless you all. A new life begins. May God grant a favorable exit. May he give me the strength to do my duty to the very last; toward Joe, toward Mr. Villard and Science.

The Bandeliers spent the night of May 24 in Albuquerque, where Adolph conferred one last time with Lummis. Leaving that city in the early morning of May 26, the couple traveled through southern New Mexico and Arizona on the Southern Pacific Railroad. They reached San Francisco on the afternoon of May 28, putting up at the Lick House. While in San Francisco, Bandelier paid a visit to the famous historian Hubert H. Bancroft. Adolph had been critical of Bancroft in the past, but on this occasion he noted in his journal simply, "Charmingly received."

Adolph and Joe left San Francisco on the steamship San Juan at noon on Monday, June 6. It would be more than eleven years before Adolph again set foot on United States soil, and Joe would never return to the country of her birth. The trip southward was pleasant for Adolph, although Joe was often seasick. By June 20, the ship was in the Bay of Fonseca, and two days later it reached the city of Panama. There, Adolph jotted down observations on the Lesseps' ill-fated attempt to build a canal. This operation, according to the scholar, had been rife with fraud and corruption.

From Panama, the Bandeliers booked passage on the Chilean steamer *Aconcagua,* departing on June 24. After a day of gentle weather, there came high seas, and Joe suffered seasickness again. Adolph, however, found time to praise the red Chilean wine served on shipboard and to make notes on butterflies that appeared on the deck. By the morning of June 28, the ship had cruised past northern Ecuador and arrived in the outer stretches of the Rio Guayes, docking at the port of Guayaquil. Adolph and Joe explored this port city, which in 1892 had a population of perhaps forty thousand. On June 30 the ship left for the final leg of the trip, down the coast of Peru. After touching at various points in northern Peru, the *Aconcagua* arrived at Callao, the port of Lima, on July 3. The Bandeliers obtained rooms at the Hotel Maury in Lima, which was managed by Maximiliano Lecaros, who—seemingly by accident— had met them at wharfside and accompanied them to Lima.

> Got very excellent suite of rooms: one parlor, two bedrooms, and two Alcoves or balconies. Everybody here is highly polite, but it is chilly. The latest census of Lima gives that city 106,000 inhabitants. The streets are not wide but they are much cleaner than those of Mexico and the people look cleaner and handsomer. The "Manta" however is an ugly garment, it makes the ladies all look like Sisters of Charity.

July, of course, is mid-winter in Lima. The climate of Peru's capital has never had a good reputation, because of coastal fogs that appear especially during the southern hemisphere's winter months.

During the next few days, Adolph and Joe explored and made contacts in the city. Bandelier began at once to investigate collections of antiquities for sale in Lima, since this was a major charge given him by Villard. On the fourth of July, Bandelier commented:

Bandelier's travels in South America, 1892–1903

In the morning I delivered my letters of introduction. Saw Duncan, Fox & Co. [and?] Thomas Dawson and sold my Gold and paper to Mr. Jacoby at 58%—He has a large collection of Antiquities, Pottery, Silver, Gold, Copper, and some very fine cloths & ca. He offered the whole collection for £800.—I shall see. The Silver is handsome, but the trouble is, that the localities are not given. Still, I may perhaps make a trade. Went there again in the afternoon with Joe, and she was very much pleased, she says however (and she is right) that it would be better to buy only the metallic objects and the cloths, and leave the Pottery out. Some of the metallic objects are very fine.

Selling "gold and paper" presumably referred to currency exchange: dollars to Peruvian soles, the sol being the national unit of currency in Peru.

In his journal, Bandelier commented at some length on the behavior of Chilean soldiers who had been barracked in Lima's Exposition Park for two and a half years during the Peruvian-Chilean War of the Pacific in 1879–83. The victorious Chileans, after taking Lima, had emptied the zoological garden, attempting to ship the animals to Chile but allowing all of them to die. The national library was looted of valuable books and manuscripts, the museum stripped of its antiquities, and the school of medicine sacked.

On July 5, Bandelier went to the Bank of London, Mexico, and South America, where he was introduced to a young man named Frederico Macedo, whose father owned the largest collection of antiquities in Lima. The same day the Bandeliers unexpectedly met an old friend and colleague from the Hemenway expedition, H. F. C. ten Kate, the Dutch anthropologist. Dr. ten Kate was returning from the Dutch East Indies and had stopped off in Peru. During these first days in Lima, Adolph also became acquainted with José Pardo, son of the first civilian president of Peru and later to become president himself. This acquaintance followed a pattern Bandelier had established in Mexico and would later repeat in Bolivia. Bandelier quickly gained entrée into the circle of political and financial powers in whatever Latin American country he found himself.

On July 11, the Bandeliers received their first letters from home. They learned that Mrs. Charles Lummis had given birth to "a healthy little girl." Letters from Papa Bandelier and from Henry Kaune in Santa Fe indicated that both were well. The city itself, however, was "in a horrible state. Murder upon murder. And no relief."

On July 20, Adolph and Joe met new and, as it turned out, very important friends. After spending part of an afternoon examining a local collection of antiquities, Bandelier noted in his journal that he "went accidentally [incidentally?] to get some beer, and dropped into the business-place of a Mr. Von [de] Ruetti, of BERNE!—the ladies there are of Zurich, their name is Ritter, and I immediately led Joe thither. They were charmed at seeing her. So she has—at last—lady friends with whom she can speak and entertain herself."

During the days that followed, Bandelier continued examining collections and arranging for their purchase. He deferred to Joe in determining the authenticity of certain of the objects. There were many examples of weaving, and Adolph seemed to feel that his wife had special expertise in this regard. Bandelier also met de Ruetti again, and Joe visited the Ritter ladies in the afternoons.

Henrietta Ritter was a widow whose husband had been a business partner in a store with de Ruetti. The Ritters had three daughters, Martha, Hedwig (familiarly called Heidi), and Fanny. The last was twenty-two at the time Adolph and Josephine first met the Ritter family; she had come with her parents from Zurich as a fifteen-year-old schoolgirl. The ages of the other daughters are not altogether clear; judging from various journal entries, however, they were younger than Fanny. Hedwig was probably nineteen or twenty in 1892, and Martha somewhere in her mid-teens.

August of 1892 saw Lima beset by an influenza epidemic, and among the ill was Hedwig Ritter. On August 14, Bandelier wrote in his journal: "In the afternoon I let Joe go out alone, and she took a walk with Fanny Ritter. It was a sunny day for a wonder, and not cold at all. . . . The influenza is increasing very rapidly here. Business is suffering from it, and many stores are compelled to close on account of the disease."

Epidemic or no, Bandelier threw himself into the work of collecting, measuring, describing, and excavating ruins in the vicinity of Lima, including the famous site of Pachacamac. By now Bandelier had begun to find fault with Lummis, whose overly enthusiastic letters grated on the older man. Indeed, the scientist seriously considered breaking off the arrangement for Lummis to come to South America. Bandelier's reaction to Lummis over the next several years ranged across the emotional spectrum from fever hot to icy cold, but it is likely that Lummis remained unaware of these emotional changes. In early September, Bandelier was offered the largest collection to date, that of Dr. Nicolás Saenz, for twenty thousand dollars. Joe, after visiting and admiring the collection on September 5, advised her husband to recommend its purchase, which Adolph did in a telegram to Villard the following morning.

In October, Joe and Adolph spent a brief time examining ruins in the Chorrillos area near Lima, returning to the city in time to celebrate Joe's fifty-sixth birthday at the Ritters' home on October 11. During the balance of October, Adolph took Quechua lessons and further excavated the ruins of Pachacamac. Around this time Bandelier contracted an ear infection, for which he received treatment from a local Chinese curer. It failed to alleviate the itching, pain, and discharge, however, so the Ritters suggested a plant called *ruda* (*Galega officinalis,* or goat's rue). It too brought no relief, so Bandelier tried the bark of the calisaya tree (*Cinchona calisaya*), which produces quinine, and then, when all else had failed, he sought out a Lima physician. This man diagnosed an infection of the tympanum, and under his treatment the ear gradually became better. By the beginning of December, it was well except for occasional itching, though in later months Adolph's ear problem flared up again. It was, perhaps, a staphylococcus infection.

Lummis, in great high spirits, arrived on the steamer *Imperial* on November 21. In spite of Bandelier's reservations, and after some initial coolness, the older man decided that his young associate might work out satisfactorily after all. Lummis, with his usual energy and enthusiasm, threw himself into the task of collecting and photographing.

At the beginning of December 1892, the world of Adolph Bandelier was satisfying and serene. His ear infection was virtually cured, news from the Santa Fe family was generally good, and Lummis seemed to be working out well. Joe's health was no worse than usual, and on this South American trip she was, atypically, working closely with her husband, helping to sort specimens and performing other archaeological duties. From later correspondence, we know that Joe had been given the primary responsibility for collecting plants to sell to Professor N. L. Britton of Columbia College. On her birthday, de Ruetti had presented her with a cake carrying the inscription, "A la intrépida viajera Señora Bandelier," something Adolph noted with approval in his journal of October 11. Apparently, in these waning months of her life, Joe *was* becoming something of an intrepid and adventurous traveler.

On Thursday, December 1, Adolph commented that his wife had

made an important discovery. While unrolling small cloth bundles from Pachacamac, she found that they invariably consisted of a string of coarse brown enclosing a small piece of gold and a yellow strip with a bit of silver. Bandelier thought they might be "medicine bundles" and remarked that Joe had effected "a very important discovery, and I am glad that She made it. She is so good."

These tranquil days ended suddenly and dramatically. The journal entry for December 1 was the last for several days. On Monday, December 5, Joe was stricken with terrible abdominal pains, quickly diagnosed as "colico miserere" (according to Adolph's notes), a stricture or blockage of the intestines. Joe was taken at once to the Ritters', where she was nursed with care and devotion. Five physicians were called, but not one was willing to operate, owing to the great weakness of the patient. Joe rallied on December 7, and Adolph noted in his journal that day:

> Under the influence of the terrible sickness of my poor dear Joe, I write now this diary for all the times past. The only important thing to record is: unhappily, her sickness. It began Monday with pain in her bowels, and increased horribly in the course of the afternoon so as to constipate her completely and cause something like the MISERERE.—What [a] time I had in consequence of it, I cannot put down in writing. I placed her at once at Ritter's where she was attended to with every possible care and devotion. But to secure the Doctors was a trial in itself. At last I got Dr. Sosa who has so far been successful. Last evening the crisis set in and now she feels relieved but very weak and downhearted. I was almost crazy until the good crisis took place. What is the cause of this terrible attack I cannot guess at all. She committed no imprudence whatever, was always quiet, modest and—so so very good to me. . . . I wrote to Papa and to Mr. Villard. Joe also, poor thing, wrote to Lizzie and to Henry. If only God grants her recovery.—She is well attended at Ritter's, her sister and mother could not do more for her than they are doing now and have always done for the poor sick darling of mine.

Another week passed without a journal entry. Then, on December 14, a weary Adolph resumed writing.

> It is almost impossible to write a journal now. Everything is, unfortunately, OVER. My darling died on Sunday morning about eleven, and I

had to bury her on Monday afternoon. The shock is still within me and I am still more or less wandering in a kind of trance. She died so sweetly. Her last audible word was: Adolf!!—Now a new and distinct life begins. I am utterly alone now, for Papa is very old and feeble and, after him, there is nothing left for me to care. Yet, I do owe the Ritter's my friendship and assistance. I am too deeply indebted to that family for what they did for Joe. They acted like Angels. Goodby my love, my past life,—but do not forsake me, now that You are in heaven. God loved you too well to leave you to me.

At the bottom of this entry were two slanting black lines, a cross where the two met at mid-page, and, underneath, the death date, December 11, 1892.

On December 15, he finally found strength to write his father the sad news, and two days later, he wrote Joe's sister, Bertha Lambelet, in St. Louis. During the following days, Bandelier worked listlessly at packing and shipping materials to Villard. A short letter dated December 24, written in German to Villard, spoke almost entirely of shipping the sketches and plans of various ruins, especially those of Pachacamac. There was only tangential mention of the personal tragedy in Adolph's life.

By Christmastime, Bandelier was beginning to recover his equilibrium, though he clung to the Ritter mother and daughters as a surrogate family. On Christmas Eve, Adolph reached a sudden and surprising decision:

I am beginning to resolve, that I should propose to Fanny. It is fearfully soon, after the catastrophe but, it seems to me, that dear Joe almost expects me to take this step. The girl is a lovely prize, worthy in every respect. Joe loved her, and why, then, did she join our hands on her deathbed. Spent the evening at OUR, now at MY folks.

And on the following day, Christmas morning:

Worked some time, then at 11 AM: I took my heart into both hands and asked Fanny. She said YES in the simplest and most charming manner. So my future is mapped out. I have somebody to love and to care for. But, dearest Joe, do not get sad, I love YOU quite as much and Fanny loves You and we shall pray to You to be our guardian Angel on high all the time. You know me thoroughly, YOU know that I must have somebody to love and care for. Therefore do not get angry at us, do not withdraw Your protection from us. We will love you and Your memory, and care for Your grave, like as if we were Your children. Dearest Joe, pardon us, but we love each other upon this earth. I love You much and more, now, than every dearest angel of mine, or ours. . . .

[On Monday, December 26] we went to the Photographer and then to the sister[s] of Charity at Monserrate. Pleasant. Dear Joe, pardon and bless us. I feel happy and yet very, very unhappy. Evening at home, Ritter's. It has been a pleasant day. At night, the mail came. Letters, mostly all for poor Joe from Bertha and all the children.

Finally, on the last day of 1892, Bandelier summed up, as was his wont, the events of the past year and his hope for the coming one.

What a year this one has been for me!—The most important events of all my life have transpired. I have lost the most loving, devoted and faithful being that ever was upon earth, and have acquired another companion, as loving and faithful, I am sure, but not as soft and sweet. Still, this may be better for me, as Joe was too good, too pure, too kind for my own bad character. Joe, dear Joe, be YOU with us. . . .

The last day of a remarkable year: heaven knows what the next will bring. God be merciful to us, HE can crush us, but Joe is with him and SHE will pray and intercede for us in heaven. . . . God be with us, with Fanny and me, during the coming year. Joe, think of us and pray for us. Good-bye 1892.

At the bottom of the page he added the handwritten notation, "A new life begins, a new leaf is turned over."

On New Year's Day, Adolph went with Fanny and Mrs. Ritter to visit Mr. Ritter's grave at the small Bellavista Cemetery, where Protestants, especially foreign-born ones, were buried. Bandelier and the Ritters then went to the home of de Ruetti, "who gave us a handsome and very pleasant dinner, Dr. Fernández Dávila, the physician who attended Mr. Ritter last, was there. I led my Fanny to and from the table. How lovely it was to have the dear girl clinging to my arm. If it is not a sin to love her, then I have hopes to become very happy. Beautiful moonlight."

The following day Fanny and Adolph paid a visit to Joe's fresh grave in the great Panteón Cemetery. A statement Fanny made to Leslie A. White in 1936 revealed that Joe had made a deathbed conversion to Catholicism, as she wanted to die in her husband's faith. If this statement is true and not a figment of Fanny's romantic imagination, it would explain Joe's burial in the Panteón rather than the Bellavista Cemetery.

After his visit to the cemetery, Bandelier, with Lummis, took ship for Pisco on the south coast, where they had all along been preparing to work. Adolph and his young companion were now easier in their relationship, so strained just a month before. As Adolph remarked in his journal on January 2, "He is so faithful and attached that I had to inform [him] of my relations to Fanny, and he was at once very happy." Adolph, however, was somewhat worried over Fanny's reaction and wrote her a note telling what he had done: "I hope Fanny will forgive me, as I shall explain everything to her in my next letter which will be from Pisco."

The two men spent several weeks in the Pisco area, collecting, sketching ruins, photographing, and so forth. Joe, now apotheosized and appealed to as a guardian angel, was never far from Adolph's thoughts. On January 6, he worried about her reaction to his coming marriage with Fanny. "I dare not recall the anniversary which this date represe[nts]: that of our marriage!—Dear, poor Joe. Be not angry with me, dearest, if now I have again provided for my happiness here."

After working most of January in the valleys inland from Pisco, Bandelier returned to that city itself on January 26. A few days later, he became ill with a recurrence of the ear infection, complicated by an outbreak of eczema. Adolph decided to seek medical help, but, as we shall see, with unfortunate results. Partially recovering from the ministrations of the local doctor, he returned to Lima, taking the French steamer *Atlantique* from Pisco on February 8 and arriving in Callao about noon the next day. Bandelier summed up these happenings in his journal on February 10: "Lummis gone to Oroya, and everybody else well and happy. Fanny only was anxious about me and angry, as I had not written to her."

Fanny had reason for anxiety. In the same journal entry, Bandelier also described the hazards of Peruvian medicine as practiced in the provinces. Writing from the Hotel Maury in Lima, he remarked that a violent flare-up of the eczema had confined him to his hotel in Pisco for a week. In addition, the ear grew worse, so finally Adolph consulted a doctor whose name I shall never forget, Vasquez-Solis—and who is a real genuine ASS and FOOL. HE treated my ear with Phenic Acid [phenol or carbolic acid]. The result is easily conceived. I was for several days in a very bad condition. Then came chills and fever and—upon that, I concluded to go back to Lima and recuperate, also and especially to cure my ear, which now is completely deaf and heavily suppurating, while the whole head is weak and painful.

Phenol does have strong antiseptic properties, but it seems an extraordinary treatment considering the irritant action of the medication. From the fact that Bandelier's ear was severely burned and became infected, it would seem that Vásquez-Solís used a concentrated phenol solution.

The researcher remained in Lima for some time, partly because he became enmeshed in the financial problems of the de Ruetti store. De Ruetti himself was ill and staying afloat with borrowed money, including loans from Bandelier, who was trying to protect the Ritters' interest in the store. Eventually, on May 3, de Ruetti was forced to declare bankruptcy. On May 14, Bandelier moved the Ritter family to new quarters, the first floor of a house at 74 Negreiro, paying $720 for a year's rent in advance.

The struggles of the widowed Mrs. Ritter and her three daughters to survive financially in an alien land, and the anxiety concomitant on such economic distress, may help explain Fanny's facile acceptance of Adolph's proposal of marriage. She had, after all, known the Bandeliers for only five months, and the proposal had come an unconventionally short time after Joe's death. But granted that economic security must have figured in Fanny's decision to marry Adolph, it surely was not the only element in that decision, and probably it was not even the most important one. This was a romantic era, and Fanny, as her later correspondence and journals amply demonstrate, was romantic to the core. To this naive and provincial young woman, Adolph Bandelier must have seemed not only a strong figure on whom to lean but also a sophisticated, glamorous, and desirable "catch" as a husband.

While trying to organize the Ritter family, Bandelier was also preparing for a long-planned trip to the north coast and highlands of Peru. Unfortunately, trouble now flared again between Adolph and Charles Lummis. Lummis planned to bring his wife to Peru and tried to persuade Bandelier to put her on the payroll, something the older man resisted.

To add to these personal problems, a serious political crisis was developing. Andrés Caceres's military government had been in power since 1886, first under his own presidency and then, after 1890, under that of a subordinate, Colonel Remigio Morales B. This government was under increasing pressure from the two large civilian political parties. Though Caceres held on to power during 1893, the upheaval was only delayed; it would come two years later, bringing with it a short civil war.

Finally, on May 16, Bandelier left (sailing once more on the *Aconcagua*) for the north coast of Peru. He reached Trujillo on May 17, and on the following day made his first visit to the great pre-Inca ruins of Chanchan, capital of the pre-Hispanic kingdom of Chimu. Chanchan, one of the largest and best known pre-Columbian sites in the New World, became the focus of Bandelier's archaeological work for two months. He offered an evaluation of the site in a letter to James Terry of the American Museum of Natural History on May 27, 1893.

> I am here, at present, before the greatest task that ever I have undertaken in any single locality: the measurement and Survey of the Ruins of CHAN-CHAN on the seaside. Chan-Chan is by far the most extensive of all American ruins, both North and South. If I succeed in mastering the monster, you will have then, such ground-plans as no other place in the world owns.

Bandelier's work at Chanchan was later recognized by archaeologists, and one of the major compounds within that huge site was named for him.

By the end of July, the scientist had finished at Chanchan and had undertaken additional explorations in the Moche and other nearby valleys. The summer was marked by increasing difficulties with Lummis, and by the time Lummis left for Lima on July 29, Adolph's journal entries were etched in acid. The "dear good boy" of the New Mexico years was now a "fellow [who] must be laboring in craziness."

From his archaeological work along the northern coast, Bandelier moved into the northern highlands of Peru, to the Cajamarca region. He was again ill with diarrhea and fever (the latter vaguely diagnosed as malaria) and another flare-up of the ear trouble. In the highlands, Adolph managed to shake off these illnesses (though the ear problem was to continue intermittently), but then he was afflicted with an eye infection that made it difficult for him to work. In the midst of these problems, on

November 5, Bandelier received word from his old Santa Fe friend, Reverend H. O. Ladd, that Villard had been

accused of a gigantic swindle of the stockholders of the Northern Pacific. I also received a letter from Villard, dated October 6 in which he declares that he cannot do anything at all for me in Washington, and a letter from Ulbricht [Villard's secretary] stating that Villard and the whole family leave for Europe in a few days, to remain there a long time. This is very suspicious.

It is not clear what Villard was supposed to have done for Bandelier in the nation's capital. Possibly it involved obtaining some sort of quasi-official status for the scholar as an aid in his negotiations for collections. At any rate, on November 10, Bandelier left Cajamarca, arriving in Lima on November 20. The Ritters were waiting for him, as was Lummis. The latter man was now planning to return to New Mexico, and Bandelier, with very bad grace, gave his companion the remainder of the monies owed him.

Saturday [November 25] I took the draft for Lummis for $350.—, a poorly earned salary indeed. He has all told, been in South America eight months [?] of which he did nothing for three months fully. And yet, he will, in all probability, derive all the public benefit from the whole enterprise. I—did all the work, and receive nothing at all, except for a few thousand Soles. But I have Fanny, and that is ample glory.

The money draft was actually mailed to Lummis on November 27, the younger man having left Peru the previous Tuesday, November 21.

Just ONE YEAR from the date on which he first arrived here, he left on the steamer Arequipa for the United States, I hope and pray—NEVER TO RETURN anymore to these countries; or at least while I am here. He has utterly ABUSED of me and *of my good will toward him*. He is an over-ambitious, greedy, reckless, and grasping spirit. He has not the slightest scientific capacity, he is not even a conscientious Photographer. All his motives are utterly selfish and of him that appear streaks of mental aberration and again some things that indicate rascality in purpose if not in action. He is gone, at last. I am rid of him, thank God.

Such bitter words, in all probability, were not spoken directly to Lummis, for within a few years Charles Lummis once again had become Bandelier's "dear good boy." The reasons for Adolph's wild swings in his relationship with Lummis are hard to understand. The younger man, from all evidence at hand today, remained Bandelier's steadfast friend throughout the older man's life and was a supporter and ally of Fanny's after Adolph's death. One wonders if Josephine's passing may not have created deep mental disturbances in Adolph. There were physical disturbances as well; during the year after Joe's death, Adolph endured an astounding variety of bodily afflictions.

Of course, Lummis was hardly perfect, and his rather Bohemian ways did attract criticism throughout his life. Witness a writer for the Albuquerque *Evening Democrat* who met Lummis when the young man passed through Albuquerque on his 1884 "tramp across the continent" from Cincinnati to Los Angeles. The Albuquerque newsman took some sort of offense, and in a March 1885 story he lashed out at Lummis:

> Young Lummis made his headquarters at *The Democrat* while here and was treated with the greatest kindness, and while he seemed to have lots of energy and not much brains, he met with no less consideration on that account. He is an ungrateful, conscienceless little scrub . . . and it can be truthfully said of him that he has traveled farther, seen less and lied more than any youth his age and inches in the country.

The article carried on for two more incoherent and abusive paragraphs without ever really explaining what the young easterner had done wrong. What the article *did* make clear was that Lummis could rub people the wrong way.

The month of December was spent arranging the wedding. Bandelier enlisted the aid of the apostolic delegate in Lima in his plans to marry Fanny in a Catholic ceremony. The archbishop of Lima, M. C. Bandini, was unenthusiastic, but under pressure from the delegate gave his permission, with the stipulation that the ceremony should not be held in a church. It was decided that the wedding should take place at the Ritter home at 74 Negreiro. Bandelier was still trying to sort out the Ritter estate matters, and with the possibility that he might lose Villard's patronage, money worries were undoubtedly troubling him once more. He found great difficulty in getting accurate information about the early days of the de Ruetti and Ritter store. "I know hardly anything about the firm in general, and especially nothing about early transactions. Neither do my people. Fanny was too young at the time and Mama knows nothing but what Mr. Ritter has told her. The poor man knew but little himself." The real villains in the case, according to Bandelier, were de Ruetti and a man named Bodmer, who seems also to have had an interest in the store and who had now filed a claim.

The last entry in Adolph's journal for 1893, as one might expect, concerned the great event of the year, his marriage to Fanny.

On the 30th of December at 8 1/2 P.M.—Fanny and I were duly MAR-RIED—. A new life begins again. May God be our guide and staff and may SHE—who has been my Angel upon earth before, remain OUR ANGEL now and watch over us and pray for us in HEAVEN—Good-bye year 1893—eventful, unlucky in part, but still very HAPPY—YEAR.
FINIS 1893

It was a wedding of deep autumn with springtime. Adolph was fifty-three; his new wife was only three months and six days past her twenty-fourth birthday.

FIFTEEN
Peru and Bolivia

If He only had charity enough to take us away from the
scene of so much misery . . .

T HE NEWLYWED let his journal lapse for weeks after his marriage to Fanny. When at last he opened his 1894 journal, it was to say
merely, "I begin this Journal of the 17th of February. As I entered upon
my second stage of married life on the last day of the past year of 1893—
it is perhaps pardonable if I neglected the Journal until now. Furthermore, our life has been a rather quiet one in the main."

Bandelier's chief worry at this time was whether he would continue to
obtain support from Villard. He received disturbing letters from Lummis
containing clippings from American newspapers that reported accusa-
tions against Villard. Already Bandelier was in contact with the American
Museum of Natural History, since Villard had contributed the Bandelier
collections to that museum. A series of letters to James Terry, curator of
the Department of Anthropology and Ethnology, outlines this relationship. Bandelier had met Terry some years before in Santa Fe and was now
renewing the acquaintance by post.

By March 1894 it had been decided by Morris K. Jesup, president of
the American Museum, that AMNH would take over the entire
Bandelier operation. A letter reached Bandelier on March 26, and he responded the following day with a letter to Terry detailing the tragedy of
Joe's death, his recent marriage to Fanny, Lummis's unsuitability for the
project, and Bandelier's own plans for the future. On May 23, Adolph

wrote again, this time to Jesup, having received the news that Terry had left the museum, apparently with unpleasantness on both sides. For the next several years, most of Bandelier's correspondence would be addressed to John H. Winser, AMNH secretary.

While waiting for details of the American Museum sponsorship, Adolph and Fanny left on May 31 for the north coast of Peru, where final arrangements were made to ship the 1893 Chanchan collections. The Bandeliers returned to Lima on June 23, and on July 1 finally received the AMNH conditions of contract. Initially, Bandelier was to get $1,000 per quarter plus extra funds for collecting and for special expenses. These monies—like earlier payments by Villard—were remitted to Bandelier via the W. R. Grace Company, an import-export, shipping, and commercial firm with large holdings in Peru.

On July 3, Adolph and Fanny visited the cemetery authorities "to see about a tablet for the permanent Nitch [*sic*] for poor, dear Joe." On November 3, Josephine Bandelier's body was placed in a perpetual niche at the Cementerio General. It is likely that Joe was originally buried in a temporary site, and now Adolph and Fanny had her remains moved to a more permanent place with an appropriate grave plaque.

Now that final arrangements were worked out with the AMNH, Adolph and Fanny left for Bolivia in July 1894. A later, whimsical story by Fanny entitled "My Introduction into Archaeological Research" tells something about those early married days. The couple landed at Mollendo in southern Peru and spent a few days exploring the beautifully preserved burials in the nitrate-soaked soil in the area. According to Fanny:

My eyes fell on one particular piece of reddish-black material which looked like exceedingly fine weaving. I lifted it, but there seemed to be a lot of it buried deep in the sand; so I pulled. . . . It slid clear off the sand . . . [and] horrors . . . it was . . . a head . . . a woman's head. The supposedly wonderfully fine fabric was her hair, woven into a fantastic design by exposure, the sand, and time, discolored by the scorching sunbeams. — Behold it, and fling it way over my shoulders into the ebbing waves of the Pacific was one! —Ouff!—I looked up into my husband's laughing eyes. "If you are going to be that kind of assistant to me, dear, I think I shall have to send you back home to mother!"—I mended my ways however and he never again had occasion to find fault with my collaboration in the ten years of hardships and wonderful experiences that follow[ed] this my initiation into digging.

Adolph and Fanny reached La Paz on the eleventh of August that year. They spent nineteen days at the enormous pre-Inca ruin of Tiahuanaco and then made an exploring expedition to the slopes of Illimani mountain, southeast of La Paz. The Bandeliers next turned to the island of Titicaca in the southern part of Lake Titicaca, landing there on January 1, 1895. The owner of the largest hacienda on the island, don Miguel Garcés, served as their host. Except for one short break, the two stayed on Titicaca until April 15, 1895. This period saw the long-threatened civil war break out in Peru. The war created problems for the Bandeliers, since the northern and western shores of Lake Titicaca were Peruvian soil. Nevertheless, the two continued work at Titicaca and at the nearby smaller island of Koati through July 2. Returning to La Paz, Adolph and Fanny spent an additional time on Illimani, rounding out their first research period in Bolivia.

In that country, Bandelier was aided not only by friends in the archaeological establishment and by political and social leaders, but also by United States government officials. The American Museum of Natural History had previously requested the United States Department of State to assist Bandelier, and the U.S. minister at La Paz, Thomas Moonlight, had agreed to do so.

In the fall of 1895, Adolph and Fanny returned to their home base in Peru, reaching Lima on November 15. By this time the brief civil war was over and the civilian leader Nicolás de Piérola was president. The Bandeliers remained with the Ritter family, working on maps and ground plans and writing the report that would eventually be Adolph's most significant South American publication, *The Islands of Titicaca and Koati*. Bandelier was to send the first sections to the AMNH within a few months. Over the years, he agitated for publication of this work, but in spite of his insistence, it was finally the Hispanic Society of America that published *Islands* long after Bandelier's return from South America.

Journal entries give some of the flavor of Bandelier's life during the Peruvian visit.

Wednesday, December 11, 1895. HER anniversary. —we celebrated it, to the hour, at Santo Domingo. Father Prios sang the Mass, & the Altar was nicely decorated. Morning as fine as it can be in Lima; just as it was clear and hot three years ago.

Sunday, December 21, 1895: Christmas is coming and I must take part in preparing for it also. Fanny has a childlike delight in all these preparations, these little secrets and mysterious hidings of presents. We hope for some quiet and innocent pleasure. . . . Night with stars out and cooler. Day very sultry indeed.

During the early months of 1896, Adolph worked on notes, ground plans, and sketches and copied from local library collections. On March 22, the family celebrated the birthday of Fanny's sister Hedwig. Four days later Adolph wrote, "Went to the theatre. Fanny for the FIRST TIME IN HER LIFE!!! —This is certainly rare in our days, for a married woman, of her education, not to go to the theatre except at her twenty sixth year."

On April 18 came the bad news that the Wedeles grocery and general merchandise firm in Santa Fe had failed and that Henry Kaune had lost his position and his savings of $500. A letter from Father Bandelier claimed that Henry and Lizzy Kaune were mistreating him, and Bandelier thought of bringing his father to South America. By May 27, however, with Papa still waiting in the wings, Adolph and the Ritter family decided that Mrs. Ritter, Hedwig, and Martha would return to Switzerland, where the girls might have a brighter future. In Adolph and Fanny's eyes, this meant that Papa Bandelier would not have a proper home base. The elder Bandelier continued to express a desire to join his son and new daughter-in-law in Peru, so Adolph finally wrote to say that "he could not stand the voyage, and since Mama and the girls return to Switzerland, it is useless to take him to Peru."

After a certain amount of delay because of the illness of both daughters, the Ritter family left Callao on July 21. On August 9, Papa Bandelier wrote again, saying that he had decided to return to Bern. Adolph was skeptical, but on September 7 came a letter from Henry Kaune giving the news. As Bandelier noted in his journal: "Papa had left promptly for Bern. It seems that he has become insufferable of late. Much worse than ever."

Adolph and Fanny themselves were planning to return to Bolivia. They had completed their major task in Lima—arranging for the purchase and shipping of the extensive Garcés collection. An internal

AMNH letter from Assistant Curator M. H. Saville to President Jessup, dated August 31, gives a rough inventory. There were, for example, 79 gold and 106 silver objects, including statuettes, masks, and jewelry.

On September 23, Bandelier noted: "Day of our departure from Lima after four Ys. —It is quite an important day. But we could not visit HER grave. I hope she will forgive us for it. Mrs. Schlutze [Schultze?— a family friend living in Lima] will deposit a wreath on her tomb in our name."

Adolph and Fanny made a somewhat leisurely journey to Bolivia, arriving at Puno on the northwest shore of Lake Titicaca on October 1. They had to wait several days for the steamer while Adolph tried to shake off a severe cold. On October 11, Bandelier forgot Joe's birthday "until it was too late to beg her forgiveness. Illness and the preparation for departure are the reasons for it." On the twelfth, the couple boarded the lake steamer and disembarked at Chililaya. From that port the Bandeliers engaged a tilbury (a two-wheeled, two-person carriage) for the trip to La Paz.

On the morning of October 14, Bandelier collected a "host of letters," including one from Alphonse telling that Papa Bandelier, though weak from a fall, had reached Bern safely. The Bandeliers spent several days visiting friends and making arrangements for work. In November, they left for fieldwork on the slopes of Cacaaca in the cordillera east of La Paz. There, in Aymara Indian country, the couple collected, sketched and measured ruins, made photographs, and gathered ethnographic and linguistic data, often working at altitudes of over fifteen thousand and sometimes over sixteen thousand feet. They occasionally complained of altitude sickness but generally seemed to be free of it. On November 18, the scholar noted that an Aymara child had had two fingers blown off by dynamite two days before. It was the occasion for a typically Bandelierian tirade about the Aymaras:

> His mother did not want to send him to La Paz. Hence it is not imposs-ible that the unfortunate child may yet lose his entire hand, if not the arm even or his life. This is a fair specimen of Aymara brutality and beastliness. These Indians are brutes of the worst kind. They are much worse than any other Indians I ever met elsewhere North Or South. Sordid, mean cupid [*sic*], thievish, filthy, and cruel. They lie and deceive, and are also cowards.

That the mother perhaps had little reason to trust outsiders seems never to have occurred to Bandelier.

At the end of 1896, Adolph and Fanny were still working in the Cacaaca region. Adolph had now begun to contrast the abilities of his two wives. "It is HER death-anniversary, and I think of Her. After all it is much better thus. How [could] SHE have come to THIS country? — It is an immense sacrifice for Fanny but then, Fanny is young and her love and enthusiasm assist her. Poor Joe would have been unable to withstand all what this country exacts from us." Three weeks later, Adolph had this to say of Fanny:

> To-day is our third wedding-day, a day for which I cannot sufficantly [*sic*] thank God for, as it gave me Fanny. She is the companion I need in these regions in fact, I could not have obtained a better wife. Joe was what I need[ed] at first. After her death, and being left alone, I could not be luckier tha[n] through having Fanny given to me. She is exactly what I need for my mission and for myself. Always ready to help, always pleasant and cheerful, always contented.

Clearly, God had done the decent thing, removing Joe just when she would have become a burden and substituting the youthful Fanny to continue the great work.

Around the first of January, 1897, the Bandeliers shifted activities to the small hacienda of Santa Ana, not far from the tin mines of Huayna Potosí, some twenty-five miles from La Paz in the Cacaaca area. They had been given permission by the owner of the hacienda, a La Paz widow named Navidad Loayza, whom the two Bandeliers had met through the United States vice-consul, Geraldo Zalles, and his father, a prominent La Paz banker.

Adolph and Fanny arrived at Santa Ana on January 2. On the evening of January 3, they found that señora Loayza had ordered that they be forced out of the hacienda. The Indians of Santa Ana had prepared a long list of charges against them, including mistreatment of the headman of the local community, abuse and misappropriation of local horses, and desecration of a community cemetery. As these charges were mostly for incidents that purportedly happened before the Bandeliers had even ar-rived in Santa Ana, it seems likely that Adolph was justified in his angry denials. His comments on señora Loayza were acerbic, branding the widow a "miserable wretch and slut in every respect." This was on January 6; in a letter to Winser two days later, Bandelier suggested that Madame Loayza was afflicted with temporary insanity due to alcoholism. In any event, this situation disturbed Bandelier greatly; he justified himself in great detail to the AMNH officials and even had Thomas Moonlight, the U.S. minister to Bolivia, write a letter attesting to his innocence.

After the Santa Ana incident, the Bandeliers remained in La Paz for a time, visiting with new friends such as Miguel Vicente Ballivian, a prominent political and social leader. In early February, the couple was on the road again, this time to the southern and eastern shores of Lake Titicaca. There they gathered information on the Aymaras, past and present, including details on current trephining practices in the area. Trephining is the removal of a portion of the skull of a living person to decrease pressure following a head fracture (or sometimes for magical reasons). It was a well-known practice in the central Andes for many centuries, and Bandelier claimed that such operations were still occasionally performed.

Another milestone in Bandelier's life came on April 11, when a letter from Alphonse in Bern announced the February ninth death of Adolphe E. Bandelier.

He passed away very quietly and gently and without any struggle. — Peace to his ashes. So I have now lost both parents. Papa has had a long and very eventful life. His last years might have been prolonged, had he remained in Santa Fe but—HE could never stay quietly anywhere. . . . So Papa has joined Mama and HER, —When will my hour strike?

It might be well to pause at this point and try to give an objective evaluation of Papa Bandelier. He was a man who made many demands on his only son, his relatives, and his associates. In good times he was a strong, admired figure, as is attested by his successful career in Switzerland and in the early years in Highland. Yet there obviously were serious flaws in Adolphe E. Bandelier's character. His ignominious flight at the time of the bank failure in 1885, leaving his family and associates to face the consequences of what must have been his own business shortcomings, hardly betokens moral strength. The elder Bandelier's bad relations with his son and daughter-in-law seem largely of his own doing—

though only Adolph F.'s side of the story remains. Father Bandelier certainly seems to have been demanding, opinionated, and inconsiderate. Of course, he existed largely on family charity in the years after the bank failure, and this he seems to have resented. In any case, Adolph Bandelier's attitude toward his father was ambivalent; theirs was a love-hate relationship that not even the saccharine sentimentality of the times could disguise.

It was around the time of Papa's death that Adolph conceived a plan to become U.S. minister to Bolivia, replacing his friend Thomas Moonlight, whose appointment was nearing an end. Apparently with Moonlight's approval and help, Bandelier solicited assistance from President Jessup of the American Museum of Natural History. In the end the plan came to nothing, and given the rampant spoils system of nineteenth-century American politics, it probably never had a real chance. The new minister had been appointed on October 8, 1897. He was Dr. George H. Bridgman, a physician from Elizabeth, New Jersey, who had never held a public position before but seems to have been active in New Jersey Republican politics.

Before all this, however, in late May 1897, Adolph and Fanny made another field trip, this time to Carabuco on the eastern side of Lake Titicaca, reaching that town on June 1. From there the couple explored parts of the Cordillera Real. At least they were keeping in good physical shape. On June 25, Bandelier recorded in his journal: "Weighed ourselves after breakfast. Fanny weighed 109, —and I 159, english pounds."

On October 6, 1897, Adolph was in a reflective mood: "Forty-nine years to-day! Since I arrived at Highland, and saw Joe for the first time. Little did I dream, then, of what the future would bring, of what Highland was to be for me, for Her! Little did I dream that, 49 years later, I would be in the heart of Bolivia, with Fanny, so very happily at work."

The Bandeliers returned to La Paz on November 7, with Fanny exhausted from the long, hard fieldwork. She was ill with laryngitis and what may have been pneumonia. On November 18, the Bandeliers met a young American painter named Charles T. Wilson, and Adolph commissioned him to paint some landscapes. In the succeeding days, Fanny gradually recovered, and the Bandeliers spent much time in house hunting and buying furniture. Finally, on December 18, they moved into their new quarters.

Adolph F. Bandelier and his second wife, Fanny Ritter Bandelier, in Peru. (Museum of New Mexico, neg. 7051.)

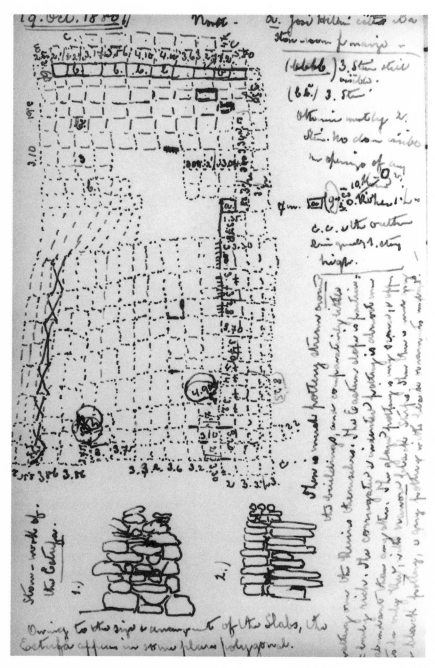

Bandelier Journal, October 19, 1880.

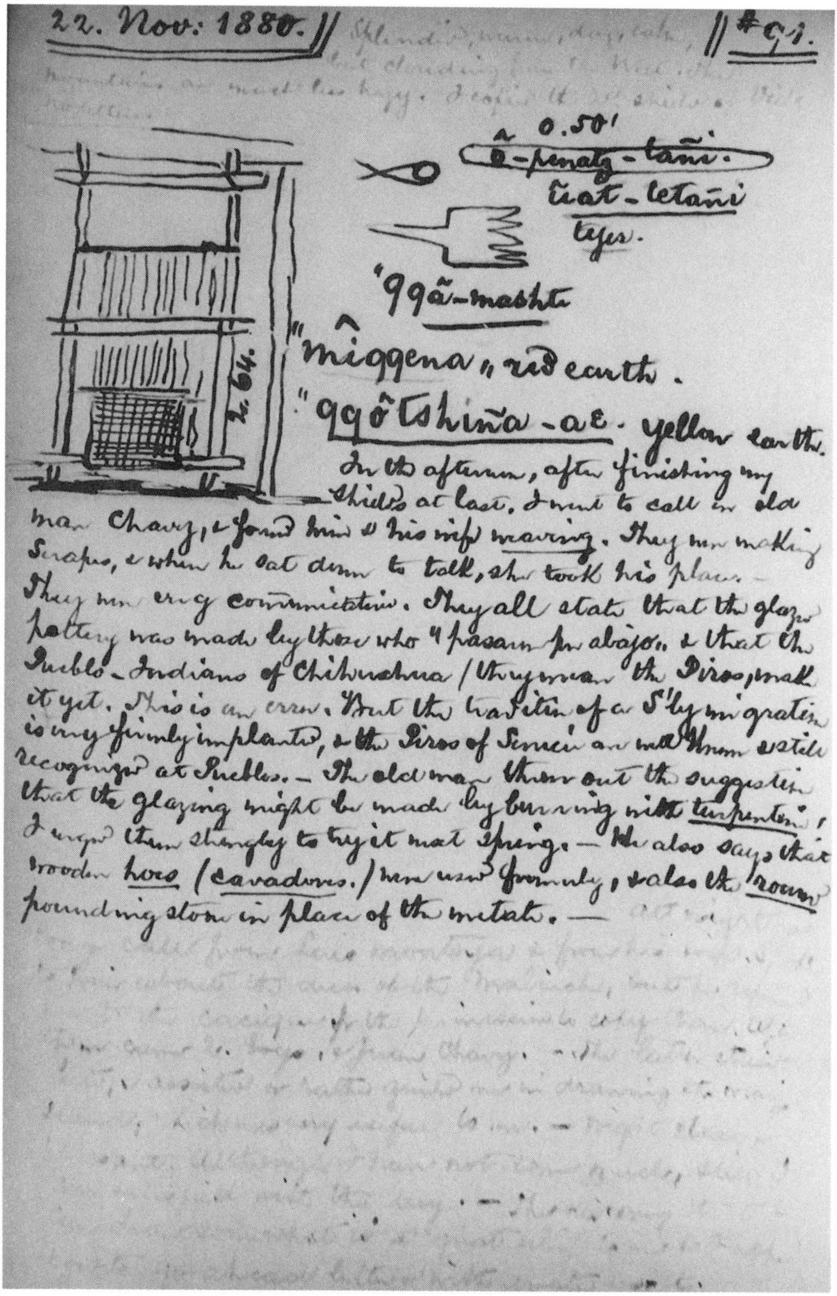
22. Nov: 1880. // #91.

0.50'
ê-penatz-tãni.
tsat-letãni
teyes.

'qqã-mashte

"mîqqena" red earth.

"qqôtshiña-ae. yellow earth.

2. 64.

In the afternoon, after finishing my sketches at last, I went to call on old man Chavez, & found him & his wife weaving. They were making Serapes, & when he sat down to talk, she took his place. — They were very communicative. They all state that the glazed pottery was made by those who "pasaron pa abajo," & that the Pueblo-Indians of Chihuahua (they mean the Piros) make it yet. This is an error. But the tradition of a S'ly migration is very firmly implanted, & the Piros of Senecú are well known & still recognized at Pueblos. — The old man threw out the suggestion that the glazing might be made by burning with turpentine! I urged them strongly to try it next Spring. — He also says that wooden hoes (cavadores.) were used formerly, & also the round pounding stone in place of the metate. —

Bandelier Journal, November 22, 1880.

Adolph F. Bandelier, portrait painted by Gerald Cassidy from a photograph, 1913, in possession of the Museum of New Mexico. (Museum of New Mexico, neg. 7006.)

(top left) Peruvian field group: Adolph (by camera), Fanny (with family dog), and four unidentified crew members. The man standing between Adolph and Fanny may be Charles Lummis. (Museum of New Mexico, neg. 9172.)

(bottom left) Adolph F. Bandelier with the family of his second wife, Fanny Ritter Bandelier (seated in front of Adolph). The identities of the two sisters at the left have not been established. (Museum of New Mexico, neg. 7045.)

Bust of Adolph F. Bandelier by Gutzon Borglum. The work was done in
New York City, 1905–06. (Museum of New Mexico, neg. 107988.)

[We eventually succeeded] with the help of Wilson who directed the decorative part in arranging our principal and most expensive rooms fairly. The parlor is particularly handsome. I bought four Gobelins [tapestries?] of Ansa and these, together with the three paintings by Wilson, make our main parlor a beautiful apartment indeed. The little parlor is crowded with Bolivian and Peruvian curiosities and also presents a pleasing aspect. . . . I perhaps go to too many expenses, but I trust GOD will forgive me—and will allow us to enjoy this splendid home for a little while at least. We have had, in fact, so little real enjoyment since we are married, and Fanny is so good, that I nourish a faint hope He will forgive my action in this instance and give me the means of keeping honorably what we have thus far acquired. And then She—to whom I would gladly have given all that and more, —once away from Highland. —She will watch over us and pray for us for His protection, aid and forbearance.

Wilson, whose artistic abilities had helped to make the home furnishing such a success, eventually married a Bolivian woman whom Adolph, at any rate, considered low class and not acceptable company. He scornfully characterized her as "a little chola of Chililaya, the daughter of a drunken Judge Mallea." Eventually, after his return to the United States in 1900, Wilson lost touch with the Bandeliers entirely. Years later, now a fairly well-known painter living in Eureka, California, Wilson somehow learned the address of the recently widowed Fanny and reentered her life with consequences to be told later.

On the very last day of 1897, Adolph Bandelier reported some good news from Europe. He was still abed when Fanny rushed in with the report that Hedwig Ritter had married a young man named Otto Masshardt. The new brother-in-law, originally from Bern, was secretary of the School of Industrial Arts in Zurich. Writing in his journal that same day, Bandelier praised the deity for his marvelous protection during the past year and added, "May He continue and MAY SHE be with us in the new year as well as in the OLD. Goodby 1897!"

The year 1898 began with a revolutionary flare-up that would lead to a liberal takeover of Bolivia the following year under José Manuel Pando. The Bandeliers remained in La Paz, waiting out the rainy season, which in 1898 lasted until about mid-April. Letters to Winser gave a running account of affairs. On January 14, Bandelier told Winser that Henry Kaune was shipping the Bandelier library to New York for eventual reshipment to Bolivia. In a letter of February 2, Bandelier explained why he had not worked at the great site of Tiahuanaco near La Paz. It was out of deference to the famous German anthropologist Max Uhle, "he having selected the spot as a sort of special field." Bandelier had seen a great deal of Uhle in South America over the previous years. His comments about Uhle were often caustic, and it would seem that the two men did not get along well.

During the early part of 1898, the Bandeliers took the new U.S. minister, Dr. Bridgman, and his family under their wing. The most dramatic event was a gala ball held at the Bandelier residence on Saturday, April 23. The previous Saturday, Adolph had written that the ball, which, "with the help of God and Her," would be given on the twenty-third, kept him from regular work. His next journal entry came exactly one month later and indicated that the ball, with 230 persons present, had been a splendid success. A letter to Winser of the AMNH, written on April 29, gave more details.

> I believe now to be able to say, that we are so established in Bolivia as to be in a position to obtain anything desirable for the Museum. We made a great "hit" by giving a large party at our house, to which the whole official world at La Paz and the cream of society contributed by their presence. As Dr. Bridgman expressed himself familiarly to my wife it was "a howling success," —He was fully aware of the purpose of this social gathering and approved it thoroughly, as the best means to consolidate our position here in the future. —The occurrence was also interpreted by the people here as being offered by us to our new Minister and wife, which is true in part, as we wished them to become well introduced in society.

In his entry of May 23, a long summation of what had happened in the previous month, Bandelier noted that the United States and Spain were at war. On June 6 he remarked, "News of Spanish victory at Santiago de Cuba. Am glad of it."

Adolph and Fanny spent most of the balance of 1898 in the field, a great deal of it along the west and south slopes of Illimani. Bandelier was becoming concerned about the manuscript for *Islands of Titicaca and Koati,* and on November 12 he wrote Winser asking that the AMNH send the remainder of the proof sheets for this publication. The Bandeliers were still in the field during the last days of 1898, and then on December 31 returned to La Paz. Around them swirled civil war.

In spite of the war, the year 1899 was relatively uneventful as far as the Bandeliers were concerned. From the beginning, La Paz had been controlled by the Liberal party, and as the year wore on, this group took over the governance of Bolivia, ostensibly with a junta, or committee, but with actual power in the hands of President Pando. Like most people in La Paz, Adolph and Fanny were Pando supporters, but they began to feel increasingly worried over the widespread Indian unrest. Partly because of his fear and dislike of the Indians, Bandelier at this time thought of moving from Bolivia to Cuzco, once capital of the Inca empire, in the central highlands of Peru. This plan, perhaps because of AMNH reluctance or lack of interest, was never carried through.

It was about this time that AMNH support became somewhat uncertain. Although monies continued to be remitted through W. P. Grace and Company, Bandelier began to feel that the museum's support could come to an end at any time. In 1899 the couple began to sell their furniture, and Bandelier asked Henry Kaune in Santa Fe to negotiate the sale of his library collections to the American Museum of Natural History. Because of the war, postal service was interrupted a number of times in Bolivia, but by the end of the year Adolph knew at least that the AMNH had received a preliminary inventory of his books.

It is not altogether clear what was going on in the Bandeliers' economic life at this time. The stipend from the museum seems often to have been delayed, or not forthcoming at all, and it looks very much as if the couple was feeling the pinch. The year 1898 had seen the crest of Bandelier's fortune in Bolivia; it was a time in which he seemed firmly ensconced in Bolivian society and economically secure. The following year saw the first indications of decline in Bandelier's fortunes, a decline that became more precipitous year by year and then month by month. With that decline came an ever-deepening paranoia. Bandelier's journal entries for the last years in South America make fascinating, if depressing, reading.

During 1899, Bandelier's anti-American and anti-British feelings came out strongly in his comments on the two wars going on at that time, the Spanish-American War and the Boer War. His journals took on an increasingly strident tone. By the end of the year, Adolph was railing at Americans, the English, and Bolivians in general, but especially at the boorish and mean-spirited people of La Paz, who failed to buy his furniture, at Henry Kaune, who failed to write, at the American Museum personnel, and most of all at the villainous Indians, whose hostility disrupted Bandelier's plan for fieldwork.

The year 1900 was gloomy for the Bandeliers. Correspondence with the American Museum of Natural History was minimal (today, only two letters from Bandelier remain in the AMNH archives for that entire year). Adolph worried more and more about his future with the museum. At one point everything seemed settled, for on May 28, 1900, Adolph wrote to the painter Eva Scott Fényes, a friend from Santa Fe days, that the AMNH directors had decided to bring the Bandeliers back to the United States.

This [is] positively my last appearance—on paper from South America. We hope to leave at last, toward the end of June, and for NEW YORK. —The Museum wants us there and we go.

Life here becomes insupportable and Mr. Indian is so completely master of Bolivia, that it is useless to remain. We intended to go to Cuzco and had taken every step toward that end, when the call from the Museum came, which we were very glad to obey.

What happened to those plans is a mystery, but their collapse left Adolph extremely unhappy. It was at about this time that Bandelier began to turn against God, blaming him for personal illnesses, financial problems, and adverse conditions in Bolivia. After several strident journal entries over two or three months, on October 21, 1900, Adolph bluntly accused God of favoritism against the Bandeliers. This was nothing compared to the tirade of October 30. After receiving bad news—a business contact named Moritz, who had made promises to the Bandeliers, failed to show up in La Paz—Bandelier had this to say about the Almighty:

Well —it is in keeping with God's will and we must submit to the meanest, lowest, most despicable doings of others. HE—will not, hence WE—CANNOT. If HE only had charity enough to take us away from the scene of so much misery but HE has not even THAAT [*sic*] charity!! —HE —wants us to suffer, to be the butt of every misery, and HE — who promises to have mercy on all his children, has no mercy upon US. WE —are his objective point for every evil, for every deception, for every suffering imaginable, and the more we pray to him, the more we are grateful to HIM for every seeming token of good, the less HE helps us. It is as if He were a heinous fiend bent upon torturing US. . . . [After a trip to the city center] I went home. Got a new dress for Fanny. Poor thing I may not even keep her fairly dressed! God prevents me from doing it. He makes her suffer, because she is good and because she loves me.

The next day Bandelier found out that the arrangement with Moritz, several months in the planning stage, had completely fallen through. It was a mining venture, details of which are unknown, in which Moritz was the advance man for a Chicago group of financiers. For some months, Adolph had blown hot and cold on this venture, expressing the idea on July 5 that Moritz was God's instrument to lure the Bandeliers into false expectation. Nevertheless, he had pinned all his financial hopes on the project. When, on October 31, it all collapsed, there was another outbreak against God, though for once Bandelier cautiously hedged his bets.

[Moritz] is a swindler and scoundrel and has merely played with us. This is the sequel of our career here. Deceived, abandoned by God as well as by men. —God is enormously cruel for us. He brought us that man and HE is responsible for his actions. He is the author of every evil. Still— perhaps not—He only tried us but He may try us merely for our best. It is very very hard to suffer.

Although God had seemingly turned against the Bandeliers, Adolph still had hope that Joe would help out. As he wrote in his journal a day later (November 1, All Souls Day), "I should think of HER, who is our angel above. She did so much for me, and she left me as a legacy, my Fanny. Poor, dear Josephine. How much have I sinned against Thee! —I Pray Thee to forgive me where Thou art now, in Heaven and to look down upon us mercifully, poor children of the earth."

Bandelier's rather odd attitude toward religion deserves a word here. Both Bandeliers, father and son, appear to have been quite devout. This was surely true also of Josephine, and probably of Fanny. Neither of the Bandelier men was involved in the rationalism that was becoming increasingly fashionable in intellectual circles in America and western Europe. This is a little surprising, for both were well read in several languages and both thought highly of German scholarship, which was in the forefront of much of the late-nineteenth-century biblical "higher criticism." There is no evidence, however, that either man ever questioned the traditional Christian faith.

But Bandelier's approach to the deity (and to his Angel, Joe) was almost eerily personalized. One cannot help thinking that for Adolph, God was a great Papa-like figure in the sky, revered but resented, and readily blamed for any and all problems. Josephine in heaven was like Joe on earth, but less self-effacing and much more powerful. Bandelier seems to have expected the angelic Joe to dress God down, just as in life she had handled a cantankerous Papa.

In 1901 Bandelier continued to receive museum support, but his contacts were now farther and farther apart. In a letter of March 28 to Winser, Adolph mentioned receiving a remittance from Grace and Company. He also wrote several short notes concerned solely with revisions to the *Islands* chapters. The last one, and the last Bandelier letter on file in the AMNH archives, was dated December 8; it complained bitterly of museum inaction on the *Islands* manuscript. The AMNH does not seem to have acknowledged these letters. A letter to Mrs. Fényes, dated December 30, talked of the increasing danger of staying in Bolivia because of the menace of the Indians and the possibility of an Indian revolt.

The year 1902 brought severe financial hardship for the Bandeliers. Adolph investigated several possible money-making schemes without any great success. Health problems plagued him, as he indicated in a short letter to Lummis dated June 23: "A few words only to explain why we have not been able to leave —I have been quite ill, and am still not all right—throat and bronchitis. . . . I am compelled to have my teeth set right before we leave; today only the impression was taken. I have lost all my upper teeth and could not well travel without eating."

By the end of 1902, Adolph and Fanny desperately wanted to leave and go to the United States, but they were uncertain how to finance the trip. At the beginning of 1903 (the first journal entry was February 11), the Bandeliers were in dire financial straits. Adolph was negotiating for some role (exactly what is unclear) in the operation of a copper mine at Corocoro in the sierra near La Paz. While waiting for these plans to reach some fruition, the Bandeliers remained in Bolivia, attempting to sell furniture and pictures to make ends meet. In February they kept the eight-year-old son of an American couple for a few days while his parents were out of the city. This lad, Lincoln Todd, seems to have touched Fanny's strong maternal instincts, and she lavished affection on him— affection that normally would have been extended only to Bandelier and the ubiquitous family dog.

By the later part of April, hopes for the Corocoro mining property were fading. Following the entry of April 29 in Adolph's journal was a typed date for April 30. The journal, however, was not actually resumed until two months later, and all subsequent entries were handwritten. It seems likely that the Bandeliers had sold their typewriter. "I write this on *June 20.*—and in the harbor of Chala on board the Chilean steamer Tucapil, going to Callao.—I shall not refer to the awful time we had to go through at La Paz. No money! But Christ got us out, leaving the town on June 4." It is unclear whether the reference to Christ was a literary convention or whether Bandelier was quietly rebuking God and Josephine for not holding up their end of things.

The Bandeliers reached Lima on June 22 and spent several weeks visiting friends and continuing to make plans for the sale of furniture. The journals do not make clear whether or not this furniture had been brought from La Paz; most likely it was property that had originally belonged to the Ritter family and that had been stored when the Ritters left Lima. On August 10, an old friend named Sevilla, a man whom Adolph had known since 1892, offered to supply Bandelier (presumably as a loan) the sum of one thousand soles. Adolph noted in his journal that day, "With that we can reach N. York. Thank God!"

The couple left at midnight on August 14, on the steamship *Limari* for Panama. On August 25, at Panama City, Bandelier wrote, "Good bye Pacific after eleven years!" That same day, the Bandeliers traveled to Colón on the Caribbean side of Panama, remarking on the scattered evidence of work on the Panama Canal. After reaching their ship, the *Seguranca,* Adolph noted, "On the Atlantic side after 18 years." This seems to be a reference to the trans-Atlantic trip the scholar took in 1885, the year of the Highland bank fiasco.

During the last days of August, the couple sailed across the Caribbean, around Cuba, and up the east coast of the United States. Bandelier's last journal entry for 1903 was made on August 31: "Are meeting steamers and sailing vessels, but not a fish, not a bird. The Atlantic is much more desert[ed] than the Pacific. At night saw many lights along the shore. Got to Sandy Hook about 10 P.M."

A dramatic segment of Bandelier's life was over. When he had sailed for Peru in the summer of 1892, with Joe at his side and Lummis soon to join them, Bandelier had planned only a limited stay in South America. Within a year, however, he had realized that in order to do significant work, he would need to stay much longer. The American Museum of Natural History, which took over Bandelier's contract from Villard beginning April 1, 1894, understood this need and supported Bandelier during the long years in Peru and Bolivia. Though his arrangement with the AMNH broke down sometime after 1900, Bandelier was still under contract, and it was to the AMNH that he returned in the autumn of 1903.

The Bandelier who reentered the United States after an absence of eleven years was a very different man from the optimistic person who, with Josephine, landed at Callao in early July 1892. Adolph was now old and tired; indeed, about this time his handwriting began to show the strong effects of age and debility. His journal entries take on a clamorous tone of hurt and outrage at the world for its mistreatment. Most extraordinary of all are the journal entries (only a few samples of which we have quoted) that hurl charges at God. The deity had deliberately decided to torment this Just Man, Adolph Bandelier, while thieves, time-servers, and liars (that is to say, most of Bandelier's acquaintances in South America and elsewhere) were lifted up and exalted. Fanny, the faithful wife, is punished by God for her loyalty and love. Among the heavenly hosts, only the bright angel, Josephine, cares, and even she may become angry at any sign of carelessness or neglect on the part of Adolph or Fanny.

Bandelier's journals during the last few years in South America reveal a man weary in both body and mind, a man gripped by what later anthropologists might have called *anomie* and what the modern generation would refer to as "burnout." His one great consolation was Fanny, his new wife. Bandelier's journals from 1892 onward are filled with praise for this wonderful woman. That Bandelier still had creative years ahead was surely due in large part to her. Perhaps it was a generous Providence after all that decreed that the final decades of Adolph's life should be spent at the side and with the constant support of the young, capable, and totally loyal Fanny.

SIXTEEN
The Urbanites

The feeling for hope is almost dead within me.

T HE BANDELIERS' SHIP docked in New York harbor at 10:00 A.M. on the first of September, 1903. Adolph wrote, "Entrance into North River quite imposing. Towering buildings and much life on the water. Went to Marlborough hotel, 37th Street and Broadway. . . . In the afternoon, went to the Museum with Fanny. Most lovely reception by [AMNH secretary] Winser and Saville. They seemed overjoyed at seeing us."

Professor Marshall H. Saville was a Mesoamericanist, educated at Harvard and the University of San Marcos in Lima, who had just joined the faculty at Columbia University and was in and out of the American Museum of Natural History. Bandelier was to see a great deal of Saville at the museum in the years ahead.

On September 8, Saville told Bandelier that a salary of $200 a month was being proposed for him. On the ninth, Saville introduced Adolph to the biologist Herman Carey Bumpus, the American Museum's current director. Adolph also had a long talk with Winser about the possibility that the financier J. Pierpont Morgan might provide funds for publishing *The Islands of Titicaca and Koati*. This plan never came to fruition, but— like Villard's earlier support for Bandelier's South American project, and like the later sponsorship of Bandelier by a member of the railroad-magnate Huntington family—it is an interesting indication of the way many wealthy people of the time were involved in scholarly philanthropy.

On September 10, Bandelier went with Fanny to the museum, where they met Mrs. Alice Le Plongeon, wife of the archaeologist whom Bandelier had seen in Yucatán in 1881. Two days later, Bandelier was allowed to check on his library, which had been shipped from Santa Fe. The books and manuscripts had arrived in relatively good condition. Over the next few hot days, the Bandeliers made brief visits to the museum and also to the Lenox Library, where Adolph showed Fanny manuscripts. Parenthetically, although Bandelier in his journals continued to refer to the Lenox and Astor libraries as separate entities, they had in fact been merged into the New York Public Library in 1895. The couple also visited the Metropolitan Museum of Art, where Bandelier remarked that the Old Masters were not very well represented, the most numerous being paintings by Franz Hals.

For several days Bandelier busied himself at arranging his books. Fanny, meanwhile, went with Mrs. Saville to look for suitable housing. On September 15 they found a two-room apartment for $60 per month. The rooms were large, "beautifully lit and with good ventilation." It was a second-floor apartment on West Eighty-second Street, close to Central Park and the museum. At about this time, Bandelier met Franz Boas, the famous German-American anthropologist. Boas was an assistant curator at the American Museum and a professor of anthropology at Columbia University. He was already well established in an illustrious career that would continue for another four decades.

Events continued to move slowly. The museum dragged its feet on Adolph's appointment, and J. P. Morgan declined to help underwrite his book. Bandelier attempted to sell the manuscript to the Lenox collections in the New York Public Library, but the officials there showed no interest. Eventually, in late October, Bandelier and Director Bumpus reached a tentative agreement whereby the Swiss-American scholar would be paid $150 per month. On October 29, Bandelier was invited to a meeting of the American Ethnological Society at the museum. A number of distinguished anthropologists attended: W. H. Holmes, chief of the Bureau of American Ethnology; American Indian experts James O. Dorsey, W. J. McGee, and Alice Fletcher; Frederic Ward Putnam, director of the Peabody Museum at Harvard; and Franz Boas. Bandelier was asked to report on his South American work and was generally well received.

Franz Boas and his wife proved especially hospitable. They entertained the Bandeliers, and Franz took Adolph as a guest to his German Scientific Society. Bandelier enjoyed himself, though he remarked cattily in his journal, "There was, of course 'Made in Germany' and german glorification all around, and in the highest degree."

Because Saville was moving to Columbia University, his office at AMNH was made available to Bandelier. Adolph now purchased a new typewriter, to the heartfelt gratitude of anyone trying to read his deteriorating handwriting.

The last months of the year saw a trip to Washington, D.C., where Bandelier continued to seek help in publishing his Titicaca manuscript, this time from Worthington C. Ford, chief of the Documents Division of the Library of Congress. This trip was authorized by Bumpus and paid for by the AMNH, so it seems that the museum still felt some responsibility for publishing the manuscript. In Washington, the Bandeliers met with Otis T. Mason, head curator of the United States National Museum. The two returned by way of Philadelphia, where they toured the collections of Peruvian artifacts at the University of Pennsylvania.

Back in New York for New Year's Eve, the scholar made his usual Bandelierian comment on the past year:

> This year which began so badly, is finally ending better, and all through the Grace of HIM, Father, SON and Holy Ghost, three in one indivisible and by the intercession of His Holy mother and St. Anthony of Padua. It is good to be a Catholic. I was cut out for one after all. But its not proper to be buoyant. At any time HE may send us sore trials and we may prove wanting after all. Goodby 1903.

It is not clear why Anthony of Padua, a thirteenth-century Franciscan and the patron saint of Portugal, was a factor in getting the Bandeliers through a troubled year. The saint's birthday (August 15) is fairly near Adolph's (August 6), but Anthony's festival, June 13, does not seem to correspond to any important date in Bandelier's career. The most striking omission in this expression of piety and dogma was any mention of Joe. Whatever else, Adolph was certainly correct about the trials ahead.

The early days of January 1904 were spent at the museum working on the exhibit hall. Bandelier made a journal entry on January 12 but did not write again until February 19:

I was discouraged about continuing on account of my hand which is becoming as good as useless. The arm is lame, and the muscles of the wrist do not function any more. Still I try again.

I gave a lecture at Brooklyn on January 28th. At the Museum on February 11th, both with fine exit[?], thank God WHOSE work it has been. Now I am pending a reply from Harper's in regard to an article on the Island. . . . Fanny now has a good seamstress, an old lady—French—Madame BONAME. She is worthy of every confidence it seems and does good work. Tomorrow we are invited to an afternoon tea at the National Art Club.—It is Adelheid Hasse's doings. She has now been to my three lectures here.

Adelheid Hasse, a New York art patron, was to see a great deal of the Bandeliers in the months and years ahead. The next day, at a National Art Club tea, Bandelier met for the first time the sculptor Gutzon Borglum, a man who later would become famous for his creation of the massive heads of American presidents at Mount Rushmore in the Black Hills of South Dakota.

Journal entries for the following days included extended commentaries on the Russo-Japanese war. It is clear from his remarks that Adolph's sympathies lay with the Russians. Of the three major wars during this period, Bandelier cheered for the loser in each one.

On February 29, the Bandeliers went to the museum to listen to a lecture by George H. Pepper, at that time on the AMNH staff, who would later serve with the Heye Foundation Museum of the American Indian. Also speaking was Marian W. Smith, a Columbia University anthropologist who also was on the museum's staff. At this evening affair, the scholar met the famous linguist Waldemar Jochelson, who had just returned from the Jesup North Pacific expedition, which the AMNH had sponsored.

The next day Adolph was back working while "poor dear Fanny colored slides alone at home." On March 11, the Bandeliers went to Washington, where they were met by Frederick Webb Hodge and taken to the Hodge home in Garetts Park. There Bandelier renewed his acquaintance with "Maggie"—Margaret Magill, the sister-in-law of Frank Cushing. The next day the Bandelier couple saw Cushing's wife, Emma, who was "grey, but otherwise looks well." Bandelier gave a lecture at the National Geographical Society's Washington headquarters, and after the lecture the scholar was elected to membership.

The next day Bandelier met again with Emma Cushing and was told of Frank Cushing's last moments. Later the scholar called on the former army surgeon Washington Matthews, a friend from New Mexico days. He found Matthews in poor physical condition but still mentally alert; Matthews would in fact live until 1905.

For the next few months Adolph and Fanny were busy rearranging their apartment and working in the Lenox collections and at the museum. Frank Bigler, a cousin of Will C. Barnes, the army telegrapher whom Bandelier had met at Fort Apache in 1883, visited the couple in April. Bigler, whom Bandelier had also known since 1883, seems to have met Fanny for the first time on this visit—a significant event for Fanny, as Bigler was to be her devoted and loyal friend after Adolph's death.

In May, Bandelier, through Boas's influence, was given a year's appointment at Columbia, and he was named to the executive committee of the newly founded Explorer's Club. Fanny helped the family finances by copying. The couple saw a great deal of Adelheid Hasse and sometimes Borglum.

In mid-September, Bandelier noted that "visitors [at the museum] are falling off considerably, in numbers." It was, Adolph thought, Bumpus's fault, because of "his ever-eagerness to 'educate' the public." A rift was beginning to develop between the Swiss-American scholar and the AMNH director.

Bandelier's great bugaboo, debt, was once again a factor, for Adolph had never managed to live within his income. In flush times he was always overextended, and in lean times he borrowed, begged, or scrounged. Adding to their financial burden, the Bandeliers moved from their rooms on Eighty-second Street because "the place became simply LOW!! —So we obtained very fine apartments at the Evelyn . . . for sixty dollars only, BUT, we had to buy our own furniture. This further reduced our resources, already small enough." Friends loaned money to the Bandeliers, "but, these are temporary reliefs only, and the final help, which must come through a sale of paintings, delays and appears further removed as ever. It is often an almost unbearable situation and yet, I have to bear it and it would be ingratitude to complain so far."

In the same journal entry, Bandelier noted that "Dr. Laufer, a Jew, who has recently come from Middle China by the way of Germany, is here. He is, of course, a German but not unusually offensive." Berthold

Laufer was, of course, the famous expert on China who joined the staff of AMNH in 1904 and who in later years was associated with the Field Museum of Natural History in Chicago. Throughout his life Bandelier was critical of Germans, perhaps the result of his Swiss upbringing. Even now, the Swiss occasionally look humorously askance at their big neighbor to the north. A distinguished architect friend of one of us (Riley) once remarked that during World War II a Jewish refugee from Hitler's Germany had stayed at the family home in Bern. "He was a really nice fellow till the war ended, and then he turned back into a German."

The paintings mentioned by Bandelier seem to have been ones salvaged from the Bolivian stay, or perhaps ones stored in Lima and then shipped back to the United States. Bandelier believed that one of these works was an original by Francisco de Zurbarán, a seventeenth-century Spanish painter of religious subjects. According to records of the period, a number of Zurbarán's paintings were in fact shipped to Lima, Peru, in the 1640s.

Bandelier's loyalties and sympathies were now clearly shifting. Bumpus, once well regarded, was now "an ass, afterall." Saville, who had helped Bandelier with loans and support at the museum just weeks before, was also "making an ass of himself." Adolph continued to meet anthropologists who would become world famous but who were at the beginnings of their careers: the Mayanist Alfred M. Tozzer and the Plains Indian specialist Clark Wissler.

On December 7, 1904, Bandelier was happily surprised when former New Mexico territorial governor L. Bradford Prince and his wife, also from Santa Fe, dropped in to meet Fanny. Later in the month, Lummis visited. Things seemed to be looking up financially, and Bandelier's New Year's Eve comments were relatively upbeat.

The new year, 1905, saw the fall of Port Arthur in China to the Japanese, which led to a rueful comment in Bandelier's journal that again reflects the scholar's strange and idiosyncratic version of Christianity: "What's the use of being a Christian, if God is so manifestly with the heathen and unbelievers." On the fifth of January, Adolph "had a long talk with Boas about the future. He says my position at the Museum will become untenable. I know it, but if God helps, I will find something besides yet." His lectures at Columbia continued, though they never seemed to draw more than a handful of students, mostly colleagues from the New York area.

Late in January, the famous Berlin anthropologist Eduard Seler and his wife visited the American Museum of Natural History. Bandelier had met the Selers some years before in Bernalillo, New Mexico. He now commented:

> He is a good, narrow-minded, German school-master, afflicted with academic and other titles.—At night we were invited at Boas'. Selers were there, Savilles and Smith.—Also Laufer.—It was a very indifferent meeting. Seler's wife is a damned overbearing, pretentious, ill-bred and conceited German wench—impertinent & rude to Fanny. I shall not forget her—in time.

Over the next few weeks, Bandelier continued lecturing at Columbia. But his AMNH position was in considerable jeopardy. On February 27, Adolph wrote that "Bumpus told me—at least, that after the first of April, I would be reduced to 300. or 400. Dollars a year.—Allright.—It is my usual reward. God arranges it thus, and I bow to it, though not without exceedingly bitter feelings! I am doomed to constant misery upon this earth.—If Huntington does not step in, then—what."

The Huntington under question was Archer M. Huntington, adopted son of the industrialist Collis P. Huntington and cousin of Henry E. Huntington of Huntington Library fame. Archer Huntington was a specialist in Spanish archaeology and in 1904 founded the Hispanic Society of America. In November of the previous year, Bandelier had had a conversation with Huntington, who seemed supportive of the scholar's attempts to remain at the American Museum. Huntington now, in late February, was on an extended trip to Europe. On March 2, Bandelier received a letter from Bumpus offering him $25 per month. After a long talk with Boas, he "concluded to accept for the present.—Shall wait and see how it works."

His journal entry of March 8 was largely taken up with Bandelier's resentment toward God: "Mama's wedding-day!—How much did God make her suffer afterwards! —And she was *so* good! Just like Fanny—for them *He* has no compassion, not a shadow of regards for her sufferings and goodness. *He*—is not our protector, neither is *He*—our true friend. *We* are too *lowly* from Him." As he had during the South American years, Bandelier subjected the deity to opprobrious comments every time he had a bad day. Curiously, Adolph's personal saint, Josephine, pretty much dropped out of the picture during the New York years. No longer was she called on to intercede with God. Many saints in Latin American folk culture have strictly limited territory, sometimes no more than a village and its environs. If Bandelier believed saints were basically territorial, he may well have felt that New York was outside Joe's field of operation.

Money problems were mounting rapidly. On the twenty-first of March, Adolph remarked that Eva Fényes wanted money that she had advanced him at some previous time. "She is right, but it is not my fault if she has had to wait so long. In the meantime it is very serious. . . . It is no use to bur[den] this Diary with our sad condition." Bandelier received a paycheck from the museum on March 29 and wondered how much longer this would last. "Complaints at the Museum becoming worse and worse. At night we went to Barnum & Bailey's Circus, the first one Fanny ever saw. It was very beautiful indeed."

Bandelier's unhappiness with his lot at the museum—as well as the betrayal and failure of God—occupied much of his thoughts (or at least his journal entries) throughout April and May. A letter from Huntington (contents not noted) cheered him up for a few days, and he continued working on manuscripts, visiting the Lenox and the Astor collections to examine documents, catching up with correspondence, lecturing at Columbia, walking with Fanny in Central Park, and making social exchanges with friends such as Adelheid Hasse. He gave his last lecture of the 1905 spring term at Columbia on the twenty-second of May. Two days later, Boas, who was having his own troubles with Director Bumpus, resigned from the American Museum of Natural History.

Bandelier's attention had for some time been shifting to the newly founded Hispanic Society of America. Not only was Huntington a power there, but Morris K. Jessup, who had earlier sponsored Adolph at AMNH, was also on the society's organizing committee. In addition, Huntington was showing increasing interest in the Titicaca manuscript. These hopeful signs were interrupted by news that the Russian fleet had been destroyed in the Russo-Japanese War. As usual, Bandelier gave a bizarre personal twist to this latest sinister act of the deity: "God, of course, protects the Japanese and tramples down his own people.! It is just like Him!—He must torture the good, martyrize the innocent, & trip the poor and helpless, but aid the unjustly rich, the scoundrels, hypocrites, and criminals. That is His policy to win souls.—It is simply a shame.—I trust to nothing [any] more."

Boas was still trying to extend Bandelier's tenure at Columbia. In late June, however, the Swiss-American scholar received a letter from Boas saying that the president of Columbia, Nicholas Murray Butler, had left town without acting on the matter.

I feared it. Well, it is only in harmony with the rest.—I do not even attempt to complain, as it is useless. His work is in all that. He does not want me to live honorably.—HE is an infernal fiend. . . . God's love-parrot, Bumpus, is back again, plastered over with academic degrees. There is nothing like being on the good side of the Almighty without believing in Him. His selections are sometimes very queer! Thus he favors the Percy wench but cruelly persecutes my poor, dear, little Fanny—only because Fanny is *my* wife.

Exactly who "the Percy wench" was remains unclear, unless Bandelier meant the poet Florence Percy. In any case, Adolph's pique with the way supernatural affairs were being run quickly subsided. On June 24 he went to see Huntington at his home in Baychester, and the two men had a long talk that turned to the subject of an appointment for Bandelier at the Hispanic Society: "Then, with great generosity, he promised to begin my salary on June 1st which is an enormous help. Thank God for it so far. We discussed plans for work. Returned home to Fanny to bring her the apparently good news. Night very fine.—The feeling for hope is almost dead within me. I accept favorable outlooks most gratefully, but without any enthusiasm."

The Bandeliers' financial affairs began to look considerably brighter. At the end of June, Adolph received a check for $100 from Huntington, and checks from Columbia and the museum. The first day of July saw a check from the Geographical Society, perhaps in payment for a lecture. At any rate, the Bandeliers were happy again.

It is not entirely clear why Adolph, after a good start, had such problems with the American Museum of Natural History. It is possible that in spite of his extraordinary amount of fieldwork and number of publications, his lack of academic degrees made him ineligible for any of the regular curatorships. It did probably bar the scholar from a permanent academic appointment at Columbia. On balance, it would seem that personalities entered into the situation at AMNH. Bandelier and Bumpus obviously did not get on well, and part of the fault may well be laid on the director, who seems also to have quarreled with Boas and Saville. Earlier we suggested that Bandelier got rid of aggressions and resentments by pouring them into his private journals. If his good friends Lummis, Hodge, and others had ever *heard* some of the things he wrote about them, they surely would not have remained faithful friends over the years. Perhaps in the case of Bumpus, Adolph allowed himself to speak out. Nevertheless, Bandelier remained on the museum's payroll until the early months of 1906.

On June 30, the Bandeliers went to see the new Hispanic Society building, under construction in uptown Manhattan. Bandelier was well pleased at the sight. "It is up as far as the roof, not large, but chaste and plain. The situation is very handsome with romantic view on the Hudson." The scholar continued to work, correcting and editing the Titicaca manuscript, almost certainly with considerable help from Fanny. He continued to be paid by Huntington, even though he does not seem to have done any particular work at the Hispanic Society itself. A part-time job at Columbia was still a possibility, although a note from Boas stated that he could do nothing on Bandelier's behalf until September.

The Bandeliers spent their days working and their evenings in Central Park, where they "sat on the self-same bench looking at the coaches and automobile riders." One of the projects Fanny had been doing on her own was a translation of *The Journey of Alvar Núñez Cabeza de Vaca,* from Cabeza de Vaca's account of his travels across the southern United States and northern Mexico from 1528 to 1536. Adolph had edited the translation and added annotations. The book, published by Barnes and Company of New York, came out during the summer of 1905. On August 5, the *New York Times* announced that Frederick S. Dellenbaugh, a popular writer of books on the West, would review Fanny's book. This infuriated Bandelier, who held Dellenbaugh in contempt. But his anger in this case was misplaced; Dellenbaugh's review was highly complimentary.

In spite of the promise of work at the Hispanic Society and at least sporadic payment from Huntington, Bandelier continued on a part-time basis at AMNH. His actual move to the Hispanic Society was likely contingent on completion of the new building. As of September 10, when the couple visited it again, the structure was "now roofed and looks very well." Bandelier, who became easily despondent, was upset over Henry Kaune's failure to write, over Bumpus's villainies, and over the lack of interest in his newly revised and edited Titicaca book. Adolph was lecturing again, but this time at the museum itself. "My lectures began on October 6th but God caused the pay to be withheld until November 4th. I had only one listener." At the end of the year, Bandelier had only this comment: "End of 1905. A most sickening year again."

It was on January 7 that Bandelier made the first 1906 entry in his journal, and it was not a happy one:

Bumpus is acting in the most infamous and the most highhanded man-ner, protected by Him above, of course.—Yesterday something tran-spired in regard to Boas, but, I do not yet know the outcome.—In the meantime Winser has fallen very sick, with pneumonia, and while in that condition, his wife died! —He is now at the Hospital, has been informed of his wife's death, and his condition is critical. Should he die [which in-deed happened a few days later] it would be another instance of God helping Bumpus.

On January 9, Bandelier made a cryptic note in his journal: "Went down to Borglum.—Sat an hour and a half about." This is the first indi-cation in the journal that Gutzon Borglum was creating a bust of Bandelier, although we know from a much later comment by Fanny Bandelier that late 1905 was the time when sittings began. The Borglum plaster bust was eventually given to the Museum of New Mexico, and thanks in large part to publicity given to the piece by the Albuquerque artist Marie Louise Martignoni, a number of bronze copies were made by the museum in the early 1990s.

Things were about to look up for the Bandeliers. On January 21, Adolph finally made contact with Huntington, who apparently had been out of town again. "He received me in the most charming manner possible. He wants us to leave the Museum and come to live up on 155th Street near the Hispanic Society. What a Godsend and surprise all this is. Went home, almost in a trance, and told my dearest little one everything. So we spent a quiet and deeply pleasant evening!"

On the twenty-third, the Bandeliers went down to Borglum's in the forenoon. "Spent a very pleasant time. Bust progressing very well." On February 10, the scholar happily noted, "A genuine miracle occurred! My journals complete, came from Santa Fé! Thank God a thousand times for it." In mid-February, final arrangements were made for Bandelier to move to the Hispanic Society.

I am to leave the Museum next week. The Zurbarán went to Huntington, who admires it and believes in its genuineness. The books are to be deposited with the Hispanic Society until the debt is extinguished, the plans are to go there also on deposit! The Museum is open to me for the use of the collections and for lectures. Thank God a thousand times. It looks as if we are safe now—at last. I communicated the news at once—to Fanny and at the Museum. Oh! how good it feels to be on my level again, at last. Thank God a thousand times and our Patron Saint. [Anthony of Padua? Or could this have been a belated mention of Joe?]

Bandelier did not explain to whom he owed the debts, but the Bandelier library was perhaps being offered as surety. The alleged Zurbarán was probably the one collected by the Bandeliers in Bolivia or, more likely, Peru. It dropped out of sight as far as Bandelier's documents are concerned, and its whereabouts today are unknown. In all probability, the painting was not genuine.

On February 17, amid other errands, Bandelier went to the Hispanic Society and arranged to move his books there. He then spent some time looking for a new apartment near the society's offices. On the twenty-fourth, Bandelier took formal leave of the American Museum of Natural History, though he still had several loose ends to finish up there. The following weeks were spent partly at the museum and partly at the Hispanic Society, where all was in chaos but "all are very nice."

On May 2, Bandelier was elected to membership in the Catholic Historical Society, which pleased him a great deal. Two days later the scholar gave his last lecture at AMNH. In June, there was a surprise meeting with Eva Fényes, who was visiting from Santa Fe. "Charmingly received. She looks better than when I saw her last, eighteen years ago. She is very happy in her second marriage. Leonor is married in New York and has two children. We arranged with Mrs. Fényes to visit the Hispanic Society to-morrow, if she has time." The debt Adolph had owed to Mrs. Fényes seems to have been paid; at least there is no further mention of it. As a note of historical interest, her daughter, Leonora Curtin, who died in 1972, was an artist and author, her writings appearing under the name L. S. M. Curtin. A few days after the Fényes visit, Bandelier had his last sitting with Borglum.

In mid-July, Lummis came to New York and managed several visits with the Bandeliers. A cousin of Fanny's, one Arthur Ritter, also showed up about this time. Adolph was very impressed with Ritter, who spoke French, German, and English. The young man had spent three years in South Africa, a year in Australia, and now had married someone from Rochester, New York. The Ritters, with their child, were living in Hoboken and "looking for a situation" in New York, which they eventually found. Ritter and his wife turned up several times in the next few months and became something of a nuisance. They eventually moved to Kentucky and dropped out of the Bandeliers' orbit.

A variety of ailments, including sciatica and sleeplessness—caused partly by the brutally hot weather—continued to plague Bandelier. A few days into August, Fanny became ill, too:

> She awoke, about one o'clock with a fearful pain in her right side. Until noon, no abatement of the sufferings. Poor, dear child. I am anxiously awaiting the Doctor. God is very hard on us. Now He plagues us with sickness and thus takes away from us what little I can earn. HIS favorites, HE of course spares and thrusts enjoyment and all sorts of blessings upon them. Poor Fanny is suffering terribly, and the Doctor is out. By a fortunate circumstance the Doctor came earlier than expected and examined her thoroughly. It is "Gravel," [a calcium deposit in the kidneys and bladder] and can be stopped at present. She lost the pain soon and fell asleep and continued sleeping. So this ugly day passed also. The heat was intense, in the night even. It is my sixty si[x]th birthday, but I am so hardened that I do not think of such dates anymore.

The next days brought little relief in either health or weather. On top of it all, the Bandeliers were house-hunting again. On September 19, they rented an apartment at the "Royal Court," 432 West 160th Street. The fall dragged on with sporadic work at the Hispanic Society and writing of articles for *Catholic Cyclopedia*. Adolph's sciatica flared up, and he was bedridden for a time. Then Fanny's gravel returned. In the midst of all this, the Bandeliers entertained a number of visitors, including the famous British anthropologist Alfred C. Haddon, of Cambridge University. Finally, in late December, seeking a temporary change of scenery, the couple, helped by a monetary gift from Huntington, moved to nearby Salisbury, Connecticut. There, Adolph and Fanny took rooms with a Mrs. Bogert.

The year 1907 opened with the Bandeliers still at Salisbury. The weather, so hot the preceding summer, was now blustery and cold, and the situation at Mrs. Bogert's inn suddenly deteriorated. "The guests have been increased and a dance was given this evening, most to the annoyance of Mrs. Bogert and ourselves. A certain family, Greenwood, of New York, simply invited about thirty people, without asking Mrs. Bogert's permission at all. It was most annoying and Fanny as well as I spent a miserable night."

Aches, pains, and sleepless nights typified the first part of January. As the days passed, Bandelier complained about the food and about Mrs. Bogert's inability to properly manage her hostelry business. The weather continued bad, with severe snowstorms. Finally, the Bandeliers left on January 16, somewhat improved in health and happy to return home.

Despite continuing pains and sleepless nights, Bandelier slowly began to resume his routine. On January 26, he noted that his benefactor "Archer Huntington has been made President of the American Geographical Soc'y. . . . This is excellent, for the Society at least." At the end of March, Bandelier noted that he had received copies of his article "for the Memorial book of Boas." This was a festschrift, or commemorative volume, presented to Boas by his students and colleagues in honor of the twenty-fifth anniversary of the awarding of his doctorate in 1881. Bandelier's article for the book was a paper entitled "La danse des 'Sicuri,' des Indiens Aymará de la Bolivie" (The "Sicuri" dance of the Aymará Indians of Bolivia). Poor Adolph could not resist the wistful comment, "Another contribution to somebody else's glory!"

Meanwhile, Mrs. L. Bradford Prince called several times. She had been asked by authorities in New Mexico to feel Bandelier out on the possibility of his taking a position with the Museum of New Mexico. Bandelier commented, "I satisfied her that I could not accept the position at Santa Fe, but would go out there for two or 3 months in summer to start the matter, provided our fare was paid. He [Governor Prince] will come up in the course of the week to talk it over." As with so many of Bandelier's plans, nothing came of this, and Bandelier never returned to New Mexico. Another honor, however, came on April 12, when Adolph received word from the Minnesota Historical Society that it was naming him a "corresponding member."

On the domestic side, Adolph and Fanny were having considerable trouble keeping household help. They had tried several young women, mostly African Americans, who either left after a short time or were dismissed. It may be that Bandelier's racial attitudes, common to all but the most sophisticated people of his day and expressed forcefully in his writings, showed a little too clearly in conversation. In late April, Adolph and Fanny hired still another cleaning woman, this one named Francisca, on whom they pinned great hopes.

With the advent of May, the Bandeliers had Huntington to lunch, with an extended conversation afterward. Adolph was very pleased to hear from Huntington that he would soon begin publication of *The Islands of Titicaca and Koati*. A few days later, Bandelier also received notice of his being appointed for another year at Columbia. All this time, both Bandeliers continued to be afflicted with assorted illnesses. On May 16, however, the printing of the Titicaca book was begun, and that was a considerable boost for morale.

Despite his ailments, Bandelier was busily scurrying about meeting with people, mainly at the Hispanic Society but also at the Explorers Club. Meanwhile, the latest maid, like her predecessors, proved erratic in coming to work and was consequently dismissed. Not too surprisingly, this was attributed to the fact that the Bandeliers were not among God's favorites.

The Bandelier couple had probably been planning a trip to Europe for some time, but the plan was first mentioned in Adolph's journal almost casually on June 30, 1907. "Now I close this part of my Journal, hoping to continue on board of our steamer, the "Moltke," Tuesday next, if possible." Reading between the lines, it is apparent that a series of sessions and visits with Huntington in the first months of 1907, although they focused on the Titicaca publication, had also concerned this European trip.

It was perhaps billed as a business trip for the purpose of collecting materials for the Hispanic Society and furthering Bandelier's researches for that organization. Nevertheless, the trip was to Switzerland, not the most likely place to search out Hispanic documents, but a place where both Adolph and Fanny had deep roots. Huntington seems to have been genuinely fond of the Bandeliers, and money for the trip may have been intended mainly as a gift.

Bandelier actually resumed his journal on July 1, 1907, while he and Fanny were still in New York awaiting the departure of their ship. The time passed slowly, with last-minute errands to the Hispanic Society and elsewhere. Fanny had completed packing—"suffering, and I too with pain." Finally, on Tuesday, July 3, the *Moltke* left the dock at 3:30 P.M.

On this sea voyage, Adolph made detailed notes on the geography of the Azores and other islands they passed. Then the seas became rougher, and the Bandeliers, especially Fanny, joined many of the other passengers in being sick. On July 14, the lighthouses of Spain came into view, and Adolph noted, "First sight of Europe, after twenty-two years." Actually, this was true for both Bandeliers, Fanny having left Europe as a teenager in 1885, the same year Adolph was in Switzerland trying to save the Highland bank.

The passengers disembarked for a short walk at Gibraltar, and then the *Moltke* entered the Mediterranean Sea. On the seventeenth of July, the ship dropped anchor in the harbor at Naples. That evening, they were on their way again, the sea as smooth as glass. On the nineteenth of July, the *Moltke* reached Genoa at 1:00 P.M. The harbor and city impressed Adolph much more favorably than had Naples.

The next morning, the twentieth, the Bandeliers left by train and passed through the Gotthard tunnel going into the Reuss valley of southern Switzerland. Emerging from the tunnel, Bandelier "found the gorge most imposing, far more so than any part of the Andes I have seen. The whole landscape is enchanting, magnificent beyond description." By 3:30 P.M., the travelers had reached Zurich, where they were met by the Ritter family.

Mama Ritter had taken a room for the Bandeliers, and they were to have meals with her. During this Swiss stay, the Bandeliers saw Hedwig again and met her husband, Otto Masshardt, for the first time. During most of August, Adolph worked in the library at Zurich, examining books and manuscripts from the early sixteenth century. Alphonse Bandelier came to visit, and late in the month the American couple traveled to Bern to see Alphonse and to show Fanny her husband's birthplace and the school he had attended as a boy.

Upon his return to Zurich, Bandelier was busy gathering materials and preparing slides for a lecture, with Fanny's assistance. The lecture was held at the schoolhouse of the Industrial Department and was quite a success. A later Zurich lecture (for the photographic society, of all organizations) failed because of a breakdown in photographic equipment.

By the beginning of September, Adolph's chronic health problems had lessened considerably, except that he began to have eye troubles, and new eyeglasses gave only minor relief. But there was a more pressing problem: the Bandeliers were again without money. Possibly they expected to finance their European trip partly with money from lectures and overestimated the amount they could make this way. If past behavior was any guide, however, Bandelier had simply overspent his limited budget. At any rate, he turned again to Huntington, writing him a plea for more money. While waiting, the couple made another trip to Bern, where Alphonse had a surprise in store. He took Adolph to meet Lisi (Lisl?), the nursemaid who had cared for him during his boyhood in Switzerland.

By the end of September, Bandelier had exhausted the resources of the Zurich library. No word had been received from Huntington, and the scholar was despondent. "Huntington ought, at least, to *refuse!* I cannot do anything, have no money left, and get no news, no relief, from no quarter. My eyes weaken almost daily."

A few days later, the emotional skies brightened: "This morning I got a letter from Gates [Huntington's agent] and remittance. Thank God, our Saint, and Huntington. Now we can leave. The Federal Bank also has a cable for money. We are overjoyed. I at once ordered passages from Genoa. Weather ugly but I do not mind it now."

Adolph was able to book passage on the SS *Hamburg* for October 16. On the fourteenth, Fanny's whole family and others came to the Zurich train station to see the Bandeliers off. The couple did some sightseeing in Genoa and then sailed for home.

With a brief entry on October 23, 1907, en route to the United States, Bandelier's journal ended. He had developed cataracts, a very serious eye problem in those days of primitive ophthalmology. There is relatively little evidence from which to reconstruct the Bandeliers' activities during the next few years. They did return to their apartment on 160th Street, but in the early months of 1909 the couple moved to a small house at 521 West 158th Street, still in the vicinity of the Hispanic Society.

Eventually Adolph had a successful operation for the cataracts. According to the rather scanty records, it was performed during the summer (probably late July or early August) of 1908. Only the left eye was operated on; according to Bandelier, the physicians expected the right eye gradually to clear. Given his age and general disabilities, Bandelier made an understandably slow recovery. As late as 1910, he still could not see well enough to read. Fanny, meanwhile, worked as secretary, taking dictation, editing, and proofreading.

Unsurprisingly, Bandelier's literary output was fairly small during his years of failing eyesight and recuperation. It is true that two major works, *The Islands of Titicaca and Koati* and *Documentary History of the Rio Grande Pueblos,* appeared in 1910. *Islands* was already in press in 1907, but *Documentary History* was a different story.

In December 1908, the Archaeological Institute of America gave Bandelier a two-year grant—$1,200—to complete *Documentary History*. The work was organized through the School of American Archaeology (now the School of American Research), the Santa Fe, New Mexico, branch of the AIA. By the summer of 1909, Adolph felt well enough to write the introduction for the volume, dictating to Fanny. At some point, permission was extended to Bandelier to use the historical documents he had collected for the Hemenway expedition two decades before. Edgar Lee Hewett, director of the School of American Archaeology, had requested that Bandelier keep the introduction to fewer than five thousand words. Predictably, he did not, as he confessed in a letter to Hewett on November 2, 1909: "There is not much left to be done on the bibliographic introduction. It has now reached about 10,000 words and what I have to add are: a short sketch on what was written on New Mexico previous to the american occupation and a glance at the distribution of Pueblo stocks in the sixteenth century."

The manuscript was mailed on November 30. While writing it, Adolph actually had the title of documentary historian, School of American Archaeology, but he resigned that position in November 1911 to take up an appointment with the Carnegie Institute, as we shall soon see. Another project that engaged the Bandeliers' attention was a plan to republish *The Delight Makers*. In 1909, Dodd, Mead and Company had given Bandelier copyright to the book and made him a present of the plates. According to Bandelier in an August 1909 letter to Hewett, influential friends (unnamed) were

busy arranging for an active and competent publisher. The new book will be profusely illustrated with landscapes from the Rito etc. etc., and with scenes of Pueblo life. In fact it will be an advertisement for the Institute and for the country. I now ask you, would the Atchison, Topeka and Santa Fe railroad and the Denver and Rio Grande perhaps take a substantial number of copies and how could I set this matter a going. Do you think Catron could or would do something toward interesting these railroad lines and would you advise me to appeal to Governor Prince also.

Nothing came of this project, although the book was reissued by Fanny some years after Adolph's death.

Four years after the last journal entry of October 1907, Bandelier—his eyesight now somewhat restored—took up the journals once more. On October 1, 1911, he wrote, "I will, after four years!—try to begin again, by entering such notes which I make for my own work." Unfortunately, this attempt was short lived. On October 2, 3, and 4, Bandelier made scattered notes on documents at the New York Public Library and at the Hispanic Society, but nothing more. Though a rejuvenated Bandelier, now with the Carnegie Institution of Washington, was to do more foreign research in Mexico and Spain, his long-time habit of keeping daily journals was abandoned.

SEVENTEEN
Journey's End

My life was simply all his and if I live now, it is only to do
his work.

BY THE END of 1911, Bandelier had sufficiently recovered from
his eye problems to be able to travel again. In October 1911, the trustees
of the Carnegie Institution of Washington made a grant to Bandelier en-
abling him to go to Mexico to copy documents from the Archivo
General. This was the main Mexican collection of documents on the
viceroyalties of New Spain (modern Mexico and much of Central
America). Under Carnegie auspices, Adolph and Fanny left for Mexico
City, arriving on Christmas Eve. They moved into the Hotel Jardín and
immediately began work on the archives.

Bandelier was pleased with certain conditions in Mexico. The national archives had been reorganized, and he thought Mexico city had
been transformed since his earlier visits in 1881, 1886–87, and 1890. It is
less clear whether he welcomed the social and political changes going on
around him.

The year 1912 saw the country in the early phases of its great revolution. The dictator Porfirio Díaz, whom Adolph had found rather con-
genial on his earlier visits, had been ousted in the Madero revolution of
1911, and the upper-class idealist and reformer Francisco I. Madero was
in power, with a government that promised democracy and social
progress.

It is not entirely clear just how long the Bandeliers stayed in Mexico.
In a letter dated January 10, 1912, Adolph expressed the desire to remain

a year. This goal was realized, and the couple returned to the United States in the spring of 1913. It was a bad year physically for Bandelier. In a letter to Eva Fényes written in 1914, Fanny Bandelier remarked that the Mexican sojourn had exhausted her husband and that he was very ill in New York after their return. The trip had been fairly successful: some five hundred pages representing seventy-two transcriptions had been made. Of these, however, about half were from printed books and may have been partly for Bandelier's own use.

Another trip, more important than the Mexican one, was in the offing. This time the Bandeliers would make the long-awaited trip to Spain. For many years Bandelier had dreamed of doing research in that country. Spain was the repository of much of the documentary data on Spanish America, and most of this vast treasure of documents was contained in the Archives of the Indies in Seville. In the early centuries of Spain's overseas empire, the Council of the Indies, a body that directed American affairs under the authority of the Spanish crown, had its headquarters in Seville and accordingly built up its archives there. Thanks to the bureaucratic nature of Spanish rule, documents were usually duplicated or triplicated, with one copy going to the Seville archives. Even today this great archive has been only incompletely examined.

It was to Seville, of course, that the Bandeliers would go first, and this city was to be their headquarters for the Spanish research. Adolph and Fanny planned to visit other important archival sources later, including those of the capital, Madrid. The Carnegie Institution sponsored this new endeavor, extending its original grant to include work in Spain.

The Bandeliers, according to Fanny's 1914 letter to Mrs. Fényes, had sold all their belongings in preparation for this trip, except for their books and a few curios from previous trips. For a "whole house full of good furniture," the Bandeliers received only $225. Seriously short of ready cash, the couple booked passage on the Italian Lines steamer *Emperor Barbarossa*, which regularly sailed the New York to Naples route via Gibraltar. All evidence indicates that the Bandeliers left New York on the late morning of October 18, 1913. For example, a letter dated October 3, 1913, from Adolph to Frank Bigler, stated that the Bandeliers planned to "Sail 18th for Gibr."

As it happens, we know quite a bit about this voyage because of two long letters written by Fanny, the first shortly after the Bandeliers' arrival in Seville, and the second, eight months later to the day.

On November 20, 1913, Fanny wrote to her dear friend Perlina (Ina) Cassidy in New York. The two couples, Adolph and Fanny and Gerald and Ina Cassidy, had become close and had seen a great deal of each other during the spring and summer of 1913. Indeed, it was during this time that Gerald Cassidy, a well-known artist who was interested in early Spanish exploration, took a photograph from which he later painted the last known likeness of Adolph Bandelier. This oil portrait is now owned by the Museum of New Mexico and is exhibited at the Palace of the Governors in Santa Fe.

The letter to Ina Cassidy shows Fanny at her whimsical best. Adolph had promised to write, but because she saw "no preparations on his part to do the stunt, I think I had better do it, even at the risk of disappointing you dear people." According to Fanny, "*poor me*" could not pretend to write such brilliant letters as could her husband. She would "simply chat with you about all the things we have seen until now and all that has happened since we saw you last."

Fanny went on to describe the voyage. The Bandeliers unpacked, and Fanny decided to take one of the packets of seasickness and indigestion powders that Mrs. Cassidy had given her for the trip, but only because "they were bound so enticingly in my favorite color! We had not yet suffered from seasickness, much less from indigestion."

At dinner the first night, "as is our habit we did not go to the steward to reserve seats, but this scramble for a preferred place is so hateful that we do not like it and would rather sit in the last little corner." From the mock humility of Fanny's tone, one expects a fairy-tale ending, and sure enough, they were seated at the captain's table because of friends from New York "who sent so many messages that the leadingman of the diningroom concern, thought we were really somebody!"

Then followed a story that obviously delighted Fanny and showed both Fanny and Adolph in a flattering light.

To the captain's left sat yours truly, alongside my Lord and Master (pray don't let him hear that, he might get stuck up) and next to him an American gentleman, with whom the funniest thing on earth happened. . . . We had been talking about travelling in general and he became interested and asked whether any of us knew something about the Southwest. Now, when it comes to talk with strangers, my dear old man shuts up like a clam and so I said he had been there many years. Then Mr. Hicks begged him to say if he knew Governor Prince . . . who had told him at one of the Pueblos there when they had been together, that he ought to get hold of a man by the name of Bandelier or at least read his books on those things. "Now," says Mr. Hicks, "do you perhaps know Mr. B? Or where can I see him?" Well, the answer was given very quietly, Dolph said: "I think, Mr. Hicks, you are as close to that man as the seats allow,." I thought Mr. H. Was going to have a fit and held a glass of water in readiness. He jumped up from his seat and declared this the nicest trip he had ever made and so on and so on. And from that moment on the two were always together and we love and loved Mr. Hicks very much, he is a fine, gentlemanly kind of man with a big heart.

Frederick Cocks Hicks, a lawyer and important Republican politician, was on a trip around the world. Unfortunately, this shipboard friendship did not carry over afterward. Fanny could have used an influential friend in the years following Adolph's death, but there is no indication that she ever saw Hicks again.

With Fanny and Adolph was the current family pet, a dog named Dodo. According to Fanny, he was "a dark brown hunting dog which was given me in Mexico where they poisoned my handsome white (Pekinese) darling you have seen. Dodo is good and very intelligent and as I love all dogs she is much company for me." This pampered creature was allowed on deck with the Bandeliers and was cared for by one of the ship's staff, who kept the dog in his room and—if Fanny is to be believed-allowed her to sleep on his bed and share all his food, down to the coffee and bread.

The Bandeliers arrived at Gibraltar on a windy, rainy day and were put abroad the tender for Algeciras, the Spanish port opposite Gibraltar, from where they would begin their journey to Seville. The sea was very rough, and everyone on the boat, with the exception of Adolph, Fanny, and Dodo, became seasick. The Bandelier couple had offered to care for two boys, aged thirteen and fourteen, who were visiting relatives in Madrid. At the hotel in Algeciras, one of the boys became ill, and Fanny, as she stated with some satisfaction, was needed to play mother.

The following day, the Bandeliers began their journey to Seville by train. They had a leisurely trip, stopping at Bobadillas for an ample lunch, and in the afternoon, joined by two other passengers from the

Barbarossa, they took a direct coach for Seville, reaching that city about sunset. The couple put up at the Hotel de Ingleterra and began making plans to find a house.

Like many other people making their first visit to the city, the Bandeliers spent a few days sightseeing. Fanny remarked on the Moorish architecture and the narrow streets of the old city. The couple visited the cathedral and the famous Moorish palace, the Alcázar, which Fanny compared to stories in the Arabian Nights. Like many visitors before and after them, the two Bandeliers admired Seville's collection of paintings by her famous native son, the seventeenth-century artist Bartolomé Esteban Murillo (1617?–1682). To Fanny, one of the great glories of Seville was Murillo's famous *Dolorosa* that hung in the Royal Chapel of the Cathedral. "It is the most marvelous expression of suffering in that sweet motherface I ever saw. There are no tears and one can see that hers is a sorrow that is beyond the shedding of tears. Oh, it is simply beyond description. I could send you a photograph of the picture but this does not give a true impression."

Adolph seems to have gotten to work almost immediately, even while the two were house-hunting. According to Fanny in a letter to Ina Cassidy:

Dolph is of course already working at the archives. I cannot yet go to help him on account of the installation in the house. We found it, this house, but not altogether at the favorable conditions we were told we would, in New York. We have to pay $25. per month, but we had to give three months as guaranteed ahead and will only get the money back when we leave the house, so you may well imagine how that fixed our poor purse, then we had to pay another sum for installation of the light, fortunately no water to pay. And with furniture we had bad luck, they only sell for cash so had to rent what we most needed for the present and got the most abject stuff, you can imagine. But it will do for a few months at least, we cannot help ourselves otherwise. If in the course of time we can furnish the house to suit our taste it will become a little jewel as it is charming; think of a big chinese lantern and you may get an idea of the house. . . . The stairs wind up along one side, giving us a little square court at the entrance closed off by an iron gate. On the ground floor are three rooms, two with windows on the street. On the next floor are four rooms, and here we shall live.

Fanny went on to describe the bedroom as very small but bright. There was a kitchen and maid's quarters on the top floor. The Bandeliers hired a mother and daughter combination, paying them together seven dollars per month. Though help was cheap, meat in the Seville was quite expensive. Still, Fanny delighted with the house on Atansio Barrón, number 2—at least until the winter wore on.

Bandelier had continued working at the archives for some weeks despite increasing malaise. In an earlier letter to Mrs. Cassidy, Fanny had mentioned that her husband was feeling good—a sense of well-being perhaps caused by the excitement of going to Spain and the sea voyage itself. It quickly dissipated once the couple arrived in Seville. Bandelier was suffering from heart trouble and chronic bronchitis; the heart condition caused him to be very weak, and he often fell asleep in the middle of a conversation.

Adolph described these last weeks of work and the winter of 1913–14 at Seville in a letter to Dr. R. S. Woodward, head of the Carnegie Institution. This letter, dated February 17, 1914, was, so far as we know, the last he ever wrote to the Carnegie. In it, Bandelier thanked Woodward for both the December and January remittances from the institution. He also mentioned that all archives and libraries in Seville had been closed for the Christmas holidays, December 12 to January 7. In any case, Adolph indicated that he had been very ill during that period. The terrible cold weather that began around the first of January contributed to his illness.

Even now, it is not yet spring, against all reasonable expectations of the inhabitants who clai[m] that for nearly half a century Sevilla has not known such low temperatures. I would have faired [*sic*] much worse yet, had it not been for the extreme kindness of a lady-friend of mine, Miss Alice Gould, who insisted upon our joining her at the only hotel in Sevilla; which is properly heated. Our household, of course [has] no heating contrivances yet, like all the rest of this town; the floors are of tiles, uncarpeted . . . so that the houses are colder than the streets. Under these circumstances my condition rapidly became critical.

Bandelier also noted in this letter that he had been ill for three months, suggesting that Fanny's comments to Ina Cassidy about his good health during the voyage had been optimistic. Adolph added that "only recently" had he been able to think of "going back to the archives."

The Miss Gould mentioned in Bandelier's letter was the Columbus scholar Alice Bache Gould, who was also working at the Seville archives. According to a later letter from Fanny to Frank Bigler, around the beginning of 1914, Miss Gould invited the Bandeliers to stay as her guests at the Hotel Oriente, where steam heat was to be found. Although Adolph felt better in these more comfortable surroundings, he missed Fanny's home cooking, and eventually, in mid-February, the couple moved back to their unheated quarters. In spite of Fanny's devoted care, Bandelier became weaker and weaker, according to one of Fanny's letters to Frank Bigler after Bandelier's death.

Fanny, who had met Adolph's old friend after the Bandeliers settled in New York, had herself become friendly with Bigler. Indeed, it was he to whom Fanny turned in the tragic times following Adolph's death. In the spring of 1914, she had written a number of letters to various friends and professional colleagues of Adolph's, and she believed that many of them had gone astray. Her letter of July 20, 1914, to Bigler was partly a request for him to provide mutual acquaintances with the story of her husband's death. Fanny also relived those final dark days and hours.

In her letter, Fanny went over certain of the main events of the trip and told the story of Mr. Hicks in almost the same words she had used in the Cassidy letter. In Seville, according to Fanny, her husband had worked until December 18 (perhaps she meant December 12, the date given for the closing of the archives). After the Christmas holidays, Adolph had managed at most only a few more days of archival research.

> I took him for drives in the warmest hours of the day and for a while, it seemed as if he was gaining. Unfortunately, his limbs began to swell, he could not walk any more but held on fast to the hope of spring coming— it never came for him again. How gladly would I have given my life for him had he been able to live without me but he wanted me every minute; I could not leave his side. I shall forever be sorry for the hour the doctor and Miss Gould made me go out on the Monday before he died. How life came back into his dear face when I came home again! You see, my life was simply all his and if I live now, it is only to do his work.

How much of this overheated prose is late-Victorian hyperbole and how much "pure Fanny" is hard to tell. It should be noted, however, that Bandelier had the knack of eliciting tremendous loyalty and devotion in people near to him. This seems to have been especially true of both his wives.

The end came in the early morning of March 18. Fanny described the scene in her letter to Frank Bigler:

On Tuesday he felt a good deal better, although I found him weakening al[l] the time; he had at times great difficulty to speak and he was not able to eat right, but he joked with the doctor who was on his last visit. That night he stayed up until the paper, the Figaro, was out, and I read it to him for he wanted to know all about the murder of Mr. Calmette by Madame Caillaux [a cause célèbre in which the wife of the French minister of finance had shot the editor of the newspaper *Figaro*]. About nine he went to bed, saying he felt quite good and now he was sure that he was going to be better. At 2 A.M. he woke for only a moment, again saying he felt good, and these were the last words I ever heard from his lips. When I woke at 5:30 he was breathing so hard that I called him, got up, put him higher on the pillow, but he never again opened his eyes, never uttered a word, and 6:30 he was no more. What I suffered in this dreadfully long hour! The doctor did not come although I sent the maid for him; nothing could I do to help him so I held his hand and spoke to him, and finally I simply held that dear hand. The doctor told me he had expected this to happen long ago, and that I should be thankful that he did not suffer for he lay there so peacefully, so quiet, with a faint smile on his lips that I really think that he did not suffer. But what do we know?

The stricken Fanny was faced with arranging burial for her husband. His body was taken to the San Fernando cemetery the following morning. Fanny arranged for a ten-year lease on a grave but hoped that she could take the body with her when she returned to the United States. This did not prove possible, and Bandelier's remains were to lie in Seville for sixty-three years.

After a few disorganized and hapless weeks, Fanny found herself at the archives, where she took up Bandelier's work. Apparently Frank Bigler and others of her friends had recommended to the Carnegie that she be appointed to succeed her husband. It may be that the institution planned to do that in any case. A later letter from R. S. Woodward to Arthur von Briesen, a prominent German-American lawyer and scholar who had befriended the Bandeliers, stated that the Carnegie grant was extended to Fanny in order to diminish the hardship caused by her husband's death. She was very lonely during this period, as the generous and solicitous Miss Gould had now completed her own archival work and was gone. Still, the Carnegie Institution provided her with a certain financial security.

Fanny (with her faithful Dodo) stayed on in Seville until the later part of 1915. The Spanish archival portion of the Bandelier documents, later published in three volumes by Charles W. Hackett, was primarily collected by Fanny alone. She later spoke of investigating archives in Madrid and possibly Simancas, but all extant documents in the Bandelier collections coming from Spain were from the Archives of the Indies in Seville. The Carnegie Institution eventually received nine hundred pages of transcripts from that archive.

Financial worries were never far from Fanny's mind. Although she was the sole beneficiary of Adolph's will, there was little for her to inherit. On April 4, 1914, officials of the Hispanic Society of America, which held Bandelier's will, sent Fanny $300, presumably representing the liquid assets from Adolph's estate. The Hispanic Society people also continued their efforts to straighten out the status of the Bandelier library. Adolph seems to have made a verbal agreement for its sale to the American Museum of Natural History, although it is not clear how much money, if any, changed hands in the transaction. Now, personnel at the Hispanic Society cautioned against completion of the library transaction in the absence of Adolph's heir. It is still not clear just what happened to Bandelier's books.

Whatever the case might have been with the library, Fanny suffered from great financial insecurity for some years to come, partly because the Bandeliers had depended primarily on the Carnegie grant for their livelihood. This grant of $2,000 per year had begun on November 1, 1911, and was renewed annually in 1912, 1913, and (to Fanny) 1914. The grant ran out on October 31, 1915, and as Woodward clearly indicated in his letter to Briesen on October 1, 1915, the institution at that time had no intention of renewing it. A little over a year later, when Fanny had returned to New York, Frederick Webb Hodge wrote that the trustees of the Carnegie Institution were considering another renewal, presumably to allow Fanny to further edit the fourteen thousand or so pages of documents. Fanny at that time believed she had a "secret enemy" at Carnegie, an idea Hodge did his best to dispel. Whether or not Fanny had real enemies in the woodwork at Carnegie, the institution never did renew the contract.

During this last year and a half in Seville, Fanny adapted herself to Spanish customs and delved more deeply into Adolph's life's work. Her long letter to Bigler gave some information on the first part of this period:

> The people begin to go way for the summer and soon Sevilla will be very quiet, relatively, of course for the lower classes do their best not to have it too quiet. They live at night, in the daytime they sleep, since in these hot summer months there is hardly any business going on.
>
> Where I live, in the small house [where] Dolph died, it is not so bad; we have the baths, "de la Florida" in our neighborhood and I am taking one every day. It is true it is quite far from the city and I have to take the car (2 or 3 cents each time) to go to my work, but I have good and pure air, and that at least I may have, may I not? I do not go out after my hours at the Archivo for I have to make myself thoroughly fit for the work I am doing, and, therefore, I am studying Dolph's many books on the subject. Of his Archaeological Tour, his Pecos, etc. I am making a complete index, and that takes all my free time. Then of course, when it is so hot now I cannot do any work after the work at the Archivo. This only lasts from 8 to 12 in the morning for they say they cannot open in the afternoon on account of the hot weather, and truely it is almost unbearable when one goes home at 12.

Fanny closed this letter with a comment on the problems she faced in getting and receiving mail. It seems that a number of her dispatches had gone astray, including, among others, letters to Bigler, the Cassidys, Mary Prince, and the librarian of the Geographical Society. At least, these people failed to respond to Fanny's earlier correspondence. For example, in a letter dated April 30, 1914, Bigler told Fanny that he had learned of Bandelier's death only that day, probably from the pages of *The Nation*. Fanny, with the aid of the postal authorities, had set a trap to catch the supposed thief in the Spanish postal service, but no such person could be identified.

In her July 20 letter to Frank Bigler, Fanny painfully reconstructed the previous one; she did not relish reliving the events of Adolph's death. "Now I will try and re-write my first letter to you telling you all I can about my dearest one's illness and death. You have no idea how much I suffer each time I have to recall all these dreadful weeks, and yet, I know that his dear, good friends are entitled to know every detail I am able to give."

Many years later, in 1940, the historian Lansing Bloom, of the Museum of New Mexico, gathered information about Fanny during that Seville period. He quoted liberally from a letter from Francis S. Philbrick, then of the University of Pennsylvania, who arrived in Seville in the early summer of 1914 and saw a great deal of Fanny. In his letter to Bloom, dated August 14, 1940, Philbrick wrote:

> Of course Mrs. Bandelier was in mourning and often depressed in spirit in the months that I spent that year in Seville, but if you knew her personally you know how vivacious she was, and how irrespressible her spirits. She continued her husband's work in the Archivo, and the company of Miss Wright and her mother and of myself—for we four were together a good deal of the time—doubtless helped her through a difficult time. . . .
>
> Mrs. Bandelier remained throughout her life one of my best friends. I never knew one more generous, and very few indeed who had led such interesting lives in different parts of the world and were so well worth knowing. She must have been a perfect companion for her husband despite the disparity in age.

The "Miss Wright" mentioned was Irene A. Wright, who also wrote to Bloom in August 1940. According to Wright, Fanny, after Bandelier's death, had no associates whatsoever, except for "Francis Philbrick, my mother, myself, and presently certain scholarship men whose identity I do not recall. We were a close and isolated group. I remember that, when, because of the war, means of communication were cut off and "money from home" became irregular in arriving, Mrs. Bandelier offered to finance all of us. She alone had 'money in the bank.'" It is uncertain where Fanny got the "money in the bank" and why the others were having more problems getting money from the United States than Fanny herself.

In spite of the new friends she made, there is no doubt that Fanny suffered from a terrible sense of loss. As she wrote to Bigler, now she lived only to do Bandelier's unfinished work. There would be happier times in the future, but it is clear that the tragic months following Adolph's death represented the nadir of Fanny's adventurous life.

EIGHTEEN
Fanny Alone

Dolfi: What shall I do? . . . Will you let me go to the wall?

THE CARNEGIE GRANT expired at the end of October 1915, and about that time Fanny sailed on a Spanish ship from Spain to the United States. She reached New York on November 12 and five days later wrote Ina Cassidy from the Hotel Arlington. Fanny was going to Washington to deliver some materials to Dr. Woodward of the Carnegie Institution and also to explore possibilities for employment. A letter dated December 29, 1915, told of her attendance at the Pan American Scientific Conference.

In Washington, Fanny unexpectedly met friends from Bolivian days — Ignacio Calderón, now the Bolivian minister to the United States, and his wife and daughter—and was invited to stay at the Bolivian legation. The job possibilities came to nothing, however, and by the end of May 1916, Fanny, virtually penniless, was back in New York and had taken a furnished room. A year or so later, she moved to an apartment at 181 Claremont Avenue, where she would live until 1925.

It may have been a blessing that Fanny Bandelier had no children and so was relieved of what might have been an additional drain on her financial and emotional resources. It might be well here to address the question of Bandelier's childlessness. So far as we know, both Josephine and Fanny were healthy young women when he married them in their early to mid-twenties; Joe's chronic illness seems to have been a mid-life phenomenon. There is no evidence that Adolph and Joe wished to avoid having children, especially since they appeared quite willing to make

Lizzie Bandelier, the young cousin, part of their family. In Fanny's case, it is clear that she loved children and gloried in the times she and Adolph could look after their friends' offspring. Moreover, Bandelier lived during a time when both Catholic and Protestant churches were opposed to birth control, and it is doubtful that the religious Bandelier family experimented with the primitive birth control measures available in the nineteenth century. One is left with the strong suspicion that Bandelier himself could not father children, perhaps due to some childhood illness that left him partially or completely sterile. It is unfortunate that the Victorian prudery of the time made such matters virtually unmentionable in letters and journals.

The chronic financial worries that plagued Fanny for most of the remainder of her life were indicated in a letter to Ina Cassidy dated July 24. Around that time Ina, who was living in Montclair, New Jersey, a few miles east of New York City, asked Fanny to give her lessons in Spanish, and Fanny was full of plans. She had purchased a book called *Cuentos Españoles* (Spanish tales) for their practice reading. A comment by Ina in the margin of Fanny's letter noted, "I think I commenced Spanish lessons about Tuesday, Aug. 1."

As early as January 22, 1916, in a letter to Eva Fényes, Fanny mentioned that she was trying to republish Bandelier's novel, *The Delight Makers,* and had approached Dodd, Mead and Company on the matter. A letter from Fanny to Ina Cassidy, dated September 21, had further news of Dodd, Mead's reissue of the book. According to Fanny, Charles Lummis asked that he be allowed to do an introduction. Fanny agreed and discussed the matter with Frank Howard Dodd. Her point to Dodd was that it might be well for both Lummis and Frederick Webb Hodge to write front matter for the book. The picturesque Lummis could give a highly spiced personal account of Bandelier, while Hodge, with his scholarly credentials, could describe Bandelier's importance in the scientific world.

> I am more than glad that Mr. Dodd accepted it. He first wanted to throw Fred Hodge's preface out, but when I explained my ideas, he quite agreed and you can bet that I will stick to my opinion. The Lummis article will be a fine asset for the sale of the book out west, do you not think so? And do you not think your little friend was wise to insist on Mr. Hodge's writing it and having it first?

Eva's "little friend" was at her coy and whimsical best. Like Bandelier, Fanny seems to have been equivocal in her relations with Lummis—not surprisingly, since she must have observed years of emotional ups and downs between her husband and his old friend. She was really quite pleased with her negotiations with the Dodd, Mead executives and could not forgo boasting a bit to Ina.

> I think I can get Dodd Mead to allow me more pictures also, I really think they do all my biddings, they have become nice and rather worldly, not at all so very *saintly*. I told Mr. Dodd yesterday a bit of my opinion of dear Lummis' outfit and he laughed himself sick. He said Mr. [Frederick C.] Hicks had told him, L: was a character and rather excentric [*sic*].

Why Fanny would have expected these tough New York businessmen to be "saintly" is not clear. In any case, a new edition of *The Delight Makers* came out in 1916 with front matter by both Hodge and Lummis. An essentially identical edition was released in 1918, the only change being that the copyright was now transferred to Fanny.

In the later months of 1916, Fanny launched a project that she was to return to several times in the next twenty years. Fanny seems always to have been obsessed with the idea that Adolph had not received proper respect and recognition from the scientific world during his lifetime. As early as May 17, 1914, in Seville, she had written Ina Cassidy of her plan for publishing a biography of Bandelier, and on May 26 she wrote again, giving more details. The biography was to contain a collection of Adolph's own writings, including "all his shorter writings just in the places when they were written, but for this I need several data only his cousin in Bern can give me. I have with me all his journals and everything I could lay hands on he ever wrote. There are many publications, though, mostly in [G]erman, which I cannot get."

By 1916, Fanny had considerably developed her plan to produce a biography of Bandelier. She wrote several people about how to fund this work. Some of her friends were dubious about the prospects. Frederick Webb Hodge, for example, in a November 1916 letter to Ina Cassidy, pointed out the difficulties of such a project. The people who would most appreciate Bandelier were scientists who, generally speaking, could not offer much monetary support. In addition, funds would be needed for travel and to visit the scenes of Adolph's work, something that would not be cheap. And Fanny herself would need twelve hundred to fifteen hundred dollars a year simply to live. Hodge suggested that in order to get the program off the ground, Fanny would have to answer some hard, businesslike questions: "How long will the preparation of the manuscript require, and what [are] the actual pecuniary needs during this period? What will the publishers be willing to do, and what will be the cost of the book? It is hardly possible to approach anyone unless these questions can be answered definitely."

Hodge added, in a handwritten, confidential footnote to Cassidy, that Fanny's case (that is, the possibility that she continue at Carnegie) was coming before the trustees of the Carnegie Institution. Hodge doubted whether anything could be done. Sadly, he was correct.

During this same period, Fanny attempted to augment her income by working as a translator. A business card of hers still exists; it is undated but probably belongs to late 1917 or 1918. On the card, Fanny advertised translations from and into Spanish, French, German, and English for commercial, technical, and literary materials.

As early as 1916, Hodge was helping Fanny get translating work: a letter of April 20 that year discussed work she was doing at the Smithsonian. At a later date (1923), Hodge, who was now with the Heye Museum in New York City, scolded Fanny in a letter because of the exorbitant amounts she demanded for her translations, saying that "it looks a good deal like killing the goose that laid the golden egg."

During the First World War, Fanny served as a volunteer with the American Red Cross, where she directed a group knitting socks. Fanny was having increasing trouble making ends meet. She put at least part of Bandelier's library up for sale, and in a letter to Ina Cassidy dated December 12, 1918, she admitted that she was having difficulty keeping up the rent payments on the Claremont Avenue apartment. Things were indeed at a low ebb:

> My own matters are not one bit better, but so far the landlord has not spoken though I am afraid that he will before the 15th. I shall simply tell him that I had made a mistake in my accounting and would have to ask him to wait a bit only a few days perhaps because I hope the books will at least net enough to pay the 38 dollars. I hope I shall never get so low. I just wish I could bury myself over these holidays, they are dreadful to me.

Ina Cassidy, perhaps responding to what she thought was a hint in Fanny's letter, invited her friend to spend the Christmas holidays with the Cassidy family. On December 18, 1918, the day Adolph's library was to have been sold, Fanny wrote back that she had accepted an invitation from a Mrs. Alice D. Jackson. The Jackson family seems to have been friends of the Bandeliers' of several years' standing. On December 27, Alice Jackson wrote a curious and revealing letter to Ina Cassidy, whom she seems to have known only formally.

Dear Mrs. Cassidy

Mrs. Bandelier was here for dinner on Christmas Day and as she said you had written her that I would tell you about her plans for the books and the Museum [of New Mexico]. I told her a little, though I didn't go into details, and I am sorry to say that she didn't seem to like the idea of leaving any of Bandelier's things to the Museum. I am afraid that it is the old difficulty about Dr. Hewett and of course she does cherish things like that terribly. just as Mr. Bandelier did. She seemed to think that he would-n't have liked any of his things to be there, and she doesn't seem to realize that his fame rests more on the work he did in and about New Mexico than on anything else. Perhaps because of her own association with it she thinks of his Peruvian work as the most important, and it may be, from some points of view, but a hundred persons will hear of his work in New Mexico in the future where one will know he ever went to Peru.

Possibly she can be convinced that Santa Fe is really the place where there will always be the most interest in his work, but at present she dis-likes Mr. Hewett so much and is so irritated at the Kaunes doings (about which I know nothing, though I daresay you do), that I am afraid that she won't be very reasonable.

A second letter from Alice Jackson, dated January 16, 1919, shed a bit more light on this matter.

Dear Mrs. Cassidy

I will be delighted to lunch with you next Thursday [January] 23rd, at the Arts Club. Perhaps I was unduly pessimistic about Mrs. Bandelier and the books. For the next time I saw her she seemed rather more inclined to the idea. Anyway, I hope so, for I think the idea a very good one.

Apparently Mr. Lummis started something of the kind, though I do not know on what scale, at Los Angeles. Do you know just what he did?

This plan, presumably to sell part or all of the Bandelier library and other items collected by Bandelier to the Museum of New Mexico, so far as we know came to nothing. A number of Bandelier items—papers, journals, the Borglum bust—did eventually go to the museum, but that was years later. The feud between Bandelier and Hewett is otherwise unknown. Possibly it was a falling out over the Museum of New Mexico negotiations with Bandelier after 1907. Why this should have been the case is not obvious, since the two seem to have been on amicable terms up to the time the Bandeliers went to Mexico in 1911, and Fanny's relationship with Hewett in later years seemed cordial enough. Just before his last trip to Mexico, Bandelier was working on the introduction to *Documentary History of the Rio Grande Pueblos*. Hewett eventually published *Indians of the Rio Grande Valley* (containing *Documentary History* as part II) in 1937, with the long-dead Bandelier as coauthor.

The problem Fanny was having with the Kaunes is also unclear. Henry Kaune was still living at the old "Bandelier" house in Santa Fe at the time. It is curious that after returning to the United States from South America, the Bandeliers seem to have had very little contact with the Kaunes. Adolph occasionally mentioned them in his journals, but as far as the record goes, the two families seem not to have met. This is especially odd since Elizabeth Bandelier Kaune had been raised partly by Adolph and Joe. One wonders whether Henry and Lizzie Kaune resented Bandelier's marriage to Fanny and were not prepared to welcome her into the family.

A romantic interlude came to Fanny in the spring of 1919, one that was to have a dramatic short-term, though apparently not much long-term, effect. It began when Fanny resumed contact with Charles T. Wilson, whom she had known in Bolivia in 1897 and 1898, when Wilson was a landscape artist living in La Paz. Wilson left Bolivia for Peru in April 1900, to set up an artist's studio there. His wife died at some point, probably in the early 1900s.

Sometime around 1906 or 1907, Wilson married a second time, this time a divorced woman with a daughter, but the marriage was, according to Wilson, a disaster; the woman was mercenary and cold. Following the death of his stepdaughter in 1913, the Wilsons separated, and at the time of his correspondence with Fanny, Charles Wilson was in the process of filing for divorce. He was now living in northern California and had achieved some recognition, especially as a painter of redwoods.

Only a portion of Wilson's correspondence with Fanny has been found; with the exception of one brief note, all the letters are from Charles to Fanny. By April 1919, the two were exchanging weekly letters, and Wilson was working on various schemes to help Fanny, the most practical being a plan to have Fanny sell Wilson's oil paintings in the New York area. Wilson flattered Fanny, sympathized with her, violently criticized people whom she described as treating her offensively, talked puppy-talk to Dodo, and gave her great dollops of his own philosophy of life. The following is an example that provides an appreciation for the rich flavor of Wilson's uncontrolled spelling, punctuation, and grammar.

In regards to Women?, I cannot see how you can call such a thing as you speak of a friend [Fanny apparently had told of some mistreatment by one of her feminine friends] if I could tell you of what has been said in my Studio at the Different times that I have taught painting: you would be shoked, how many times that I have told them that their Husbands have sent them to my place to learn painting only, I have made more than one sit and cry, telling their duty to their Husbands and family, and is it a wonder that I have so little use for women in general? for I have found them out to be lyars, deceitfull, malicious, vicious, unreliable and infact perfectly devoid of principal, such is my opinion of woman in general, and you could not blame me if you have had the experence with them as have I?, infact I have off the Jury two or three times in my answer to question asked by Lawyers in challenging the Jurors they ask "Will your verdict be governed by the testimony of witnesses?." I have answered "Not if their any Wemen witnesses."

This blatant misogyny seems not to have perturbed Fanny. She was, after all, used to living with a dominant and opinionated male. In any case, Wilson was also rather sharp with his own sex.

So you can see how I feel in regards to them, and I am not surprised at what you tell me of the way that this woman has done for you, there is more real and true friendship in a Man's little finger than their is in TEN wemen's whole body, that is most men? but their are many would could not help a women in distress with wanting to drag down to his own level, such men are CURS. I do not understand how they can be so? it is natual to suppose that they have or [had] Mothers, and sisters. . . . I have the greatest respect for Wemen's virtue, and when they have not that I have no use for them,. you do well to not confide your joys and sorrows in them, they are to friveles, could not understand you in your own feeling and then repeat what you have told them all backwards.

By late May the salutation "My dear Mrs. Bandelier" had become "My very dear Friend," and on June 27 it was "My very, very, very Dear little Friend." Wilson confessed that he had been attracted to Fanny from the first time he saw her in Bolivia, though at the time it seemed an impossible love. But now times had changed! Wilson dropped briefly into a greater formality in a letter simply dated "Monday the same day as my last letter," which was probably written on June 30. Here Wilson wrote:

I have posted, what may be the fatal letter to my happiness and as the ice is broken it canot be any more fatal to pour out to you my beloved Fannie, my very Soul tell you all, tell you that I kiss the stamps on your letter and the paper that your letters are written on, kiss them because your beloved hands have touched them, I am allways talking to your picture, calling endearing names to you, you are the last thought at night when I retire, and the first in the morning, you are allways in my mind even when I am painting I am thinking of you my dear Fannie.

Wilson went on to beg that Fanny "let me call you my own." Another short letter, apparently written the same day, was headed "ALMA de MIO."

You know Dear Heart that a man is never a fellon untill sentence has been passed on him, so I am making hay while the sun shines, so I will make love to my ALMA for at least two weeks as it will take that time for you to get my last three letters and me their answer's and if the verdict is against me I will have to close my mouth forever, as I love you to much ever to write a word that would be disagreeable to you my love.

Fanny's reply seems to have been equivocal, and Wilson hesitated over going to New York. He had a sister, Minnie, there, and by June 27 she was already in contact with Fanny. Wilson's movements after July 1919 are not very clear, but a brief notice in volume 2 of *Artists of the American West* reveals that he did, indeed, go to New York for an exhibition at about that time. There he died on January 3, 1920. A brief obituary the next day in the *New York Times* read, "Wilson—Charles Thel[l]er, beloved husband of Fanny Bandelier Wilson, suddenly; on Jan. 3. Services The Funeral Church (Campbell Building) Broadway at 65th St. Tuesday Jan. 6 at 3 PM."

Existing documents reveal little about Fanny's second marriage, but of course it was one of at most a few months' duration. On April 25, 1920, Camilla Lackman, a friend of Fanny's, wrote a note addressed to Mrs. F. Bandelier Wilson, but the salutation was to "My dear Mrs. Bandelier." There was no direct mention of Charles Wilson, but the note does speak of Fanny's loneliness.

A letter from Dr. Nicolás León, a friend in the anthropological establishment in Mexico, written on March 18, 1921, referred obliquely to Fanny's situation. León was apparently responsible, a few years later, for Fanny's last extended stay out of the country, but at that date he was writing mainly about manuscripts. Fanny and Adolph had known León from their 1911 visit to Mexico, and Fanny was on warm terms with the Mexican anthropologist.

Her marriage to Wilson does not seem to have given Fanny any financial security. She did receive some of his paintings and as late as 1924 was trying to sell certain of them to the American Art Works at Coshocton, Ohio. There is no record that anything came of this. Eventually, she seems to have sold or given away whatever of Wilson's paintings and other belongings she possessed, for at her death the only Wilson mementos remaining were the bundle of letters he had written before their marriage.

Why did Fanny marry Wilson, and why, after his death, was she so silent about the matter? He was some years older than Fanny, who was herself fifty or fifty-one when the marriage took place. Possibly Fanny found this aging, romantic artist attractive. Perhaps with Wilson she could relive something of the glory days in Bolivia when she and Adolph had furnished a house and invited the cream of La Paz society to lavish social functions. Or she may have seen Charles Wilson as an economic lifeline. If so, the lifeline was cut by Wilson's sudden death, and Fanny returned to an obsessive loyalty to Adolph Bandelier's memory. Perhaps Hodge and others did not mention Wilson in their letters because she did not wish to hear about him. It is even possible that some of her friends never knew of the second marriage.

Fanny tried her hand at a number of activities in the years following Charles Wilson's death. A letter from Brandt and Kirkpatrick (apparently literary agents), dated July 29, 1921, informed Fanny that the firm could not place her short story, "Adios Carmencita." The agents did encourage Fanny to try publishers directly and also offered to look at any other stories she might have.

The early 1920s, obviously, were years of struggle for Fanny. She copied manuscripts, enrolled in a hotel training course (which she never completed), and even sold chain-store stock on commission. In 1922, she was still living in the Claremont Avenue rooms. On June 25 of that year, she wrote Hewett in Santa Fe that the tenth anniversary of Adolph's death was approaching and again raised the question of a memorial volume. Probably in the fall of 1923, her beloved Dodo died.

On December 18, 1923, Fanny received a long letter from Francis S. Philbrick, the scholar who had befriended her in Seville after Adolph's death and who was now at the University of Illinois Law School. He was attempting to find employment for Fanny and had written to say that he had not been very successful. Frank (as Fanny called him) had been in touch with the Carnegie Institution and thought there might possibly be a job there—but nothing came of it.

On November 12, 1924, Fanny, signing herself both Fanny R. Bandelier and Mrs. Adolph F. Bandelier, wrote Hodge a curious note: "This is to certify that I have this day sold to Frederick W. Hodge for $1.00 and other valuable consideration all my personal effects, the books and furnishings of my home and everything else I own at present and may acquire in the future nobody having any claim on it whatever." Probably realizing that Hodge might jump to conclusions about her mental state, Fanny wrote the next day assuring him that she was not mortally ill or thinking of doing away with herself, but that she had long intended to do this "in case I should suddenly be called away, Dolph's journals and other papers are with you." She went on to say that she had been ailing from a general breakdown but would soon be well.

The next information regarding Fanny is found in the *New York Times*

(December 31, 1924) and the *New York Herald Tribune* (February 1, 1925). According to both these items, Fanny was helping to organize an expedition to Cuzco and was trying to interest the American Museum of Natural History. The *Times* story, quoting Fanny, had it that "President Augusto B. Leguia of Peru has approved and 'through his goodwill and that of [Peruvian] Secretary of the Navy Casanave we would have a clear field.'"What the Peruvian navy had to do with Cuzco, which lies far inland, was not explained. The *Herald Tribune* story covered essentially the same ground, emphasizing the interest that Leguia and Casanave took in the expedition. It added that before starting to Cuzco, Mrs. Bandelier planned to transport Adolph's body from Seville to Bandelier National Monument in New Mexico to "bring it to rest." Many years later, Bandelier's cremated remains would indeed be scattered at Bandelier National Monument, but by that time Fanny had long been dead.

The Cuzco trip came to nothing, and in May of 1925 Fanny went to Mexico instead—planning to stay only the summer, visiting with Mexico City residents Herbert and Jenny Gerber and Herbert's mother, who was an old friend of Fanny's. In January 1926, Mrs. Gerber died, and her body was taken back to New York for burial. Fanny offered to stay with the Gerber children at the family's home in San Angel on the eastern edge of Mexico City, and she remained there for at least a year.

Meanwhile, she began to teach a course in South American archaeology, under the sponsorship of Dr. León, at the Museo Nacional de Arqueología, Historia y Etnografía in Mexico City. The course started on October 27, 1925, and was listed through May 1927, but it seems actually to have been offered only from late 1925 through the early part of 1926. In addition, Fanny took on a number of Spanish students, including the American consul general, Alexander W. Weddell, and the Episcopal bishop, Frank W. Creighton, and his wife.

Fanny left the Gerbers, perhaps in 1927; an undated (but probably spring or summer 1928) letter to Ina Cassidy discussed the move without really explaining it. Perhaps working as a nanny to the Gerber children had proved too confining as well as too far from Fanny's real interests.

I live in a nice house, having taken just a room, and eat downstairs in the restaurant owned by the same people. As he is a French Chef, the cooking is very good and I am well taken care of. It would be foolish for me to take an apartment for I would have to have at least one servant and that always means more trouble and not so much security. It is true, servants are cheap enough, but they are also bad enough. It is all a matter of luck. I cannot complain for whosoever I had as servants here, while I lived at San Angel, in the house of my friends Gerber, were rather nice and took good care of me. And yet, only lately have I found out that the little maid stole all the money out of my safety bank leaving only the small coin. . . . I am really better off in a room with service, my meals etc. As I am not often home during the whole day I feel freer this way too. The meals are good the room is clean and airy, so what more can one wish.

Fanny was unhappy, however, with the regime of President Plutarcho Elías Calles in Mexico, especially with the war between church and state. This was the period of the *cristero* troubles, when gangs of religious extremists, devoted to restoring the Catholic church's power in Mexico, roamed the countryside murdering schoolteachers and other agents of government change, especially in the western mountainous regions. The Calles government retaliated with brutal reprisals. The *cristero* revolt did not finally end until the presidency of Lázaro Cárdenas in the early 1930s. Agitated by the unsettled conditions in Mexico, Fanny planned a return to the United States and finally managed to get back there in the summer of 1928. She also found permanent employment, as she explained in a 1929 letter to Ina Cassidy.

Last summer Dr. [Paul] Radin was in Mexico and persuaded me to come as his assistant in the Dept. of Anthropology at Fisk, Nashville and so there I am officially. As for this year we had no courses for the last Quarter. . . . I like my work at Fisk and am very happy as it is the work I have been longing for. Only a few days ago I was offered an additional course or two in the French Dept. where they are hard pressed on account of illness of one of the professors.

Paul Radin was a well-known anthropologist whose work on Midwestern Indians and on native religious and philosophical systems is still highly regarded. Radin had received his Ph.D. at Columbia in 1911, studying with Boas, and it is conceivable that the Bandeliers might have known him as a graduate student, perhaps as one of Boas's circle. In the same letter, Fanny mentioned that her status as an American citizen had been clarified, thanks to the good offices of the American consul in

Mexico City. "Mr. Weddell spoke directly to Mr. Kellogg and after a few days the latter wired back an O.K. so now there is no longer any doubt. Dr. Radin was most helpful and pushed the matter so it came through in a comparatively short time." It should be remembered that Fanny had been giving Spanish lessons to Weddell. The Kellogg mentioned was Frank Billings Kellogg, a later Nobel Peace Prize winner, who at that time was secretary of state in the Coolidge administration.

During her Mexican stay, Fanny seems to have gone through an especially active mystical phase in her life. She had always been a believer in such things as prophetic dreams and had related in letters and stories how she and Adolph had been saved from murder at the hands of Bolivian Indian villagers by a dream. Even more dramatic was a dream she had on the island of Titicaca, when a mysterious stranger appeared to her and showed her the site of many precious objects. These were found the next day by native workmen under Adolph and Fanny's direction.

It was during her Mexican period, however, that Fanny turned to automatic writing. This "spirit" writing, in which a person allows his or her hand to produce a script while attention is focused elsewhere, enjoyed a great vogue from about 1850 to 1900 and was generally assumed to be the result of supernatural intervention. Fanny would probably have known about the system in her youth, and indeed, in the 1920s there was a reawakening of interest in automatic writing, both by psychologists who were delving into the subconscious and by spiritualists who continued to maintain that it was a supernatural phenomenon.

Fanny saved samples of her automatic writing, done mostly on cheap or scrap paper, sometimes with other matter written on the reverse side. Several of the samples have dates, and the original writing on the documents can also be used to date the incidents approximately. Most of the papers are marked on the tops or sides with a curious symbol, thirteen upright marks in a row with a long horizontal mark connecting them through the middle. What this sign represented, and whether it had cabalistic meaning, is not known.

Much or all of her automatic writing (about twenty-five examples remain) seems to have been done in 1927; at least, the dated letters are all from the late spring and summer of that year (with one exception, dated 11/31/20 [*sic*]). The entries are mostly in English, though an occasional one is in German, and one is partly in French. Though Fanny must have been using Spanish in everyday discourse, none of the remaining examples are in that language. Many of the messages are from Bandelier him-self—for example, the following (the asterisks within brackets [★] indi-cate unintelligible words):

My love—I am so glad you came I happy to have you come at any time—dont you know you must *not* worry God's ways are wonderful and *he* can help you when you think there is no help—No ill can come to you no one can hurt you do your work cheerfully and well you are so brave and all goes well. No one can play with you—we will not permit it. You are well taken care of I watch and all your friends we who are your heavenly guides go on being brave happy and smiling all our efforts are for your good—faith faith—you must have much faith and you must not think sad and disruptive thoughts—do pray and be true to yourself [★] good music [★★] We sing much to the glory of god Come again my own come [★].
    love love Dolfie

A letter on yellow scratch paper that continued from one side of the page to the other was likely from Charles Wilson. If so, death had made considerable improvement in his spelling:

From one who loves you very much—I am always near you my lady love—I have needed a long time till I could believed that I was no longer with you—but now I know and realize the great distance that separates me from you who is my dream of everything lovely—I am allowed to be near you at times and watch over you [continued on back of page] when *he* is not able to do so. Do not hate me for what I did—it was my great love and here I learn that to love is the best of all. I love you sweet queen of all favors. I love you my heart was yours and is still yours as is possible from here I want you to be happy—
    Chas

What Wilson had done to earn Fanny's hate is not clear—perhaps it was his dying so soon after the wedding.
    Most of the letters, however, were from Adolph (none were from Joe, nor was she ever mentioned). One of them reminisced about Bandelier's own 1881 trip to Cholula. It would seem that Fanny had recently visited the Cholula area.

We are together my love you we on the road to the place where the Indians wanted to stone me it was at San Pedro de Jenancingo Cholula you walked over the same ground I walked so often and I was with you did you not feel me? I was so close so close—my own you must go again do—do Please for then we will be close still and we will be able to commune and be together go with your good friend and do the things I shall tell you—it will be so beautiful—do go some day soon you will know what I mean—I was most happy to have you go to all those places—We are always watching over you my love.

A message dated June 19, 1927, was cryptic in several respects:

My love good evening you see how quickly I come whenever you call because I am always here near you—yes yes you are going to have one and very soon—he is very busy poor fellow and you must forgive him you will see in his letter how he feels no I shall not tell you you must read it for yourself my love—you are going to marry yes yes but you must save [?] me I am not going to say whom not yet I do not want you to be alone all your life—no no [**] very good night [**]

Another letter delivered from Adolph via automatic writing a week later, on June 26, 1927, seems to have been a follow-up to the previous one.

My darling I am here and thank you for calling me yes I know the letter [?] came and you are very happy yes yes he is always the same and he works hard and he is lonesome for you you will find out when you return home. We can [?] not do much tonight darling everyday if you can—I am going to give you [★] soon but try seriously my dear now goodnight my love [★] ever I am yours my love all yours.
Dolfie

An undated scrap of message said: "My wife [?] you will be very happy with Fred Hodge and I bless you both."
Two themes run consistently through the automatic writing: Fanny's loneliness and her need of protection. That Fanny had romantic dreams about *somebody* in the world of the living seems clear, but in spite of Bandelier's statement about Hodge—which seems unequivocal

enough—just who that person was is not at all certain. A draft letter on a piece of white typing paper, included with the sheets of automatic writing, is rather a mystery. For one thing, it is undated, though its inclusion with the automatic writing collection suggests that it belonged to the 1927 period, as did a segment of automatic writing—largely gibberish—at the top of the page.

> All there is to it I can say that I love you and you cannot alter or change that it is quite impossible now, the damage is dose [*sic*] I feel so stronlgy [*sic*] for you as I ever felt for my beloved Dolph and Frank dear you must not get angry with me, promise never never to get angry because it hurts more than I can say and I am sure you donot really wish to hurt me, do you? My heart aches and aches when I think of the possibility of you changing your mind and I know I would die if should you ever do that. So please donot do it. I am lonesome enough as it is I need my dear friends to cheer me up and give me courage to Live which I would not have had had I not such dear ones to think of. And you are the very first one I am always thinking about, you need not be proud of that at all it is so natural and so necessary for me to love you and to think of you and to cherish you as I evr [*sic*] Dolph. He brought you to me so why should I not love you, tell me.

If this strange letter was meant to be copied and mailed, it could hardly have been meant for Frederick Hodge. Fanny may have had fantasies of marrying Hodge (as per Bandelier's message to her). Living in Mexico as she was, she may not have known that Hodge was married or about to be wed to Zahrah E. Proble. The addressee of the letter, however, was "Frank," a name she would hardly have used for Frederick Hodge. In any case, this draft letter does not actually mention marriage, only love and loyalty.

But who was Frank? Francis Philbrick (whom Fanny did call Frank) does not seem to fit the statement in the last line, since Fanny seems to have met him *after* Bandelier's death. Frank Bigler, cousin of Will Barnes, the author and old Bandelier friend, is a stronger possibility, since Fanny certainly leaned heavily on him immediately after Adolph's death. But there is no evidence that Fanny was in touch with Bigler at this time, nor is it even certain that he was still alive.

All in all, it seems that much of this dramatic romanticism, like the automatic writing, was simply wish fulfillment. It does show something of the deep loneliness that, notwithstanding the determined cheerfulness of her correspondence with Ina and others, welled up in Fanny during this period. It is probably best summed up in the one letter included with the automatic writing that seems to be an answer from Fanny. Written both in English and German, and decipherable only in part, it rings with despair and desolation.

Dolfi: What shall I do?

I cannot help myself any more.

Will you let me go to the wall

NO, I know your love I know you will help me, do let me know that you will not do that you will help me and will I ever be happy again? byn da me [?]

Dolfi hilf mir ich bitte dich! [Dolfi, help me; I beg you!]

If the stay in Mexico represented an emotional nadir for Fanny, the next few years in the United States were perhaps somewhat brighter. Living at 1915 Blakemore Avenue in Nashville, she received considerable support from Fisk University, an important center of higher education for African American students since the late nineteenth century. She also occasionally lectured on her archaeological specialties at Vanderbilt University. In 1932, the first volume of Fanny's projected translation of *A History of Ancient Mexico,* by the sixteenth-century Franciscan Bernardino de Sahagun, was published by Fisk University Press. On October 3 of that year, Fanny sent Hewett a copy of the newly published book, and she received a friendly reply from Hewett, who by this time was at the University of Southern California. The enmity that Fanny earlier felt for Hewett seems now to have vanished.

The following year, on March 27, 1933, Fanny drew up her will and had it witnessed by neighbors, Mr. and Mrs. L. B. Smelser, apparently friends she had made since moving to Nashville. Her executors were Mr. Smelser and a Mr. J. H. Simpson of Nashville. The will left all of her money, investments that she might own, and the proceeds of her group life insurance policy to her two sisters equally. Mama Ritter was not mentioned, and it seems likely that she had died sometime earlier. There were a number of small bequests, including books, curios, and Spanish antiques to the Social Science Department at Fisk.

The paintings were distributed among friends. Perhaps the key bequest was the following: "All pictures of my late husband and myself, his bust, his books (written by him) and his and my personal documents, I bequeath to the Research Library of Anthropology (Museum) at Santa Fe, New Mexico."These items are currently in the Bandelier collection in the History Library of the Museum of New Mexico.

Fanny resigned her position at Fisk University, probably at the end of the spring semester, 1935. Why she left Fisk is not clear, but it may have been simply that she had reached retirement age (she was 65 at the time). Meanwhile, Fanny had been trying for some years to dispose of Adolph's journals. At some time while she was still at Fisk, she had offered to let the American Museum of Natural History have the South American journals. There is also a letter from Clark Wissler of AMNH dated July 3, 1935, concerning Fanny's last project, the publication of parts of Adolph's southwestern journals:

> I am grieved to note that you are out of a job at present and sincerely hope that some[thing] may be found to readjust the matter.
>
> It so happens that we have made arrangements for the year which practically exhaust our small budget. And so at present I see no way to finance further work upon the journals.

The project Wissler referred to was Fanny's attempt to publish the Hemenway expedition segment (1886–89) of Bandelier's southwestern journals. As early as 1934, the Press of the Pioneers in New York had issued a four-page prospectus on these journals. The project was an ambitious one, with Mary Austin producing an introduction and Warren King Moorehead "an appreciation." Fanny had typed and edited the journals for these years, her editing often taking the shape of suppression, especially when Bandelier had been critical of his father or had commented unfavorably on other family members or matters. The journal project failed for lack of money, as Fanny's correspondence with Wissler indicates. Bandelier's southwestern journals were eventually published in four volumes by the present authors and Elizabeth M. Lange in the years between 1966 and 1984.

Fanny was still living at the Blakemore address in 1936, and there, on November 10, she died. There was little notice in the newspapers and virtually none in the anthropological and historical journals of the time. According to Fanny's obituary in the *Albuquerque Journal:*

> Word of the death of Mrs. Fanny Bandelier, widow of the late historian and anthropologist, Adolph F. Bandelier, at Nashville, Tenn., was received here Tuesday.
>
> Mrs. Bandelier who had been working on translations from the Spanish for the second volume of her work "Sahagun," at Fiske University died Nov. 10.
>
> She was the second wife of Professor Bandelier, well-known in New Mexico for his discoveries several decades ago and for his book, "The Delight Makers."

Fanny's death led to a lively struggle over the manuscripts of the Bandelier journals (probably only those of the Hemenway years) and transcripts, which were in the hands of a company called Wilson-Erickson in New York. This company had done some work on the journals, was out of hand sixty dollars, and so did not wish to release them. A compromise with Hewett allowed the School of American Research and Wilson-Erickson to split this amount, and the journals were returned to New Mexico.

On March 16, 1938, Frederick Webb Hodge, at the Southwest Museum in Los Angeles, wrote a letter to Hewett suggesting that he had a right to the journals and included copies of the bill of sale and accompanying letter Fanny had sent him in 1924. Hodge proposed that the journals eventually go to the Southwest Museum. Hewett was not amused by this (presumably tongue-in-cheek) suggestion. In a reply dated April 23, he said rather stiffly that the bill of sale was probably never recorded and since no claim was made under it when the will was probated, the bill would have no legal standing. In any case, the Museum of New Mexico ended up with the journals, which would seem to be what Fanny had intended some years previously.

In a sense Fanny's life ended on a note of anticlimax, with various institutions squabbling over her collections of documents. Though in the 1940 centennial celebration of Bandelier's birth held in Santa Fe, New Mexico, there was praise of Fanny, she remained (and remains to this day) very much in the shadow of her famous husband. Had she been born a half-century later, Fanny's life might have been more assertive, and she might well have been famous in her own right. Her power to charm and draw (one might almost say manipulate) people was tremendous, and her flair for language, her ability to work long and hard hours, and her strong sense of historical methodology might well have made her an independent scholar of considerable stature.

There was also in Fanny's make-up a strong desire to serve. Her perceived role vis-à-vis her husband was that of loyal assistant; indeed, loyalty was Fanny's overwhelming virtue. How much of this was due to the Victorian romanticism of her birth and upbringing in a middle-class German-Swiss home, and how much to her own personality, cannot now be known. But as we said earlier in this book, Adolph Bandelier was an exceptionally charismatic figure and one who demanded and received loyalty.

Although she certainly depended on and identified with her husband, Fanny Bandelier had strengths of her own. She was at ease in the academic worlds of archaeology and history, especially in archival studies. Adolph and Fanny worked together constantly, and an appreciable amount of the later writing that has gone under Bandelier's name likely was the result of close collaboration with his wife. But at the end, in the final two decades of her life, Fanny was forced to stand alone.

Epilogue

IN THE YEARS following Fanny's death, other portions of the Bandelier story moved slowly toward resolution. One of the major projects of Bandelier's southwestern years, his "Histoire de la colonisation et des missions de Sonora, Chihuahua, Nouveau-Mexique et Arizona jusqu'a l'annee 1700"—1,400 foolscap pages of text and four large volumes of 502 sketches, photographs, and watercolors, plus an atlas—had been sent to the Vatican in the autumn of 1887. The text, however, had somehow disappeared. So far as we know, Bandelier never saw it again, nor did Fanny ever see it.

Over subsequent decades a number of scholars, including ourselves, attempted to locate this important manuscript. One such person, the historian Ernest J. Burrus, S. J., who was doing extensive work in the Vatican archives in Rome after World War II, continually reminded his co-workers to be on the alert for the manuscript. Finally, at the end of June 1964, an archival worker named Alberto Magistri came upon the document stacked in a storeroom together with a group of other uncatalogued manuscripts. Father Burrus immediately began planning publication of the "Histoire." In 1969, the Jesuit Historical Institute in Rome published volume one of Burrus's projected multivolume *A History of the Southwest*. It appeared in both hardback and paperback and included an introduction in English and a catalogue of the illustrations with texts in French and English. A supplement to volume one, also printed in 1969, included thirty sketches in color and ten maps as well.

A second volume of the *History*—parts I and II of the "Histoire"—

contained the French text with annotations and summaries in English. Burrus published this volume in 1987, in collaboration with Madeleine Turrell Rodack. At the time of his death in 1991, Father Burrus had completed the manuscript containing parts III through VII of the "Histoire." It is now in the hands of the Jesuit Historical Institute, and we understand that publication in two volumes is planned for the near future.

Meanwhile, Dr. Rodack prepared an English translation of the "Histoire" manuscript. Three chapters of it were published in the *Journal of the Southwest* (vol. 30, no. 1, Spring, 1988), and the entire text will be published as a separate book when funds become available.

In addition to publishing Burrus's edition of the "Histoire," Vatican scholars have produced sets of Kodachrome slides of the 502 illustrations—photographs, watercolors, maps, and so forth. These sets have been acquired by the Pius XII Library at St. Louis University; by the University of Arizona Library in Tucson; by the Bancroft Library at the University of California, Berkeley; by the Amerind Foundation in Dragoon, Arizona; and perhaps by other institutions as well.

Another bit of unfinished business regarding Adolph F. Bandelier was the ultimate disposition of his remains. Immediately following his death in March 1914, Bandelier had been buried in the Municipal Cemetery of San Fernando in Seville, Spain. Fanny Bandelier had wanted to take Adolph's body back to the United States for reburial, possibly at Bandelier National Monument, but the cost was quite beyond her means. She had also considered taking Adolph to Bern to be buried alongside Papa Bandelier. Bandelier, however, remained in the San Fernando grave for the next thirteen years. In the summer of 1927, Dr. France V. Scholes, of the Carnegie Institution, happened to be working in the Seville archives. At Fanny Bandelier's request, Scholes arranged for Bandelier's bones to be transferred to a crypt, on which he paid a ten-year deposit.

As this ten-year period neared its end, there was some feeling among Bandelier's friends and colleagues that his remains should be returned to the United States and perhaps be reburied at Bandelier National Monument. Edgar Lee Hewett of the School of American Research (SAR) in Santa Fe, however, opposed this plan, and the United States Park Service was similarly lukewarm to the idea. In addition, Spain was in the midst of a savage civil war, which made the actual movement of the bones difficult. Hewett did provide for a permanent crypt and marker to be purchased. The marker was to read, "Adolph F. Bandelier, born Switzerland, August 6, 1840, died Sevilla, March 18, 1914, a great American Scholar."

The placement of the bones in a permanent repository with the engraved marker was arranged for during the turmoil of war, and it is uncertain whether or not the reburial was actually carried out. In the decades following the Spanish Civil War, various people, including one of the present authors (Riley), visited the San Fernando cemetery but were unable to locate Bandelier's crypt.

Finally, in 1974, at the urging of various influential people, Douglas W. Schwartz, president of the School of American Research, reopened the matter of Bandelier's remains. Booker Kelley, attorney for SAR, visited Seville and attempted to find the crypt. Like previous searchers, Kelley initially failed—the records were nowhere to be found. Eventually, after considerable political pressure was placed on the Seville authorities, cemetery workers identified an unmarked crypt as Bandelier's burial place, the marker having disappeared, perhaps during the Civil War. Finally, on March 3, 1977, the remains arrived at SAR in Santa Fe.

Several years of indecision and delays followed. The United States National Park Service (NPS), citing its general policy against burials on park property, refused to have a Bandelier grave at Bandelier National Monument. A number of alternative suggestions were made: that Bandelier be buried on the SAR grounds, that he be interred at the old Bandelier residence on East de Vargas Street, or that the burial take place in the "Bandelier Garden" at El Zaguán on Canyon Road in Santa Fe. All these places were eventually deemed unsuitable for one reason or another. During these months, Bandelier's remains resided in a simple wooden chest under a table in the SAR boardroom.

The matter was at last resolved in 1980, when NPS authorities conceded that although the regulations banned burials on NPS land, they said nothing about cremations. Accordingly, Bandelier's bones were cremated, and on October 16, 1980, a small group—Schwartz and Mrs. Jeton Brown of the SAR staff; John D. Hunter, superintendent, and Kevin McKibben, chief ranger, of Bandelier National Monument; Dan Murphy of the Southwest regional office of NPS, and Charles H. Lange—participated in scattering the scholar's ashes near the north wall of Frijoles Canyon, between the visitors' center and the ruined pueblo of Tyuonyi. Fanny's wish, after sixty-six years, was finally fulfilled.

Appendix
Adolph F. Bandelier's Bibliography

WORKS BY ADOLPH F. BANDELIER
(ALSO ADOLPHE F., ADOLF F., AND AD. F.)

1858   "Switzerland and the Swiss." St. Louis *Republican,* February 23.

1870   "Brief an Prof. Wolf betreffend Temperatur, Gewitter und Polar-lichter, mit Diagrammen, datiert Highland, den 4. August, 1870." *Vierteljahrschrift der Naturforschenden Gesellschaft Zurich,* pp. 380–95. Editor, Dr. Rudolf Wolf, Professor of Astronomy, Zurich.

1871   "History of Helvetia Township, Madison County, Illinois." Printed in German translation as "Geschichte des Townships 'Helvetia,' Madison County, Illinois," *Highland Union,* 1876, translator Jakob Machtleu [Machtlin].

1873   Letter to Lewis Henry Morgan in regard to the dependability of the statements of authors of early works on Spanish America, dated Highland, Illinois, Dec. 20, 1873. Original letter in archives, University of Rochester, New York. Reprinted 1931 in *Lewis Henry Morgan, Social Evolutionist,* by Bernhard J. Stern, pp. 112–15. University of Chicago Press.

1874–78   "Highland, Illinois." Article in *Johnson's New Universal Cyclopedia.*

1876   "Uber einige Spuren von Verbindungen zwischen Amerika und den ostlichen Erdteilen vor der Zeit des Columbus." *New Yorker Staatszeitung,* May 1–Aug. 15.

1876–77   "Uber die Sage des 'Dorado' in nordlichen Sud-Amerika." *New Yorker Staatszeitung,* April 16, 23, 30, 1876–July 1877.

1877   "On the Art of War and Mode of Warfare of the Ancient Mexicans." *Tenth Annual Report of the Peabody Museum of American Archaeology and Ethnology,* Cambridge, Massachusetts, pp. 95–161.

1877   Review (unsigned) of E. G. Squier's *Peru: Incidents of Travel and Exploration in the Land of the Incas. The Nation,* vol. 24, June 21, pp. 367–69, and June 28, pp. 383–84.

1877   Review of Lewis Henry Morgan's *Ancient Society. The Nation,* vol. 25, July, pp. 92–93, and Dec., pp. 107–108.

1877   Letter to Lewis Henry Morgan on the probable reception of Morgan's *Ancient Society* by anthropologists, dated Highland, Illinois, Aug. 8, 1877. Original letter in archives, University of Rochester, New York. Reprinted 1931 in *Lewis Henry Morgan, Social Evolutionist,* by Bernhard J. Stern, p. 196. University of Chicago Press.

1878   "Comment on the Work of Aug. Le Plongeon." *The Nation,* vol. 26, p. 135.

1878   "Comment on Dr. Gustav Bruhl: *Die Culturvolkes Alt-Amerikas.*" Cincinnati *Volksfreund,* February 11, 1878.

1878   "On the Distribution and Tenure of Lands, and the Customs with Respect to Inheritance, among the Ancient Mexicans." *Eleventh Annual Report of the Peabody Museum of American Archaeology and Ethnology,* Cambridge, Massachusetts, pp. 385–448.

1878   "Comment on Ph. Valentini and His *The Mexican Calendar Stone.*" *The Nation,* vol. 27, no. 684, p. 84.

1878   "Comment by Ph. Valentini on *The Mexican Calendar Stone,* with Rebuttal." *The Nation,* vol. 27, no. 690, pp. 176–77.

1878   Comment (unsigned review) on E. B. Tylor's *Researches into the Early History of Mankind,* 1878 edition. *The Nation,* vol. 27, August 8, p. 840.

1879   "The National Museum of Mexico and the Sacrificial Stone." *American Antiquarian and Oriental Journal,* vol. 2, no. 1, pp. 15–29.

1879   "Des Calpullis mexicains; de leur administration de leur origine et du principe communiste qu'ils impliquent." *Proceedings of the Third Annual Meeting of the International Congress of Americanists,* Brussels, vol. 1, pp. 58–60.

1879   "On the Sources for Aboriginal History of Spanish America." *Proceedings of the American Association for the Advancement of Science,* 1878 (St. Louis), pp. 315–37. Salem, Massachusetts.

1879   Review (unsigned) of E. B. Tylor's *Researches into the Early History of Mankind,* 1878 edition. *The Nation,* vol. 28, p. 170.

1879   "Sources of Spanish American History," signed "A. D." *The Nation,* vol. 28, p. 265.

1879   Review (unsigned) of Ad. Bastian's *Die Culturlander des Alten Amerika. The Nation,* vol. 28, pp. 357–58.

1879   "An Important Discovery for Mexican Antiquities." *The Nation,* vol. 29, Nov. 20, pp. 347–48.

1880   "On the Social Organization and Mode of Government of the Ancient Mexicans." *Twelfth Annual Report of the Peabody Museum of American Archaeology and Ethnology* (1879), Cambridge, Massachusetts, pp. 557–699.

1880   Review of *Primitive Manners and Customs,* by J. A. Farrer. *The Nation,* vol. 30, pp. 33–34.

1880   Review (unsigned) of Charles Rau's *The Palenque Tablet in the U.S. National Museum. The Nation,* vol. 30, pp. 423–25.

1880–92   Daily journals. (An earlier journal for the years 1877–79 has been mentioned but never found.) The 1880–92 journals are in the Bandelier collection of the History Library, Museum of New Mexico, Santa Fe. Journals for 1892–1911 are also in this collection: Box 71, 1880–89, and Box 72, 1890–1911.

1881   "Historical Introduction to Studies among the Sedentary Indians of New Mexico." *Papers of the Archaeological Institute of America,* Boston, American Series, vol. 1, no. 1, pp. 1–33. Second edition, 1883. Reprinted 1976, together with "A Visit to the Aboriginal Ruins in the Valley of the Rio Pecos," by AMS Press and Kraus Reprint Company.

1881   "A Visit to the Aboriginal Ruins in the Valley of the Rio Pecos." *Papers of the Archaeological Institute of America,* Boston, American Series, vol. 1, no. 2, pp. 34–133. A "second edition," in one volume with "Historical Introduction to Studies among the Sedentary Indians of New Mexico," was published by Cupples, Upham, and Company, Boston, and by N. Trubner and Company, London. This volume was reprinted in 1976 by AMS Press and Kraus Reprint Company.

1881   "Bandelier's Researches in the Southwest." *The Nation,* vol. 32, p. 94.

1881   "Letter regarding Cochiti." *Second Annual Report of the Executive Committee of the Archaeological Institute of America,* Cambridge, Massachusetts, pp. 19–20.

1882   "Kin and Clan." Address delivered before the Historical Society of New Mexico, Santa Fe, April 28, 1882. Reprinted, Santa Fe *Daily New Mexican,* April 29, 1882, and *New Mexico Historical Review,* vol. 8, no. 3, July, 1933, pp. 165–75.

1882   "Notes on the Bibliography of Yucatan and Central America." *Proceedings of the American Antiquarian Society,* Worcester, Massachusetts, new series, vol. 1, 1880–81, pp. 82–118.

1882 "Reisebriefe aus dem sudwestlichen Nordamerika. I. La Junta (Colorado), den 16. Marz 1882." *Das Ausland,* 1882, no. 37, pp. 726–30.

1882 "Reisebriefe aus dem sudwestlichen Nordamerika. II. Santa-Fé (Neumexiko), den 21. Marz 1882." *Das Ausland,* 1882, pp. 790–94.

1882 "Reisebriefe aus dem sudwestlichen Nordamerika. II. (Schlusz.)." *Das Ausland,* 1882, pp. 812–16.

1882 "Reisebriefe aus dem sudwestlichen Nordamerika. III. Pueblo 'San Buenaventura de Cochiti,' County von Bernalillo, Neumexiko, den 22. April 1882." *Das Ausland,* 1882, no. 47, pp. 923–29.

1882 "Historical Introduction: Part II." Manuscript, 100 pp.; majority of pages have associated notes and citations on back side of sheet. Bandelier collection, History Library, Museum of New Mexico.

1883 "Vocabulary of the Keres Language of Cochiti." Mentioned by Bandelier in *Bulletin of the Archaeological Institute of America,* I, Boston, 1883, p. 17. Manuscript (Ms 970.69B) now in Charles F. Lummis collection, Southwest Museum, Los Angeles.

1883 "Report by A. F. Bandelier on His Investigations in New Mexico in the Spring and Summer of 1882." *Bulletin of the Archaeological Institute of America,* I, Boston, pp. 13–33.

1883 Letter dated Fort Apache, Arizona, 29 April 1883. *Die Westliche Post,* St. Louis. Addressed to "Lieber Herr Preetorius," the letter mentioned various pueblos and pueblo remains.

1883 "Die indianischen Ruinen des Westens." *Anzeiger des Westens,* Mittwoch (St. Louis), Sept. 26.

1884 *Report of an Archaeological Tour in Mexico in 1881.* Papers of the Archaeological Institute of America, American Series II, University Press, Boston. Identical second edition printed as *An Archaeological Reconnaissance into Mexico.* Cupples and Hurd, publishers, Boston. The Algonquin Press. Reprinted 1976 by AMS Press and Kraus Reprint Company.

1884 "Reports by A. F. Bandelier on His Investigations in New Mexico during the Years 1883–1884." Appendix in *Fifth Annual Report of the Executive Committee, Archaeological Institute of America,* Cambridge, Massachusetts, pp. 55–98. A reprint of Bandelier's Casa Grande account appears in "Casa Grande, Arizona," by J. W. Fewkes, *Twenty-eighth Annual Report of the Bureau of American Ethnology,* pp. 71–72, Washington, D.C., 1912.

1884 "Ein Brief uber Akoma von Adolf F. Bandelier. Pueblo von San Estevan de Akoma (Valenzia County), Neu-Mexiko, den 20. Mai [1882]." *Das Ausland,* 1884, no. 13, pp. 241–43.

1884   "Reisebrief aus dem sudwestlichen Nordamerika. San Buenaventura de Kochiti, Bernalillo County, Neu-Mexiko, den 22. April." *Das Ausland,* 1884, no. 31, pp. 601–607.

1884   "Reisebriefe aus dem sudwestlichen Nordamerika. (Schlusz.)" *Das Ausland,* 1884, no. 32, pp. 625–33.

1885   "The Romantic School in American Archaeology." Paper read before the New York Historical Society, Feb. 3, 1885, New York. Reprinted by Trow's Printing and Book Binding Company, 1885.

1885   "Cibola I [I–VIII]." *New Yorker Staatszeitung,* May 24, 31; June 7, 14, 21, 28; July 5. "Cibola II (Zweite Serie) I–IV." *New Yorker Staatszeitung,* Oct 25; Nov. 1, 8, 15.

1885   "Ancient Pueblos in and about Santa Fe." In *Aztlan,* by W. G. Ritch, 6th ed., pp. 199–202, Boston. French translation in *Six mois dans les Montanges-rocheuses,* by H. Beaugrand, pp. 146–53, Montreal, 1890.

1885   Letter to W. G. Ritch, secretary of the Territory of New Mexico, at Santa Fe, dated Fort Huachuca, Arizona, February 15, 1884, relating to the prehistory of Santa Fe, 1885. French translation in *Six mois dans les Montanges-rocheuses,* by H. Beaugrand, pp. 146–53, Montreal, 1890.

1885   "Ein Brief von Adolf F. Bandelier uber seine Reisen im sudwestlichen Nordamerika. Highland Illinois, V. St. N. A., 12 Oktober 1883." *Das Ausland,* vol. 58, pp. 974–75.

1885   "Der Indianer Ausbruch in Arizona und der Feldzug gegen die Apaches in Neu-Mexiko." *Die Westliche Post,* St. Louis, 21, 28 June.

1885   "The Apache Outbreak." *The Nation,* vol. 41, no. 1044, pp. 8–9.

1885(?)   "Po-se (A Tale of San Ildefonso)." *New Mexico Historical Review,* vol. 1, July 1926, pp. 335–49. Edgar F. Goad noted, "This ms. was left by Bandelier with Mrs. Samuel Eldodt of Chamita, N. M., probably written in 1885."

1885   "The Progressive Indian: What Advanced Civilization and the Winchester Have Done for the Red Man." St. Louis *Globe-Democrat,* December 26, p. 12.

1885(?)   "Die Grenzgebiete der Vereinigte Staaten und Mexiko." *Verhandlungen der Gesellschaft fur Erdkunde zu Dresden,* Berlin, 1885, nos. 5–6.

1885–86   "Uber die Sage des 'Dorado' in nordlichen Sud-Amerika." *New Yorker Staatszeitung,* continued from 1876–77. According to Frederick W. Hodge, this was the German original of *The Gilded Man* (1893).

1886   "Why New Mexico Does Not Flourish." *The Nation,* vol. 42, pp. 70–71.

1886   "Must We Have Another Indian War?" *The Nation,* vol. 42, pp. 397–98.

1886   "San Bernardino Chalchihuapan. Ein mexikanisches Abenteuer." *National Zeitung,* Berlin, vols. 581, 593, 595.

1886   "Die neu-mexikanischen 'Pueblos.'" *New Yorker Staatszeitung,* Jan. 10, 17, 24, 31.

1886   "Quivira, I–IV." *New Yorker Staatszeitung,* Feb. 21, 28; Mar. 7, 14.

1886   Review of John G. Bourke's *An Apache Campaign in the Sierra Madre . . . 1883. The Nation,* March 11, 1886, no. 1080, p. 222.

1886   "Alvar Núñez Cabeza de Vaca, the First Overland Traveler of European Descent, and His Journey from Florida to the Pacific Coast—1528–1536." *Magazine of Western History,* Cleveland, vol. 5, July, pp. 327–36.

1886   "Das Alter der Stadt Santa Fe, Neu-Mexiko." *New Yorker Staatszeitung,* June 20.

1886   "Southwestern Pine Timber." *The Nation,* vol. 43, no. 1096, p. 8.

1886   "La decouverte du Nouveau-Mexique par le moine franciscain frere Marcos de Nice en 1539." *Revue d'Ethnographie,* Paris, vol. 5, pp. 34–38, 117–34, 193–212. Published in Spanish as "Historia del descubrimiento de Nuevo Mexico por el monje franciscano Fray Marcos de Niza en 1539," *El Boletín Popular,* Jan. 17–Mar. 7, 1889. Translated by Dr. L. Zabala.

1886   "The Discovery of New Mexico by Fray Marcos de Nizza." *Magazine of Western History,* Cleveland, vol. 5, Sept., pp. 659–70. Reprinted in *New Mexico Historical Review,* Santa Fe, vol. 4, no. 1, Jan. 1929, pp. 28–44. Condensed reprint in *Masterkey,* Los Angeles, vol. 2, no. 8, April 1929, pp. 5–15.

1886   "Geronimo." *New Yorker Staatszeitung,* July 5, 12, 17. Three letters written at Santa Fe in June and July 1886.

1886   "Archaeological Chronology." *The Nation,* vol. 43, pp. 132–33.

1886   "Das Gemetzel von Cholula (1519)." *New Yorker Staatszeitung,* Sept. 5, 12, 19.

1886   "Removal of the Apaches from Arizona." *The Nation,* vol. 43, no. 1106, Sept. 9, pp. 208–9.

1886   Review (unsigned) of John F. McLennan's *Studies in Ancient History. The Nation,* vol. 43, no. 1119, p. 483.

1886   "Briefe aus Neu-Mexiko. I. Santa Fe (Neu-Mexiko), 5 Juli 188★ [*sic*]." *Das Ausland,* 1886, pp. 451–56. (Includes accounts of the Fourth of July, Navahos, Acoma, Chaco.)

1886   "Briefe aus Neu-Mexiko (Fortzetzung.)" *Das Ausland,* 1886, pp. 476–79. (Includes Acoma, history.)

1886   "Briefe aus Neu-Mexiko (Fortzetzung.)" *Das Ausland,* 1886, pp. 498–99; II. Ojos Calientes von Las Vegas (Neu-Mexiko), 17 Juli 188★ [*sic*], pp. 499–500. (Includes Pueblo Revolt, reconquest, Hot Springs.)

1886   "Briefe aus Neu-Mexiko (Fortsetzung.)" *Das Ausland,* 1886, pp. 516–17. (Includes Hot Springs, Las Vegas, Rio Grande, Bernalillo.)

1886   "Briefe aus Neu-Mexiko (Fortsetzung.)" *Das Ausland,* 1886, pp. 535–38. (Includes Bernalillo, Albuquerque, Ladrones, Belen, Socorro, Piros.)

1886   "Briefe aus Neu-Mexiko (Fortsetzung.)" *Das Ausland,* 1886, pp. 555–58. (Includes San Marcial, Mesilla, Jornado del Muerto, Santa Fe, Galisteo, Gran Quivira.)

1887   "Irrigation in the Southwest." *The Nation,* vol. 45, no. 1172, p. 474.

1887–88 "Histoire de la colonisation et des missions de Sonora, Chihuahua, Nouveau-Mexique, et Arizona jusqu'a l'annee 1700." Manuscript, 1,400 foolscap pages, 400 watercolor drawings by the author, in four volumes, with an atlas; in Vatican library, Rome. Manuscripts, Vat. Lat. 14112–14116.

1888   Letter on Gran Quivira, addressed to S. B. Evans, dated Belen, New Mexico, Jan. 21, 1883. *Saturday Evening Post,* Dec. 1.

1888   Review of Daniel G. Brinton's *Ancient Nahuatl Poetry. The Nation,* vol. 46, no. 1179, pp. 102–103.

1888   "Die Kirchen und Kirchen-Ornamente von Neu-Mexiko aus der spanischen Zeit." *New Yorker Staatszeitung,* Jan. 1, p. 8.

1888   "Letter on the Progress of Archaeological and Ethnological Research in America, Especially in the United States, by Ad. F. Bandelier, Santa Fe, New Mexico, May 4, 1888." *Ninth Annual Report of the Archaeological Institute of America,* Cambridge, Massachusetts, pp. 55–61.

1888   "The Betrayer of La Salle." *The Nation,* vol. 47, pp. 166–67.

1888   "Preliminary Report on the Most Valuable INSCRIPTIONS Still Visible at the Rock 'EL MORRO.'" Manuscript (917,89B), Southwest Museum, Los Angeles; another copy in the archives of the Peabody Museum, Harvard University.

1889   "Archaeological Work in Arizona and New Mexico during 1888–89." *Tenth Annual Report of the Archaeological Institute of America,* Cambridge, Massachusetts, Appendix 3, pp. 106–108.

1889   "New Mexican Spanish Antiquities." *The Nation,* vol. 48, pp. 265–66.

1889   "Jean L'Archeveque." *New Yorker Staatszeitung,* Mar. 24.

1889   Review of Justin Winsor's *Aboriginal America. The Nation,* vol. 49, pp. 134–35.

1889 "Quivira, I and II." *The Nation,* vol. 49, Oct. 31, Nov. 7, pp. 348–49, 365–66.

1889 "Datos historicos sobre Paso del Norte." *El Centinela,* Ciudad Juárez (Paso del Norte), Oct. 20–27.

1889(?) "Ein Hexenprozess in Neu-Mexiko vor vierunddreissig Jahren." *Belletristisches Journal,* New York.

1889 "Historia del descubrimiento de Nuevo Mexico por el monje franciscano Fray Marcos de Niza en 1539." *El Boletín Popular,* Jan. 17–Mar. 7, Santa Fe. Translated by Dr. L. Zabala from the original French publication (*Revue d'Ethnographie,* 1886).

1889 Review (unsigned) of C. N. Starcke's *The Primitive Family in Its Origin and Development. The Nation,* vol. 48, no. 1250, June 13, pp. 493–94.

1889(?) "Memoranda of Investigations Required." Unpublished ms., 2 pp., Hodge-Cushing collection, folder #174, Southwest Museum, Los Angeles.

1890 *Contributions to the History of the Southwestern Portion of the United States.* Papers of the Archaeological Institute of America, American Series, V, Cambridge, Massachusetts. Reprinted 1976 by AMS Press and Kraus Reprint Company. Includes the following parts: Part I, "Sketch of the Knowledge which the Spaniards in Mexico possessed of the Countries north of the Province of New Galicia, previous to the return of Cabeza de Vaca, in the Year 1536," pp. 3–23. Part II, "Alvar Núñez Cabeza de Vaca, and the Importance of his Wanderings from the Mexican Gulf to the Slope of the Pacific for Spanish Explorations towards New Mexico and Arizona," pp. 24–67. Part III, "Spanish Efforts to penetrate to the north of Sinaloa, between the Years 1536 and 1539," pp. 68–105. Part IV, "Fray Marcos of Nizza," pp. 106–78. Part V, "The Expedition of Pedro de Villazur, from Santa Fe, New Mexico, to the Banks of the Platte River, in search of the French and the Pawnees, in the Year 1720," pp. 179–206.

1890 "Die Koshare. Eine Erzahlung aus dem Leben der Pueblo-Indianer von Neu-Mexiko." *Belletristisches Journal,* New York, Jan. 1–May 14.

1890 *The Delight Makers.* Dodd, Mead and Company, New York. Reprinted 1916 by Dodd, Mead; 1918 by Mrs. Fanny R. Bandelier; 1946 by Dodd, Mead; and 1971 by Harcourt Brace Jovanovich.

1890 "The Historical Archives of the Hemenway Southwestern Archaeological Expedition." *Proceedings of the Seventh Annual Meeting of the International Congress of Americanists* (1888), Berlin, pp. 450–59.

1890   "The Unification of Mexico." *The Nation,* vol. 50, pp. 409–10.

1890   "The Industrial Condition of Mexico." *The Nation,* vol. 50, pp. 427–29.

1890   "The Ruins of Casa Grande, I and II." *The Nation,* vol. 51, pp. 166–68, 185–87.

1890   "The Siege of La Paz . . . I." Reprinted from *U.S. Catholic Historical Society Record,* pp. 243–64.

1890   "Fray Juan de Padilla, the First Catholic Missionary Martyr in Eastern Kansas, 1542." *American Catholic Quarterly Review,* Philadelphia, vol. 15, no. 59, pp. 551–65.

1890   "Die Mineral-Quellen von Jemez, im westliche Theile Central-Neu-Mexiko." *Die Westliche Post,* St. Louis, Jan. 26.

1890   "Huaynopa." *Die Westliche Post,* St. Louis, Mar. 23.

1890   "Die literarischen und historischen Schatze in Santa Fe, Neu-Mexiko." *Die Westliche Post,* St. Louis, May 25, June 1.

1890   "Three Thousand Volumes: Hon. T. B. Catron Purchases a Much Treasured Library in the City of Mexico." Santa Fe *Daily New Mexican,* April 21.

1890   "Kingdom of New Mexico." Santa Fe *Daily New Mexican.* Part I, "Its Settlement, Occupation and Government by the Spaniards. An Interesting and Complete Historical Sketch from A.D. 1539 to the Year 1800," April 26, vol. 27, no. 56. Part II, "Its Antiquities and Population of the Pueblos; the Habits, Buildings and Doings of the First Inhabitants Prior to and During the Spanish Occupation," May 3, vol. 27, no. 62.

1890   "Indigenous Medicinal Plants of New Mexico." Santa Fe *Daily New Mexican,* May 6, vol. 27, no. 64, p. 2.

1890   "The Franciscan Sepulchres in the Cathedral at Santa Fe." Santa Fe *Daily New Mexican,* May 10, vol. 27, no. 68, p. 2.

1890   "Storming of the Rock and Pueblo of Acoma by Vicente de Zaldívar, 22d, 23d, and 24th of January, 1599." Santa Fe *Daily New Mexican,* May 17, vol. 27, no. 74, p. 2; May 24, vol. 27, no. 80, p. 2.

1890   "The Siege of Santa Fe." Santa Fe *Daily New Mexican,* June 21, vol. 27, no. 103, p. 2; June 28, vol. 27, no. 138, p. 2; and August 9, vol. 27, no. 144, p. 2.

1890   "Historia de la imprenta en Mexico y en Nuevo Mexico." *El Boletín Popular,* Santa Fe, June 5.

1890(?) Eighty-six articles in *Catholic Cyclopedia.* Listed by title in *Pioneers in American Anthropology: The Bandelier-Morgan Letters, 1873–1883,* edited by Leslie A. White. University of New Mexico Press,

Albuquerque, 1940, vol. 1, p. 98. Also listed in *The Southwestern Journals of Adolph F. Bandelier,* vol. 4, by Charles H. Lange, Carroll L. Riley, and Elizabeth M. Lange, 1984, pp. 680–81.

1890–92 *Final Report of Investigations among the Indians of the Southwestern United States, Carried on Mainly in the Years from 1880 to 1885, Parts I and II.* Papers of the Archaeological Institute of America, American Series, III and IV, Cambridge, Massachusetts, pp. 1–319 and pp. 1–591. Reprinted with 1942 index in 1976 by AMS Press and Kraus Reprint Company.

1891 "The Southwestern Land Court." *The Nation,* vol. 52, p. 437.

1891 "Existing Cave Dwellers." *The Nation,* vol. 53, pp. 408–409.

1891 "Historic San Miguel Chapel." Santa Fe *Daily New Mexican,* vol. 28, no. 223, Nov. 7, p. 4.

1892 "The 'Montezuma' of the Pueblo Indians." *American Anthropologist,* old series, vol. 5, Oct., pp. 319–26.

1892 "An Outline of the Documentary History of the Zuni Tribe." *Journal of American Ethnology and Archaeology,* Cambridge, Massachusetts, vol. 3, no. 4, pp. 1–115.

1892 Review (unsigned) of Frank Wilson Blackmar's *Spanish Institutions of the Southwest. The Nation,* vol. 54, no. 1388, p. 94.

1892 Review of H. O. Ladd's *The Story of New Mexico. The Nation,* vol. 54, p. 237.

1893 *The Gilded Man (El Dorado) and Other Pictures of the Spanish Occupancy of America.* D. Appleton and Company, New York. Reprinted 1962 by Rio Grande Press, Chicago.

1897 "Bandelier's Researches in Peru and Bolivia," by F. W. Hodge, based on a report written to him by Bandelier. *American Anthropologist,* old series, vol. 10, Sept., pp. 303–11; also issued separately.

1903 Review of F. C. Nicholas's *Around the Caribbean and Across Panama. The Nation,* vol. 77, p. 411.

1903 Review of W. H. Johnson's *Pioneer Spaniards in America. The Nation,* vol. 77, p. 473.

1904 "Aboriginal Myths and Traditions Concerning the Island of Titicaca, Bolivia." *American Anthropologist,* new series, vol. 6, pp. 197–239; also issued separately.

1904 "Aboriginal Trephining in Bolivia." *American Anthropologist,* new series, vol. 6, pp. 440–46; also issued separately.

1904 Review of G. W. James's *The Indians of the Painted Desert Region. The Nation,* vol. 78, pp. 156–57.

1904 Review of Rollo Ogden's *William Hickling Prescott. The Nation,* vol. 78, p. 357.

1904   Review of A. J. Burdick's *The Mystic Mid-region. The Nation,* vol. 78, p. 391.

1904   Review of Mary Austin's *The Land of Little Rain. The Nation,* vol. 78, pp. 391–92.

1904   Review of G. P. Winship's *The Journey of Coronado. The Nation,* vol. 78, pp. 439–40.

1904   Review of G. A. Dorsey's *The Arapahoe Sun Dance. The Nation,* vol. 78, p. 497.

1904   "Boundary Readjustments in South America." *The Nation,* vol. 79, pp. 155–56.

1904   Review of E. H. Thompson's *Account of Yucatan Ruins. The Nation,* vol. 79, p. 357.

1904   Review of L. H. Morgan's *The League of the Ho-De-No-Sau-Ne, or Iroquois* (a new edition by H. M. Lloyd). *The Nation,* vol. 79, pp. 362–63.

1904   "On the Relative Antiquity of Ancient Peruvian Burials." *Bulletin of the American Museum of Natural History,* New York, no. 20, pp. 217–26.

1904   "The Cross of Carabuco in Bolivia." *American Anthropologist,* new series, vol. 6, pp. 599–628; also issued separately.

1904   Letter to William H. Holmes. National Anthropological Archives, Letters Received: #560.4.

1905   "The Aboriginal Ruins at Sillustani, Peru." *American Anthropologist,* new series, vol. 7, pp. 49–68; also issued separately.

1905   "The Basin of Lake Titicaca." *Bulletin of the American Geographical Society,* no. 37, pp. 449–60.

1905   "Narratives of the Career of Hernando de Soto." *The Nation,* vol. 80, p. 197.

1905   "Introduction." In *The Journey of Alvar Núñez Cabeza de Vaca,* translated by Fanny R. Bandelier, pp. v–xxii. Barnes and Company, New York.

1905   "Letter of Mendoza and Report of Father Marcos of Nizza.— Introductory Note." In *The Journey of Alvar Núñez Cabeza de Vaca,* translated by Fanny R. Bandelier, p. 195. Barnes and Company, New York.

1905   Review of O. T. Mason's *Indian Basketry. The Nation,* vol. 80, p. 219.

1905   "Father De Smet." *The Nation,* vol. 80, pp. 274–75.

1905   Review of B. J. Clinch's *California and Its Missions. The Nation,* vol. 80, p. 404.

1905   "Traditions of Precolumbian Landings on the Western Coast of South America." *American Anthropologist,* new series, vol. 7, pp. 250–70; also issued separately.

1905 "The Truth about Inca Civilization." *Harper's Monthly,* vol. 110, no. 658, pp. 632–40.

1906 "La danse des 'Sicuri,' des Indiens Aymara de la Bolivia." *Boas Anniversary Volume,* New York, pp. 272–82.

1906 Review of Lowery's *Spanish Settlements in the United States. The Nation,* vol. 82, pp. 225–26.

1906 "Traditions of Pre-columbian Earthquakes and Volcanic Eruptions in Western South America." *American Anthropologist,* new series, vol. 8, pp. 47–81; also issued separately.

1906 "Uber Trepanieren unter den heutigen Indianern Bolivias." *Proceedings of the Fourteenth Annual Meeting of the International Congress of Americanists* (1904), Stuttgart, pp. 81–89.

1907 "The Indians and Aboriginal Ruins near Chachapoyas in Northern Peru." *Historical Records and Studies of the United States,* Catholic Historical Society, New York, vol. 5, part 1; also issued separately, 51 pp., 13 plates.

1910 "Documentary History of the Rio Grande Pueblos of New Mexico. I. Bibliographic Introduction." Archaeological Institute of America (Lancaster, Pennsylvania), *Papers of the School of American Archaeology,* no. 13, pp. 1–28. Expanded and reprinted in *Indians of the Rio Grande Valley,* by Bandelier and E. L. Hewett, 1937, pp. 115–241.

1910 *The Islands of Titicaca and Koati.* Hispanic Society of America, New York. Reprinted 1969 by Kraus Reprint Company, New York.

1911 "The Ruins of Tiahuanaco." *Proceedings of the American Antiquarian Society,* Worcester, Massachusetts, no. 21, pp. 218–65.

1913 "Letter to E. L. Hewett on the Age of Santa Fe." *El Palacio,* vol. 1, no. 1, Nov., p. 7.

1914 Extracts from two letters addressed to Charles Eliot Norton, one of which was written at Cochiti in 1880. *El Palacio,* vol. 1, no. 67, April–May, p. 8.

1923, 1926, 1937 *Historical Documents Relating to New Mexico, Nueva Vizcaya, and Approaches Thereto, to 1773.* Three volumes. Collected by Adolph F. A. Bandelier and Fanny R. Bandelier. Spanish text and English translations. Edited with introductions and annotations by Charles Wilson Hackett. Publication 330, Carnegie Institution of Washington, Washington D.C.

1926 "Po-se, a Tale of San Ildefonso Pueblo." *New Mexico Historical Review,* vol. 1, July, pp. 335–49. Probably written in 1885.

1927 Certification regarding facsimiles of two war-god idols of San Juan Pueblo, New Mexico, in the handwriting of Bandelier, who signed as one of the witnesses. Dated San Juan de los Caballeros, March 1, 1889. *Indian Notes,* Museum of the American Indian, Heye Foundation, New York, vol. 4, no. 4, Oct., p. 397.

1929–30 "Documentary History of the Rio Grande Pueblos, New Mexico." *New Mexico Historical Review.* Part I, 1536–1542: vol. 4, Oct. 1929, pp. 303–34; vol. 5, Jan. 1930, pp. 38–66; Apr. 1930, pp. 154–85. Part II, 1542 to 1581: vol. 5, July 1930, pp. 240–62. Part III, 1581 to 1584: vol. 5, Oct. 1930, map, pp. 333–85.

1937 (With Edgar L. Hewett) *Indians of the Rio Grande Valley.* Includes appendix by F. W. Hodge. University of New Mexico, Albuquerque, and School of American Research, Santa Fe. Reprinted 1973 by Cooper Square Publishers, New York.

n.d. "Notes on various inscriptions, primarily from El Morro." Unpublished manuscript. Catron collection (PC 29 807), Archives, Special Collections, University of New Mexico library.

Sources

This biography of Adolph F. Bandelier has been deliberately written with little of the scholarly apparatus common to such books. Except for an inclusive list of Bandelier's own writings, which appears as the appendix, we have used neither a formal bibliography nor footnotes. This does not mean that our scholarship has been hasty or careless. Research on Adolph Bandelier has been part of an agenda covering half our lifetimes, and this biography reflects our considerable insights into Bandelier's life and character. The analysis presented here represents our best judgment of the man, his family, and his associates and grows out of our long exposure to Bandelieriana of all descriptions.

With this book we hope to attract a general as well as a professional audience. We would especially like to introduce a new generation of readers to a man who, for all his miscellanea of virtues and faults, was one of the great scholars and genuinely interesting human beings of his time. His story is full of high adventure, and his journals and letters provide the reader with an intimate look into large segments of his life. Because of Bandelier's habit, for more than three decades, of writing down what concerned and interested him each day, we know the man better than most historical figures are known. But he left much unsaid, and like most biographers, we must choose and judge in attempting to present a coherent picture of Bandelier's life.

The sources discussed here are not intended to be exhaustive but, rather, to indicate major collections of materials we used for this book. The first chapters owe a great deal to scholars who have worked to shed light on the ancestry of Adolph F. Bandelier. Madeleine T. Rodack, especially, has done much to elucidate the origins of the Bandelier family. Particularly valuable has been her collection of Bandelier material obtained through correspondence with Simone Bandelier Sarasin and Eric Rufener and from other contacts in Switzerland; the collection includes letters to and from Adolphe Eugene Bandelier, Marie Senn Bandelier, and Alphonse Bandelier.

A book by Eric Rufener, *Adolphe Francois Bandelier, 1840–1914: Un promoteur de l'archéologie américaine* (Intervalles Editions, Cahier no. 1, 1982), also gives data on the Bandelier family, both in Switzerland and in Highland, Illinois. Adolph Bandelier himself gave two interviews concerning his life, one to former New Mexico territorial governor William G. Ritch in 1882, now contained in the Ritch collection in the Huntington Library, San Marino, California. A second biographical sketch was elicited by the anthropologist George H. Pepper sometime around 1906 or 1907; it presently is among the George H. Pepper papers at Tulane University, New Orleans. Both interviews were published in the fourth volume of *The Southwestern Journals of Adolph F. Bandelier.*

An English version of Solomon Koepfli and Johann Eggen's book, *New Switzerland in Illinois,* was translated by J. L. Kaeser and M. H. Driesner and edited by R. J. Spahn and B. A. Spahn (Southern Illinois University Foundation, Edwardsville, Illinois, 1977). Betty S. Coats and Raymond J. Spahn wrote a history of Highland, *The Swiss on Looking Glass Prairie: A Century and a Half, 1831–1981* (Southern Illinois University at Edwardsville and Highland Historical Society, 1983), which contains much factual information as well as an excellent bibliography. A study of Bandelier's early life by Edgar F. Goad was presented as a 1939 Ph.D. dissertation at the University of Southern California, Los Angeles.

Other sources for Bandelier's early years come from obituaries that followed the scholar's death in 1914. These include pieces by Edward Albes (*Bulletin of the Pan-American Union,* 1914), Will C. Barnes (*Old Santa Fe,* 1915), Frederick W. Hodge (*American Anthropologist,* 1914, and also a later biographical sketch of Bandelier in *New Mexico Historical Review,* 1932), Charles F. Lummis (*El Palacio,* 1914), Randall D. MacIver (*Man,* 1914), and Clark Wissler (*El Palacio,* 1914). Extremely valuable information came from an interview by Hulda Hobbs with Mrs. Elizabeth (Lizzie) Bandelier Kaune at Santa Fe, New Mexico, in 1942. This material is in the Bandelier collection of the History Library, Museum of New Mexico, Santa Fe. Another valuable source for Bandelier's life is the introduction by Ernest J. Burrus, S. J., to his first volume of Bandelier's *A History of the Southwest* (Jesuit Historical Institute, vol. 8, Rome, 1969). Father Burrus was the discoverer of the famous "Histoire" manuscript in the Vatican archives, and *A History of the Southwest* is a publication of the first portion of that manuscript.

For Adolph Bandelier as a young adult, there are two important collections of letters. One is Leslie A. White's *Pioneers in American Anthropology: The Bandelier-Morgan Letters* (University of New Mexico Press, Albuquerque, 1940), which contains a short biography of Bandelier. The letters themselves cover the period from 1873 to 1883. There are 158 letters from Bandelier to the American anthropologist Lewis Henry Morgan, and 5 to Mrs. Morgan during Morgan's final illness and after his death.

A second collection of letters covering a somewhat longer period is Bandelier's correspondence with the great Mexican historian and archivist Joaquín García Icazbalceta, which began in 1875 and continued until 1891. Sixty-six letters from Bandelier and copies of six replies can be found in the García papers. The first twenty-five letters were written in French; then Bandelier gradually switched to a rather ungrammatical Spanish. The Spanish letters have been edited and the French ones translated into Spanish in a volume edited by Leslie A. White and Ignacio Bernal, *Correspondencia de Adolfo F. Bandelier* (Instituto Nacional de Antropología e Historia, México, 1960).

Undoubtedly the most important of the documents we used in compiling this life of Bandelier were the daily journals he kept from 1880 through 1907 and then for a brief period in 1911. The 1880 and 1882–92 journals were edited and annotated in four volumes by Charles H. Lange, Carroll L. Riley, and Elizabeth M. Lange (for the third and fourth volumes) under the title *The Southwestern Journals of Adolph F. Bandelier* (University of New Mexico Press, Albuquerque, 1966, 1970, 1975, and 1984). Readers who wish to find detailed sources for Bandelier's life are referred to the bibliography in the fourth volume of that set.

Bandelier's journals for his year in Mexico, 1881, for his South American period, 1892–1903, and for his years in New York, 1903–1907, plus the few entries for 1911, are in manuscript form only in the Bandelier collection at the History Library, Museum of New Mexico, Santa Fe.

Two briefer collections of Bandelier correspondence have been published. One was by the anthropologist Paul Radin, *Unpublished Letters of Adolphe F. Bandelier* (Southwestern Archaeologica, Charles P. Everitt, New York, 1942). It included letters from Bandelier to his friend Thomas A. Janvier, the travel writer, concerning publication of Bandelier's novel, *The Delight Makers*. A second series of letters was published by George P. Hammond and Edgar F. Goad, *A Scientist on the Trail: Travel Letters of Adolph F. Bandelier, 1880–1881* (The Quivira Society, vol. 10, Los Angeles, 1949); the letters concern the early southwestern years.

There are a number of archival collections, including letters, memoranda, and other documents, that pertain to various periods in Bandelier's life. Files of the Archaeological Institute of America, Boston—now at the John M. Longyear Museum at Colgate University—contain much information on Bandelier, especially for the years 1879–97, and include the voluminous correspondence of Bandelier and others with Charles Eliot Norton. The various printed reports of the AIA for that period are also valuable source documents.

A file of letters from Bandelier to Francis Parkman can be found in the library of the Massachusetts Historical Society, Boston. At the Huntington

Library in San Marino, California, and at the Southwest Museum in Los Angeles, there are files of correspondence between Bandelier and Frank Hamilton Cushing, Washington Matthews, and other contemporaries.

In the Bandelier archive of the American Museum of Natural History in New York are a series of letters from Bandelier to Henry Villard. These date primarily, but not exclusively, from the South American period. This archive contains other documents as well—collection lists, inventories, and a journal of Fanny Bandelier's written in German. The Hispanic Society of America, in New York, also has a few Bandelier documents, mostly letters and notes from the years 1907 to 1911.

Much of the documentation for Fanny Bandelier's life, both before and after her husband's death, comes from the Bandelier collection at the History Library, Museum of New Mexico. Her letters from Charles A. Wilson are in that collection, as are her automatic-spirit writings dating from the late 1920s. Earlier material can also be found in this archive—for example, Fanny's account of her initiation into archaeological excavation in northern Chile, quoted in part in chapter 15. There is, in addition, a considerable amount of correspondence from both Adolph and Fanny to Frank Bigler, Ina Cassidy, Eva Fényes, E. L. Hewett, F. W. Hodge, and others. The important letter Fanny wrote to Ina Cassidy describing the voyage to Spain, extensively quoted in chapter 17, was published as "Bandelier's Last Journey" (*El Palacio,* vol. 56, no. 8, pp. 241–51, 1949).

Madeleine Turrell Rodack translated and edited the English version of "The Discovery of New Mexico by the Franciscan Monk Fray Marcos de Niza in 1539," which was published by the University of Arizona Press, Tucson, in 1981. This work had initially been published in French in 1886, and a Spanish edition was published in 1889.

Two miscellaneous sources that cover portions of Bandelier's life are scrapbooks consisting primarily of newspaper clippings on Adolph and Fanny Bandelier. One was sent to us by Professor Fred Eggan of the University of Chicago and is now in the History Library of the Museum of New Mexico. The second, also housed in the History Library, was prepared by Ina Sizer Cassidy.

Index